THE WITCHCRAFT SERIES MAQLÛ

Society of Biblical Literature

Writings from the Ancient World

Theodore J. Lewis, General Editor

Associate Editors

Daniel Fleming
Theo van den Hout
Martti Nissinen
William Schniedewind
Mark S. Smith
Emily Teeter

Number 37
The Witchcraft Series Maqlû
Volume Editor: Martin Worthington

THE WITCHCRAFT SERIES MAQLÛ

by

Tzvi Abusch

SBL Press
Atlanta, Georgia

THE WITCHCRAFT SERIES MAQLÛ

Library of Congress Control Number: 2015932765

ISBN: 978-1-628370-81-2

Printed on acid-free, recycled paper conforming to ANSI/NISO Z39.48-1992 (R1997) and ISO 9706:1994 standards for paper permanence.

For my very dear friends
Benjy, Steve, and Kathryn

CONTENTS

Series Editor's Foreword	ix
Preface	xi
Abbreviations	xiii
Introduction	1
Maqlû I	44
Maqlû II	54
Maqlû III	70
Maqlû IV	84
Maqlû V	100
Maqlû VI	114
Maqlû VII	126
Maqlû VIII	140
Maqlû Ritual Tablet	150
Notes	169
Bibliography	197

SERIES EDITOR'S FOREWORD

Writings from the Ancient World is designed to provide up-to-date, readable English translations of writings recovered from the ancient Near East.

The series is intended to serve the interests of general readers, students, and educators who wish to explore the ancient Near Eastern roots of Western civilization or to compare these earliest written expressions of human thought and activity with writings from other parts of the world. It should also be useful to scholars in the humanities or social sciences who need clear, reliable translations of ancient Near Eastern materials for comparative purposes. Specialists in particular areas of the ancient Near East who need access to texts in the scripts and languages of other areas will also find these translations helpful. Given the wide range of materials translated in the series, different volumes will appeal to different interests. However, these translations make available to all readers of English the world's earliest traditions as well as valuable sources of information on daily life, history, religion, and the like in the preclassical world.

The translators of the various volumes in this series are specialists in the particular languages and have based their work on the original sources and the most recent research. In their translations they attempt to convey as much as possible of the original texts in fluent, current English. In the introductions, notes, glossaries, maps, and chronological tables, they aim to provide the essential information for an appreciation of these ancient documents.

Covering the period from the invention of writing (by 3000 B.C.E.) down to the conquests of Alexander the Great (ca. 330 B.C.E.), the ancient Near East comprised northeast Africa and southwest Asia. The cultures represented within these limits include especially Egyptian, Sumerian, Babylonian, Assyrian, Hittite, Ugaritic, Aramean, Phoenician, and Israelite. It is hoped that Writings from the Ancient World will eventually produce translations of most of the many different genres attested in these cultures: letters (official and private), myths, diplomatic documents, hymns, law collections, monumental inscriptions, tales, and administrative records, to mention but a few.

The Society of Biblical Literature provided significant funding for the Writings from the Ancient World series. In addition, authors have benefited from working in research collections in their respective institutions and beyond. Were it not for such support, the arduous tasks of preparation, translation, editing, and publication could not have been accomplished or even undertaken. It is the hope of all who have worked on these texts or supported this work that Writings from the Ancient World will open up new horizons and deepen the humanity of all who read these volumes.

Theodore J. Lewis
The Johns Hopkins University

PREFACE

My edition of Maqlû has been in the works for a long time. I started studying the tablets and fragments of Maqlû and searching for new texts around 1970 and have pursued this endeavor, on and off, for many years. With few exceptions, I have examined all the original tablets and/or their photographs.

I cannot emphasize strongly enough how much the edition has benefited from the assistance and cooperation of a number of colleagues and institutions. The reader interested in the details of my indebtedness should consult the preface to my full scientific edition *The Magical Ceremony Maqlû: A Critical Edition* (Ancient Magic and Divination; Leiden: Brill). All the same, here I would mention by name those who made repeated contributions through identifications, photographs, transliterations, and collations that they generously shared with me. They are the late Rykle Borger, Markham J. Geller, the late Wilfred G. Lambert, Erle Leichty, Christopher Walker, and especially Daniel Schwemer.[1] I would be remiss if I did not mention here also the late Frederick W. Geers, among whose copies at the Oriental Institute I identified some Maqlû fragments.

Maqlû tablets and fragments are found in a number of museums, and I express my gratitude to the Middle East Department (formerly Western Asiatic Antiquities) of the British Museum; the Vorderasiatisches Museum, Berlin; the Oriental Institute, University of Chicago; the Babylonian Collection, University of Pennsylvania; the Ashmolean Museum, Oxford; the Anadolu Medeniyetleri Müzesi, Ankara; the İstanbul Arkeoloji Müzeleri, Istanbul.

I am indebted to and express my sincerest thanks to several graduate students in the Bible and Ancient Near East program of Brandeis University who

1. I would also mention here that some of the translations in this volume are the result of my collaboration with Daniel Schwemer some years ago on a German translation of Maqlû for TUAT NF 4 (2008).

worked with me on the WAW edition of Maqlû. They are Molly DeMarco,[2] Bronson Brown-deVost,[3] Sung-Chun Kim,[4] and Robert McChesney.[5] Their work was supported by the Theodore and Jane Norman Awards for Faculty Scholarship of Brandeis University, the GTR/GSFR fund of the Department of Near Eastern and Judaic Studies, and the graduate fellowship program; I thank Brandeis University for its support.

I thank Martin Worthington, the editor of the volume, for his careful reading of the manuscript and for his numerous editorial notes. Those of his suggestions (as well as the suggestions of others) that I have incorporated have improved the volume. Any mistakes or defects in this volume are my responsibility alone.

I thank Theodore Lewis, the series editor of WAW, for inviting me to contribute an edition of Maqlû to WAW. I very much appreciate his patience and support. I am grateful to Billie Jean Collins and the SBL WAW production team for their work on this volume.

---

2. Molly DeMarco reviewed with me the transcription and translation and did most of the inputting and formatting of the transcription; she also worked with me on a preliminary bibliography.

3. Bronson Brown-deVost completed inputting and formatting the transcription, kept track of the many things that had to be included in the volume, and assisted with proofreading.

4. Sung-Chun Kim formatted the bibliographies and reviewed them for omissions and mistakes.

5. Robert McChesney read through the first and second proofs of the volume.

ABBREVIATIONS

AfO	*Archiv für Orientforschung*
AfOB	Archiv für Orientforschung Beiheft
AHw	Wolfram von Soden, *Akkadisches Handwörterbuch*. 3 vols. Wiesbaden: Harrassowitz, 1959–81
AMD	Ancient Magic and Divination
ANEM	Ancient Near Eastern Monographs
AnOr	Analecta Orientalia
AOAT	Alter Orient und Altes Testament
ArOr	*Archiv Orientální*
AS	Assyriological Studies
ASSF	Acta Societas Scientiarum Fennicae
BA	*Beiträge zur Assyriologie (und semitischen Sprachwissenschaft)*
BaF	Baghdader Forschungen
*BAL*²	Rykle Borger, *Babylonisch-assyrische Lesestücke*. 2nd ed. AnOr 54. Rome: Pontifical Biblical Institute, 1979
BibInt	Biblical Interpretation Series
BibOr	Biblica et Orientalia
BJS	Brown Judaic Studies
BPOA	Biblioteca del Proximo Oriente Antiguo
CAD	*The Assyrian Dictionary of the Oriental Institute of the University of Chicago*. Chicago: The Oriental Institute of the University of Chicago, 1956–2010
CM	Cuneiform Monographs
CMAWR	Tzvi Abusch and Daniel Schwemer, *Corpus of Mesopotamian Anti-Witchcraft Rituals*. Vol. 1–. AMD 8/1–. Leiden: Brill, 2011–
CNIP	Carsten Niebuhr Institute Publications
CTN	Cuneiform Texts from Nimrud
GAG	Wolfram von Soden, *Grundriss der akkadischen Grammatik*. 2nd ed. Rome: Pontifical Biblical Institute, 1969

HSS	Harvard Semitic Studies
HTR	*Harvard Theological Review*
JCS	*Journal of Cuneiform Studies*
JNES	*Journal of Near Eastern Studies*
JSRC	Jerusalem Studies in Religion and Culture
KAL	Keilschrifttexte aus Assur literarischen Inhalts
KAR	E. Ebeling, *Keilschrifttexte aus Assur religiösen Inhalts.* WVDOG 28 and 34. Leipzig: Hinrichs, 1915–23
LSS	Leipziger semitische Studien
PSBA	*Proceedings of the Society of Biblical Archaeology*
OECT	Oxford Editions of Cuneiform Tablets
Or	*Orientalia*
RGRW	Religions in the Graeco-Roman World
RlA	*Reallexikon der Assyriologie und Vorderasiatischen Archäologie*
SAAS	State Archives of Assyria Studies
SEL	*Studi epigraphici e linguistici sul Vicino Oriente antico*
SHR	Studies in the History of Religions
SMSR	*Studi e materiali di storia delle religioni*
StOr	Studia Orientalia
TAPS	*Transactions of the American Philosophical Society*
TCS	Texts from Cuneiform Sources
TStR	Toronto Studies in Religion
TUAT	Texte aus der Umwelt des Alten Testaments Neue Folge
UET	Ur Excavation Texts
WVDOG	Wissenschaftliche Veröffentlichung der Deutsche Orient Gesellschaft
ZA	*Zeitschrift für Assyriologie*

INTRODUCTION

This volume presents a transcription and translation of Maqlû, "Burning," the longest and most important magical ritual against witchcraft from ancient Mesopotamia. I should preface my presentation of this Akkadian composition and ceremony with a few words of introduction about Mesopotamian magic and witchcraft and about the ancient literature that centers upon such concerns.

It is particularly important to start out with definitions, especially here in an SBL WAW volume, because magic and witchcraft are treated somewhat differently in Mesopotamia and in biblical literature. I understand as magical those Mesopotamian rites that address the human needs, crises, and desires, especially of the individual but also of the king. In contrast to some later western societies, magic in Mesopotamia was regarded as legitimate and as part of the established religion. Therefore, in a Mesopotamian context, witchcraft (e.g., *kišpū*, *ruḫû*, *rusû*, *upšāšû lemnūtu*, etc.) refers not to magical behavior as such, but to inimical behavior, that is, to the practice of magic for antisocial and destructive purposes.

Over the course of some 2,500 years (ca. 2600–100 BCE), numerous cuneiform texts written in both the Sumerian and Akkadian languages refer to personal crisis and individual suffering (e.g., letters, curses, and literary compositions that treat the problem of theodicy); but, by and large, the most important sources detailing ways to cope with illness, danger, and personal difficulties are the various types of texts that describe symptoms, provide etiological or descriptive diagnoses, and prescribe ways to deal with evil and suffering. These treatments include medical therapies, ritual prescriptions, and oral rites (prayers and incantations). Therapeutic acts on behalf of an individual may be undertaken either by the individual himself or by a professional healer. Procedural texts prescribe the treatment of problems either by means of various ritual or ceremonial therapies (*āšipūtu*) or by means of traditional herbal therapy (*asûtu*).

In the main, our texts are guides to actual performances that were consulted by magicians and herbalists and studied by scholars. The texts usually present in varying combinations the elements crucial to the actual ritual activity or performance (oral and manual rites and preparation or applications of ceremonial/medical materials) as well as a statement describing the circumstance and purpose of the activity. At first, only the incantation was committed to writing; subsequently, instructions regarding the time, place, and manner of ritual performance as well as other types of information (particularly, an objective description of the problem, a diagnosis, and a statement of purpose) were added.

Two typical ways of recording the content of an individual ceremony are: 1) the text of an incantation followed by a rubric (an ancient classificatory label) and ritual instructions; and 2) a description of the patient's symptoms followed by a diagnosis (e.g., "that man suffers from ..."), ritual or medical instructions (e.g., instructions to create a sacred space such as a reed hut or altar, to prepare salves or potions, and/or to recite an oral rite as well as the text of the oral rite itself), and finally, a prognosis (e.g., "the man will live").

Incantations are found in various written contexts: 1) as part of short rituals; 2) in short collections of incantations (with some ritual instructions); 3) and in standardized scribal series—some of which were collections, while others represented complex lengthy ceremonies, such as Maqlû.

The personal crises that stand at the center of the therapeutic texts may play out on the physical, psychological, psychosomatic, or social plane. Especially when treated by an exorcist/incantation-priest (*āšipu*), such distress will usually be understood to be the result of the action or inaction of supernatural powers or agencies; that is, the cause of distress will be located in either personalistic or mechanistic powers within the supernatural universe. Some of these agencies are gods, demons, ghosts, tutelary gods, witches, evil omens, curses, and sins. These forces and their nefarious deeds are described in detail in the oral rites themselves.

The larger body of Babylonian and Assyrian antiwitchcraft texts—of which Maqlû is a member, actually its most important member—is itself part of this larger corpus of therapeutic texts. The relationship in Mesopotamia of antiwitchcraft texts to the larger corpus of therapeutic texts, on the one hand, and to witchcraft itself, on the other, is not dissimilar to what Stuart Clark has said about the relationship of magic and *maleficium* in early modern Europe:

> One of the key reasons for the popularity of magical practices was that they were deployed to detect and counteract the harmful effects of witchcraft. Only the curing of illnesses occupied as important a place in the tasks for which magic was singled out—and, of course, many of these were attributed to *maleficium* anyway. Indeed, so intimate was the relationship between protective (or remedial) magic and malevolent witchcraft that historians have

> come to see them more and more as the two inseparable halves of the world of popular culture in this period.[1]

The branch of the written therapeutic tradition that is directed against witchcraft includes a large body of very significant and interesting prayers, incantations, magical rituals, and medical prescriptions. These magical and medical texts attribute misfortune and ill-health to the machinations of people designated as witches and prescribe the means of combating the witch and witchcraft. They set out the various ceremonies, devices, and treatments that are to be used to dispel witchcraft, to destroy the witch (symbolically), and to protect and cure the patient.

Personal distress ascribed to witchcraft includes the individual's experience of physical, psychological, and/or social difficulties. Texts may focus on specific symptoms, such as gastrointestinal, respiratory, sexual, or psychological difficulties, on life-threatening circumstances such as childbirth and infancy, on more generalized illnesses involving systemic physical and/or psychological breakdown, or on situations involving socioeconomic loss of wealth and status as well as social isolation.

The Mesopotamian witchcraft corpus (or, rather, antiwitchcraft corpus, since we have no texts composed by witches) comprises hundreds of magical and medical texts that contain many different elements. The constituent parts of traditional antiwitchcraft documents are oral rites (prayers, incantations, utterances), symbolic rituals (e.g., burning of figurines), medical treatments (e.g., preparation of potions), descriptions of symptoms, diagnoses, and prognoses.

These traditional texts come from the early second millennium through the late first millennium BCE. A few texts are Old Babylonian; a somewhat larger number come from late second-millennium collections, mainly those of Boghazkoi and Assur. But by far, the largest number come from first-millennium collections. Pride of place goes to the royal collections of seventh-century Nineveh; but, in addition, major groups derive from both the Assyrian sites of Assur, Kalhu (Nimrud), and Sultantepe and the Babylonian ones of Uruk, Ur, Nippur, Babylon, and Sippar.[2]

1. Stuart Clark, "Witchcraft and Magic in Early Modern Culture," in *Witchcraft and Magic in Europe: The Period of the Witch Trials*, ed. Bengt Ankarloo and Stuart Clark (Philadelphia: University of Pennsylvania Press, 2002), 112.

2. For an edition of the full corpus of Mesopotamian texts concerned with combating witchcraft (with the exception of Maqlû), see Tzvi Abusch and Daniel Schwemer, *Corpus of Mesopotamian Anti-Witchcraft Rituals*, vol. 1– (AMD 8/1–; Leiden: Brill, 2011–).

MAQLÛ

I turn now to the Akkadian magical series Maqlû itself. The text of Maqlû was previously edited by Knut L. Tallqvist and Gerhard Meier.[3] This series is the longest and most important Mesopotamian text concerned with combating witchcraft. Maqlû comprises eight tablets of incantations and a ritual tablet. The Incantation Tablets record the text of almost one hundred incantations; in the Ritual Tablet, these incantations are cited by their incipit, their opening line, and alongside each citation appropriate ritual directions are prescribed.

Long thought to be a random collection of witchcraft materials, an important breakthrough in the understanding of Maqlû came with my discovery that it was a single complex ceremony. It was performed during a single night and into the following morning at the end of the month Abu (July/August), a time when spirits were thought to move back and forth between the netherworld and this world. The primary participants were the exorcist and his patient. The ceremony is even the subject of a letter written by the exorcist Nabû-nādin-šumi to King Esarhaddon in early August 670 BCE. Here it should be mentioned that in almost all instances, the patients on whose behalf witchcraft rituals were performed were members of the male elite.[4] Although lists of witches include both male and female forms, the witch is usually depicted as a woman.

In the main, the incantations and rituals of Maqlû are directed against witches and witchcraft. The ceremony was intended to counteract and dispel evil magic and its effects, to protect the patient, and to punish and render ineffectual those responsible for the evil. The witch was to be executed. Overall in Maqlû she was not to be buried; rather fire and/or animals were

3. Knut L. Tallqvist, *Die assyrische Beschwörungsserie Maqlû*, 2 vols., Acta Societatis Scientiarum Fennicae 20.6 (Leipzig, 1895); Gerhard Meier, *Die assyrische Beschwörungssammlung Maqlû*, AfO Beiheft 2 (Berlin, 1937), and "Studien zur Beschwörungssammlung Maqlû. Zusammengestellt nach hinterlassenen Notizen," *AfO* 21 (1966): 70–81 and pls. 11–12. My edition will be published as volume 10 in the Brill series Ancient Magic and Divination.

In the introductory portion of this volume, I present a number of Maqlû incantations in translation. Generally, these translations are without notes. The incantations will all be found in the body of the volume, where such notes as might be useful to the reader will be included.

4. For the ceremonial nature of the series, see Tzvi Abusch, "Mesopotamian Anti-witchcraft Literature: Texts and Studies, Part I: The Nature of *Maqlû*: Its Character, Divisions, and Calendrical Setting," *JNES* 33 (1974): 251–62. For a collection of my studies on witchcraft, see Tzvi Abusch, *Mesopotamian Witchcraft: Toward a History and Understanding of Babylonian Witchcraft Beliefs and Literature*, AMD 5 (Leiden: Brill/Styx, 2002).

to destroy her corpse, thus depriving her of any possibility of burial—the ritual was intended to destroy both the body and ghost of the witch.[5] The series (and ceremony) was composed of three major subdivisions. The first two divisions (Tablets I–V // Ritual Tablet 1–95; Tablets VI–VII 54 // Ritual Tablet 96–137) were performed during the night, the third (VII 55–VIII // Ritual Tablet 138–179) during the early morning hours of the following day.[6]

The present form of Maqlû is, I believe, a creation of the early first millennium BCE, though a divergent proto-form may have already existed in Assur towards the end of the middle Assyrian period. Actually, this long ritual with its nearly one hundred incantations grew out of a much shorter ritual. This earlier form had been known for some time but was thought to be an extract from the longer text. But some years ago I demonstrated that the standard long text had developed from the short form by means of a series of sequential changes. This mode of composition helps explain the complexity of our present text. So, perhaps the simplest way to undertake an examination of the lengthy version would be to begin from the earlier short form, precisely because that form is shorter and less complex. Also, beginning with the short form will serve as a demonstration of how texts and ceremonies expanded and changed in the course of time. Accordingly, I shall begin with an explication of the short version.[7]

Early Short Version

There are ten incantations in the short version—ten incantations instead of the one-hundred of the longer version. Actually, the incantations of the short version are among the most important incantations found in Tablets

5. See Tzvi Abusch, "The Socio-Religious Framework of the Babylonian Witchcraft Ceremony *Maqlû*: Some Observations on the Introductory Section of the Text, Part I," in *Riches Hidden in Secret Places: Ancient Near Eastern Studies in Memory of Thorkild Jacobsen*, ed. Tzvi Abusch (Winona lake, IN: Eisenbrauns, 2002), 12–19, and "Ghost and God: Some Observations on a Babylonian Understanding of Human Nature," in *Self, Soul and Body in Religious Experience*, ed. Albert I. Baumgarten, Jan Assmann, and Guy G. Stroumsa, SHR 78 (Leiden: Brill, 1998), 374.

6. For a description of the ritual and incantation blocks, see Tzvi Abusch, "*Maqlû*," in *RlA* 7 (1987–1990), 346–51.

7. For a reconstruction of the earlier short version, see Tzvi Abusch, "An Early Form of the Witchcraft Ritual *Maqlû* and the Origin of a Babylonian Magical Ceremony," in *Lingering over Words: Studies in Ancient Near Eastern Literature in Honor of William L. Moran*, ed. Tzvi Abusch, John Huehnergard, and Piotr Steinkeller, HSS 37 (Atlanta: Scholars Press, 1990), 1–57. Cf. Daniel Schwemer, *Abwehrzauber und Behexung: Studien zum Schadenzauberglauben im alten Mesopotamien* (Wiesbaden: Harrassowitz, 2007), 53–55.

I–V, the first division of the standard text of Maqlû. But in contrast to the longer work, this shorter ceremony was performed during the morning and contained most of the important ritual actions found in the first division of the longer work.

A magical ceremony is a performance, a lyrical and dramatic cycle. My presentation of the short ceremony will simply outline it in summary form and provide short sketches of the incantations. But even this short version can be better understood if it is simplified still further and reduced to basic actions: judging the witch, burning her representation, dousing the fire with water, and disposing of the remains. The blend of action and speech that makes up the ceremony of the short version seems to fall into four sections.

Section One

This section centers on the judgment and burning of the witch. Figurines of the witches are set out in a crucible.

Incantation One. *Šamaš annûtu ṣalmū ēpišiya*, "O Šamaš, these are the images of my sorcerer" (I 73–121).

The victim of witchcraft on whose behalf the ceremony is being performed points to the figurines[8] and recites the incantation, which would have read:

73 O Šamaš, these are the figurines of my sorcerer,
74 These are the figurines of my sorceress,
75 The figurines of my warlock and my witch,
76 The figurines of my sorcerer and the woman who instigates sorcery against me,
77 The figurines of my enchanter and my enchantress,
78 The figurines of my male and female inseminators,
79 The figurines of the male and female who are enraged at me,
80 The figurines of my male and female enemies,
81 The figurines of my male and female persecutors,
82 The figurines of my male and female litigants,
83 The figurines of my male and female accusers,
84 The figurines of my male and female adversaries,
85 The figurines of my male and female slanderers,

8. So the Ritual Tablet, but based on the incantation itself and other rituals it is likely that originally he raised up the figurines while reciting the incantation and then placed them in the crucible.

86 The figurines of my male and female evildoers,
87 Whom, you, Šamaš, the judge, know, but I do not know,
88 Who against me have performed, have had performed, have sought, have had sought
89 witchcraft, spittle, enchainment, evil machinations,
90 Sorcery, rebellion, evil word, love(-magic), hate(-magic),
91 Perversion of justice, Zikurrudâ-magic, muteness, pacification,
92 Mood swings, vertigo, madness.
93 These are they, these are their figurines.
94 Since they are not present, I bear aloft their figurines (and say):
95 You, Šamaš, the judge, vanquisher of the wicked and the enemy, vanquish them so I not be wronged,
96 (Those) who have made my figurines, reproduced my facial features,
97 Seized my mouth, made my neck tremble,
98 Pressed against my chest, bent my spine,
99 Weakened my heart, taken away my sexual drive,
100 Made me turn my anger against myself, sapped my strength,
101 Caused my arms to fall limp, bound my knees,
102 Filled me with fever, stiffness, and debility,
103 Fed me bewitched food,
104 Given me bewitched water to drink,
105 Bathed me in dirty wash water,
106 Rubbed me with a salve of harmful herbs,
107 Betrothed me to a dead person,
108 Laid the water of my life in a grave,
109 Caused god, king, noble, and prince to be angry with me.
110 You, O Girra, it is you who are the burner of warlocks and witches,
111 The annihilator of the wicked, seed of warlock and witch,
112 The destroyer of the evildoers.
113 I call upon you:
114 Judge my case, render my verdict.
115 Burn my warlock and my witch,
116 Devour my enemies, consume the ones who would do evil to me!
117 Let your raging (fire-)storm vanquish them.
118 May they come to an end in a trickle like water from a waterskin.
119 May their fingers be cut back as if smashed by stones.
120 By your preeminent command that cannot be altered
121 And your affirmative assent that cannot be changed.

The plaintiff identifies the figurines as representations of witches who have unjustly harmed him through acts of witchcraft. He then appeals to

Šamaš, the omniscient judge, to find and overwhelm these evildoers. Šamaš, the judge, the illuminating and killing sun, is asked to pronounce a sentence of death by fire, and the fire god Girra, here the hypostatization of Šamaš's destructive heat rays, is asked to execute the sentence.

Because the plaintiff does not know who the witch is, he cannot prosecute the alleged criminal in a regular court of law; instead, he appeals to Šamaš, who as an omniscient judge knows the actual identity of the witch. But the sun god appearing in this type of incantation is not the commonly met and rather colorless judge. The sun here is both an omniscient judge and a relentless executioner, a god who is able not only to identify but also to locate and destroy the culprit who has taken refuge outside the bounds of the settled community. The natural force personified is the brilliant desert sun whose bright burning rays, called here (line 117) *ūmu ezzu*, Sumerian U$_4$.ḪUŠ, "raging (fire-)storm,"[9] can ferret out the criminal wandering in the steppe and overwhelm and kill him. This wilderness background is further reflected in line 118: "May they come to an end in a trickle like water from a waterskin!" This natural force provides the images of the judge and executioner that dominate our incantation and others of its type; its ritual is most naturally that of burning.

Incantation Two. ^{d}*Nuska šurbû ilitti* ^{d}*Ani*, "O Grand Nuska, offspring of Anu" (I 122–134).

After the sentence is pronounced over the bound figurines of the witches, a stalk that will be used to set the images of the witch ablaze is lit. The speaker turns to the god Nuska, the lamp, and asks him to cause the witchcraft to rebound and seize those who sent it.

122 O Grand Nuska, offspring of Anu,
123 Likeness of the father, scion of Enlil,
124 Reared in the *apsû*, creation of Enanki.
125 I raise up a reed torch and set you yourself alight.
126 A warlock has bewitched me; bewitch him with the witchcraft with which he bewitched me,
127 A witch has bewitched me; bewitch her with the witchcraft with which she bewitched me,

9. I have generally replaced my earlier translation of *ūmu ezzu* in Maqlû ("brilliant red light/fiery red light/fierce rays") with "raging (fire-)storm." However, I am still not fully convinced that *ūmu* here must refer to storm (so, e.g., *CAD* s. *ūmu*) rather than to rays or light.

128 A sorcerer has ensorcelled me; ensorcell him with the sorcery with which he ensorcelled me,
129 A sorceress has ensorcelled me; ensorcell her with the sorcery with which she ensorcelled me,
130 A woman who instigates sorcery has ensorcelled me; ensorcell her with the sorcery with which she ensorcelled me.
131 (Those) who have made figurines corresponding to my figurines, reproduced my facial features,
132 Taken my spittle, plucked out my hair,
133 Cut off my hem, collected a clump of dirt (over which) my feet (had passed),
134 May Girra, the warrior, release their incantation.

In this incantation, Nuska is evoked neither as a judge nor as an executioner but as a protective night light: "I raise up a reed torch and set you yourself alight." (I 125). Nuska frequently appears in this role in Mesopotamian literature. In magical texts, he is said to protect the sleeping household against marauders of the night, particularly evil dreams. The incantation takes for granted that Nuska had acted as a guardian during the night, keeping a vigil over the speaker and staving off all assaults of witchcraft sent in the form of evil dreams. The incantation had its original setting in the early hours of the morning and was recited by the patient upon greeting the new day.

The victim's impassioned request to Nuska to cause the nighttime witchcraft to recoil is the central theme of the incantation. It is repeatedly expressed in a forceful alliterative style in a series of lines that convey the meaning and force of the speaker's wish:

126 *kaššāpu ikšipanni kišpī ikšipanni kišipšu*
127 *kaššaptu takšipanni kišpī takšipanni kišipši*
128 *ēpišu īpušanni ipšū īpušanni epussu*
129 *ēpištu tēpušanni ipšū tēpušanni epussi*
130 *muštēpištu tēpušanni ipšū tēpušanni epussi*

126 A warlock has bewitched me; bewitch him with the witchcraft with which he bewitched me,
127 A witch has bewitched me; bewitch her with the witchcraft with which she bewitched me,
128 A sorcerer has ensorcelled me; ensorcell him with the sorcery with which he ensorcelled me,

129 A sorceress has ensorcelled me; ensorcell her with the sorcery with which she ensorcelled me,
130 A woman who instigates sorcery has ensorcelled me; ensorcell her with the sorcery with which she ensorcelled me.

Thus, with the coming of morning, Nuska is asked by the patient he had protected to perform one last service: to inflict the consequences of the evil dreams that he had kept at bay during the night upon the very witches who had sent them.

Incantation Three. *Anašši dipāru*, "I raise up the torch" (I 135–143).

After freeing himself of the terrifying experiences of the night, the speaker turns back to the figurines of the witch. The crucible is set ablaze. The speaker sets the figurines on fire and recites the incantation *Anašši dipāru*.

135 I am raising the torch and burning their figurines,
136 (Those) of the *utukku*-demon, the *šēdu*-spirit, the lurker-demon, the ghost,
137 Lamaštu, *labāṣu* (disease), *ahhāzu*-jaundice,
138 *lilû*, *lilītu*, *ardat-lilî*,
139 And any evil that seizes mankind,
140 Melt, dissolve, drip ever away!
141 May your smoke rise ever heavenward,
142 May the sun extinguish your embers,
143 May Ea's son, the exorcist, cut off the terror that emanates from you.

In this incantation, the speaker executes the verdict. He states that he is putting the figurines to the torch and expresses the hope that they melt, that their smoke rise up and be lost in the sky, that the sun shine its rays upon them and thus dim their glow, and that Asalluḫi, the magician of the gods and son of the water god Ea, quench their embers and thus cut off their emanations. The witches are executed, and in this incantation as well as in the eighth and tenth incantations, *Ezzētunu šamrātunu* (V 132–141) and *Isâ isâ* (V 158–175), they are addressed as demonic shades. In origin, these incantations belong to the stock of general antidemon incantations but have been adapted here for use against malevolent ghosts.

Section Two

This section centers on the release of witchcraft and the liberation of the victim.

Incantation Four. *Ša* ^{d}*Šamši mannu abušu*, "Of the Sun, who is his father?" (IV 107–114).

Three knots are tied in a band of white wool; the knots are then undone, and the band is cast into the crucible.

107 Of the Sun, who is his father, wh[o is his mother],
108 Who is his sister? He is the judge.
109 Of the S[u]n, Sîn[10] is his father, [Nik]kal is [his] mother,
110 Ma[nzâ]t[11] is his sister: He is the judge.
111 Šamaš [destroys] the w[itchcraft], releases the spittle,[12]
112 And she, M[anz]ât, breaks the bon[ds].
113 (So) I destroy the witchcraft, I rele[ase] the spittle,
114 I cause the wind$^{!}$ to carry off sorcery, rebellion, evil word.

Šamaš is the central figure in this incantation. In the opening lines, the speaker picks up on the mention of the sun in the preceding incantation and reiterates emphatically that Šamaš's role and identity in our incantation, as in the rest of the short version, is that of judge. While wool is being tied and untied and then thrown into the fire, the speaker states that he is unraveling and destroying the tangle of witchcraft (IV 113–114).

Incantation Five. *Šaruḫ lānī šaruḫ zīmī*, "Splendid is my countenance, splendid is my appearance" (V 83–88).

The parched roasted flour cited in the ritual instructions for this incantation serves either as a representation of witchcraft (in which case it will be cast into the crucible) or more likely as a mixture to be used for apotropaic purposes at the end of the ritual.

83 Splendid is [my appearance, splendid is my countenance].
84 Mighty [raging Girra],
85 Burner o[f the warlock and the witch].

10. The moon.
11. The rainbow.
12. That is, the effects of the spittle.

86 [My] sorcerers, [my sorceresses, and the women who instigate sorcery against me],
87 [My] warlocks [and my witches],
88 To N[uska and] Girra [(the judges) you are handed over!]

The splendor referred to in the opening statement may reflect the light of the ritual flames; it is more likely, however, that it derives from the rays of the rising sun, for the incantation was originally part of a morning ritual and would have been recited as the rays of the sun struck the speaker's face. Immediately afterwards the speaker invokes the fire god Girra; if the speaker had in fact likened himself to the sun, then it is the sun's authority that he draws upon to invoke Girra, the hypostasization of the burning rays of the sun. In any case, the speaker calls on the dying fire to consummate its work of destroying the witches in a final destructive blaze.

Incantation Six. *Šerʾānī tukaṣṣirā* ^{d}*Ea uptaṭṭir*, "Ea has (now) unbound the ligaments that you have bound up" (V 89–97).

As the crucible in which the figurines have been burning is stirred with an ashwood branch and the fire comes forth in a final climactic blaze, the victim speaks this incantation and recalls that everything that the witches have done has been undone and has rebounded against them, that Ea and Asalluḫi, gods of water and magic, have cleansed and unbound him, and that Girra and Nuska have protected and avenged him. The incantation reads:

89 [Ea has (now) unbound] the sinews that you have bound up,
90 [Asalluḫi has (now) released] the figurines that you have twisted and fettered.
91 The knot that you have knotted against me, the pl[ot that you have plotted against me]
92 May blazing Girra ca[use the wind to carry off],
93 May Nuska, the judge, the [master of exorcism],
94 [Turn back] up[on your head] the sorcery that you have performed against me.
95 My witchcraft is released, [my enchainment is] c[leared],
96 With spring water, [I undo your "spitt]le,"
97 I have (now) become pure, cl[ean, and innocent in the presence of Nuska] and Girra, [the (divine) judges.]

The stirring of the fire both concludes the burning and prepares for the act of extinguishing. The incantation incorporates the theme of releasing or undoing the effects of witchcraft, a theme that occurred previously in the fourth incantation, "Of the Sun, who is his father?" In the present incantation, the undoing of witchcraft is accomplished not only by fire gods, but also by water gods; moreover, the incantation incorporates the theme of cleansing water. This incantation seems to link the preceeding fire ritual and the following water ritual, thereby concluding the second section of the ceremony and introducing the third.

Section Three

This section centers on extinguishing both the fire and the witch's life. The smoldering figurines are drenched in water.

Incantation Seven. *Ēpišū'a ēpišētū'a*, "My sorcerers, my sorceresses" (V 112–131).

As water is poured onto the glowing coals, the speaker in the first of the two incantations of the section describes the witches' harmful actions and recalls that having first gone at the command of the water gods Ea and Asalluḫi to the fire god Girra to burn the witches, he has now returned to the water gods in order to quench their smoldering remains.

112 My sorcerers, my sorceresses,
113 My warlocks, my witches,
114 You whose heart has planned evil against me,
115 You keep on seeking malicious spells against me,
116 You have bound my knees with not good machinations.
117 In order to release the witchcraft and spittle against me, having (first) turned to Girra at the word of Ea and Asalluḫi,
118 (Now) with spring water, I quench your heart,
119 I extinguish your mood,
120 I remove the ardor of your heart,
121 I confound your understanding,
122 I unravel your thinking,
123 I burn your witchcraft,
124 I cause you to abandon the plots of your heart.
125 You shall not cross over the Tigris and the Euphrates to me,
126 You shall not cross over dyke and canal to me,
127 You shall not climb over wall and battlement to me,
128 You shall not come in through the city gate and its entranceways to me!
129 May your witchcraft not approach me,
130 May your words not reach me—

131 By the command of Ea, Šamaš, and Marduk, and the princess [Bēlet]-ilī.

Fire and water are completing their tasks, and the speaker states that he has gone back to Ea and Asalluḫi, now that Girra has completed the task assigned to fire, in order to make sure that any spark of life and malicious impulse left in the witches are extinguished and that they are completely deprived of life and power. In the last part of the incantation (125–130), these defeated witches, who have now been turned into nefarious ghosts, are then forbidden to approach the settled community and the person of the speaker.

It is of interest to note the importance accorded to Ea and Asalluḫi in the short version, for in the long one they have been pushed to the side by the emphasis placed there on other gods. Here, in any case, Ea and Asalluḫi overshadow the judgment in the fullest sense of the word;[13] for just as they initiated it by sending the victim to Girra (cf., e.g., Maqlû III 58–60, IV 1–12), so, too, do they themselves carry out the final stages of its execution.

Incantation Eight. *Ezzētunu šamrātunu*, "Raging, furious are you" (V 132–141).

Water is poured on the glowing coals. The speaker addresses the witches as if they were demonic or ghostlike.

132 Raging, furious, strong, cruel,
133 Overbearing, tough, hos[tile], wicked are you!
134 Who but Ea can calm you?
135 Who but Asalluḫi can soothe you?
136 May Ea calm you,
137 May Asalluḫi soothe you.
138 My mouth is water, your mouth is fire:
139 May my mouth extinguish your mouth,
140 May the spell of my mouth extinguish the spell of your mouth,
141 May the plots of my heart extinguish the plots of your heart!

The seventh and eighth incantations center on the final divesting of any shreds of human form that the witches still retain and the squelching of their remaining life force. The witches are pacified and become harmless ghosts,

13. For Ea as a god who guarantees judgements, see Thorkild Jacobsen "The Good Life," *Before Philosophy: The Intellectual Adventure of Ancient Man*, ed. Henri Frankfort et al. (Penguin: Middlesex, 1949), 222, and idem, *The Treasures of Darkness: A History of Mesopotamian Religion* (Yale University Press: New Haven, 1976), 112.

their evil power quenched by the power of water, Ea and Asalluḫi. The witch has been transformed into a noncorporeal being.

SECTION FOUR

This last section centers on the disposal of the witches' remains and the permanent expulsion of their ghosts.

Incantation Nine. *Šadû liktumkunūši*, "May the mountain cover you" (V 149–157).

A mountain stone is set atop (the censer which had previously been placed on) the opening of the brazier containing the charred and sodden remains of the figurines. The speaker here expresses the wish that the mountain confine and pulverize the witches, whose separation from the living is herewith demanded:

149 May the mountain cover you,
150 May the mountain hold you back,
151 May the mountain pacify you,
152 May the mountain hide you,
153 May the mountain enshroud you,
154 May the mountain turn you back,
155 May the mountain cover you over,
156 May a strong mountain fall upon you.
157 From my body you shall indeed be separated!

Present in the ritual in the form of a mountain stone, the mountain signifies some form of the world of the dead and may even be reminiscent of the cosmic Ekur. In any case, it here suggests a burial mound heaped on dead enemies in the open country, rocks piled over bodies or graves.

Incantation Ten. *Isâ isâ*, "Be off, be off" (V 158–175).

In this, the last incantation of the early version, the speaker commands the witches' ghosts to depart and adjures them never to return:

158 Be off, be off, begone, begone,
159 Depart, depart, flee, flee,
160 Go off, go away, be off, and begone!
161 May your wickedness like smoke rise ever heavenward!
162 From my body be off,
163 From my body begone,

164 From my body depart,
165 From my body flee,
166 From my body go off,
167 From my body go away!
168 To my body turn back not,
169 To my body approach not,
170 To my body reach not!
171 By the life of Šamaš, the honorable, be adjured,
172 By the life of Ea, lord of the underground springs, be [adju]red,
173 By the life of Asalluḫi, the magus of the gods, be adjured,
174 By the life of Girra, your executioner, be adjured!
175 From my body you shall indeed be separated!

The ban is imposed by the authority of the very gods who had previously participated in the ritual: Šamaš, the judge, Ea, lord of the deep, Asalluḫi, the magus of the gods, and Girra, the executioner. The remains of the witches are then cast out through the gate, and magical drawings are made around the entrances. Thus, the witches are separated from the human community and condemned to exist beyond the pale.

Here the short version ends. The ceremony is designed both to destroy the witch and her witchcraft and to protect the victim. Building upon the basic ritual of burning, drowning, and burial, the ceremony has taken up and integrated the additional themes of destruction and release of witchcraft as well as protection against future witchcraft attacks and the turning back of such attacks against the witch.

Standard Long Version

Resuming our study of the standard long version of Maqlû, we immediately note that the ceremony has been significantly expanded and changed into a nighttime ceremony. The main activities of the ceremony are the recitation of incantations and the performance of such rites as burning of figurines, fumigation, salving, washing, disposal, and protection against future attack. Each of the three divisions of the long version centers on a different set of rites: division one (Tablets I–V // Ritual Tablet 1–95) centers on burning and dousing figurines of the witch; division two (Tablets VI–VII 54 // Ritual Tablet 96–137) centers on fumigation, protection of the patient's house, and massaging the patient; division three (VII 55–VIII // Ritual Tablet 138–179) centers on washing the patient over representations of the witch. The incantations of each division have common themes; they thus develop a set of ideas that parallel or derive from the rites of the division, thereby reiterating the central ideas and ritual activities of the division. The bulk of the material of each incantation division is set out in blocks of "similar" incantations, each block reiterating a theme linked to a standard ritual act, and these blocks in turn follow one another in accordance with standard ritual patterns. The work as a whole has introductory, connecting, and concluding sections, as do the individual divisions. Thus, the work has both a ritual and conceptual structure as well as a narrative progression that impart a coherence and a distinctive character and tone to the ceremony.

Having followed the short version, let us now sample the material of the standard version by reviewing several of the more characteristic and important incantations of each of the three ceremonial divisions (excepting those already presented as part of the short version).

The **first division** opens with the patient's invocation of the gods of the cosmos—that is, the gods or powers of the night sky, of the netherworld, and of nature. In this new introduction (I 1–72), the patient asks these gods to assist him in his struggle against the witch. In line with its new ceremonial context, this section begins with the justly famous address to the Gods of the Night, Tablet I 1–36.

1 I call upon you, Gods of the Night,
2 With you I call upon Night, the veiled bride,
3 I call upon Twilight, Midnight, and Dawn.
4 Because a witch has bewitched me,
5 A deceitful woman has accused me,
6 (Because) she has (thereby) caused my god and goddess to be estranged from me
7 (And) I have become sickening in the sight of anyone who beholds me
8 (And consequently) I am unable to rest day or night,
9 (Because) a gag that is continually filling my mouth
10 Has kept food distant from my mouth
11 (And) has diminished the water which passes through my drinking organ,
12 (Because) my song of joy has become wailing and my rejoicing mourning—
13 Stand by me, O great gods, and give heed to my suit,
14 Judge my case and grant me an (oracular) decision!
15 I have made a figurine of my warlock and witch,
16 Of my sorcerer and the woman who instigates sorcery against me,
17 I set (it) at your feet and am now pleading my case:

18 Because she has performed evil against me and has constantly conjured up baseless charges against me,
19 May she die, but I live.
20 May her witchcraft, her spittle, her enchainment be released.
21 May the tamarisk that is copious of crown clear me,
22 May the date palm that withstands all winds release me,
23 May the soapwort that fills the earth cleanse me,
24 May the cone that is full of seeds release me.
25 In your presence I have (now) become pure like grass,
26 Clean and innocent like nard.
27 Her spell being that of an evil witch,
28 Her word has been turned back into her mouth and her tongue constricted.
29 On a(c)count of her witchcraft, may the Gods of the Night strike her,
30 May the three Watches of the Night release her evil spell.
31 Her mouth be tallow, her tongue be salt:
32 May that which uttered an evil word against me drip ever away like tallow,
33 May that which performed witchcraft against me dissolve like salt.
34 Her bonds are broken, her deeds nullified;
35 All of her words fill the steppe—
36 By the command pronounced by the Gods of the Night.

This opening incantation draws together magical and legal imagery; it is an indictment of the witches.[14] The incantation is a speech that accompanies a ritual act and gives expression to a dynamic situation; the text thus reflects the changes in state undergone by the patient and the witches from the beginning of the incantation to its end.

The incantation is in the form of a first person speech made by the patient, who invokes heavenly powers of the night, the gods of Anu (1–3). He first presents his plaint in the form of a description of the acts that the witch performed against him and of his resultant state (4–12). These facts clearly establish that he has suffered injuries at the hand of the witch and therefore that he has a right to a court hearing. Consequently, he asks the gods to take up his case (13–14). Then, having caused the accused witches to be present at the judgment in the form of figurines (15–17), he asks that they be punished because they have sought (perhaps by means of accusations) unmo-

14. In its present context as the opening incantation of Maqlû, I 1–36 is to be understood as a preliminary hearing, though an earlier form of the incantation might well have represented a stand-alone hearing.

tivated evil against him, and that their bewitchment be released (18–20). He asks to be cleared (of bewitchment and any guilt imputed to him) by means of a standard set of plants—these plants usually serve to purify, but here they function also as a form of juridical ordeal (21–24). Having proved his innocence and having been cleared (25–26), he rightfully asserts that since the witch's utterance belongs to an evil witch, her accusation has been refuted (27–28). He is now able to request that the Gods of the Night bring the witch to justice and indict her and that the Night Watches release the witchcraft (29–30). By means of magical associations and acts, the patient now destroys the organs of speech of the witch (31–33). Finally, he asserts that the witch's actions and accusations have been wholly nullified (34–35) by the Gods of the Night (36).[15]

Subsequent to the introduction (I 1–72), the ceremony turns to its main concern—the judgment, execution, and expulsion of the witch. The witch is destroyed by fire (I 73–IV) and water (V 98–141 // RT 83′–85′); these symbolic acts of burning and drowning are performed ritually on figurines representing the witch.

In our examination of the short version, we have already examined the primary statement of judgment (I 73–121) and witnessed the beginning of the burning process (I 135–143); so we may turn directly to the continuation of the burning theme in Tablet II. Incantations against the witch in Maqlû (as incantations generally in the Mesopotamian tradition) are based on various themes and take various forms. One of the most striking and important themes is the destruction of the witch. In keeping with a ritual in which burning is a repetitive and central act, the destruction of this evil enemy achieves concrete form in various incantation types that center upon burning. The motif of burning the witch, in various permutations and elaborations, occurs in almost every incantation in I 73–IV 151. Not surprisingly, the fire-god Girra is a primary actor in this division; many of the incantations invoke him and are recited alongside the ritual burning of images of the witch. A well-known type is the address to the fire god (Girra) in which he is described and called upon to destroy the witch (see especially II 19–149). Here, destruction

15. For an analysis of the opening incantation of Maqlû (I 1–36), see Tzvi Abusch, *Babylonian Witchcraft Literature: Case Studies*, BJS 132 (Atlanta: Scholars Press, 1987), x–xii and 85–147, and "Divine Judges on Earth and in Heaven," in *The Divine Courtroom*, ed. Shalom Holtz and Ari Mermelstein, BibInt 132 (Leiden: Brill, 2014), 6–24. For a classroom version, see my "An Incantation-Prayer: Gods of the Night 1" (ch. 7) in *Reading Akkadian Prayers and Hymns: An Introduction*, ed. Alan Lenzi, ANEM 3 (Atlanta: Society of Biblical Literature, 2011), 157–67. See also Daniel Schwemer, "Empowering the Patient: The Opening Section of the Ritual *Maqlû*," in *Pax Hethitica: Studies on the Hittites and Their Neighbours in Honor of Itamar Singer*, ed. Yoram Cohen, Amir Gilan, and Jared L. Miller (Wiesbaden: Harrassowitz, 2010), 311–39.

by fire has been joined to the motifs of judgment and execution. The incantation "O powerful Girra, wild (fire-)storm" (II 127–134) and the first part of the incantation "O blazing Girra, warlike son of Anu" (II 105–125) are short and simple addresses that exemplify this type of address:

127 O powerful Girra, wild (fire-)storm,
128 You give correct decisions to gods and rulers,
129 You provide justice for the oppressed man and woman.
130 Stand by me in my judgment like Šamaš, the warrior,
131 Judge my case, render my verdict.
132 Burn my warlock and my witch,
133 Devour my enemies, consume the ones who would do evil to me!
134 Let your raging (fire-)storm vanquish them.

105 O blazing Girra, warlike son of Anu,
106 Indeed you are the fiercest among your brothers.
107 As you decide lawsuits in the stead of Sîn and Šamaš,
108 Judge my case, hand down my verdict.
109 Burn my warlock and my witch,
110 Girra, burn my warlock and my witch,
111 Girra, scorch my warlock and my witch,
112 Girra, burn them,
113 Girra, scorch them,
114 Girra, vanquish them,
115 Girra, consume them,
116 Girra, confound them!

A more literary version of the request to consume the evildoer is found in the incantation "O blazing Girra, firstborn of Anu" (II 77–103).

77 O blazing Girra, scion of Anu,
78 It is you who renders judgment, the secret speech,
79 You illumine darkness,
80 You set straight confusion and disorder,
81 You grant decisions for the great gods,
82 Were it not for you, no god would deliver a verdict,
83 It is you who gives instruction and direction.
84 You alone speedily capture the evildoer
85 (And) speedily overcome the wicked and the enemy.

86 I, [so-and-so, the son of so-and]-so, whose god is so-and-so, whose goddess is so-and-so—
87 I have been attacked by witchcraft, and so I enter into your presence,
88 I have been made detestable in the presence of god, king, and lord, and so I come toward you,
89 I have been made sickening in the [sight of anyone who b]eholds me, and so I bow down before you.
90 Grand Girra, pure god,
91 Now in the presence of your great godhead
92 Two bronze figurines of the warlock and the witch I have fashioned with your power.
93 In your presence I cross them, and to you I hand them over.
94 May they die, but I live,
95 May they be bound, but I be acquitted,
96 May they come to an end, but I increase,
97 May they weaken, but I become strong.
98 O splendid Girra, preeminent one of the gods,
99 Vanquisher of the wicked and the enemy, vanquish them so I not be wronged.
100 May I, your servant, live and be well so that I may stand before you (and declare):
101 You alone are my god, you alone are my lord,
102 You alone are my judge, you alone are my aid,
103 You alone are my avenger!

The last several lines of this incantation are particularly interesting. The declaration "You alone are my god, you alone are my lord, you alone are my judge, you alone are my aid, you alone are my avenger!" at the very end of this incantation (II 101–103) is the equivalent of the promise of future praise found in many prayers. This statement focuses upon a mutual relationship between man and god. It expresses the speaker's gratitude should he be rescued by the god in the latter's capacity of god, lord, judge, help, champion. The supplicant hopes that the god will champion him, thereby either fulfilling the terms of an already existing relationship or creating a new one. In return, the human recipient will assert his thanks and recognition in the form of a statement of praise, allegiance, and devotion. Given this context, as well as other formulations, the speaker's wish to stand before the god, should the god rescue him (II 100), signifies a pledge of loyalty and a commitment to service.

Having examined the witch's execution by fire, we may move directly to the middle of Tablet V, where the smoldering remains of the effigies are doused with water (V 98–141 // RT 83′–85′). The two incantations V 112–131 and 132–141[16] make it clear that the evil beings are thereby deprived of the power to perform evil. Figurines of the witch are then trampled; thus concrete expression is given to the defeat of the enemy and the attainment of victory (V 142–144 // RT 86′):

142 I trample down my foe, I destroy my evildoer,
143 I slaughter my opponent, I repeatedly annihilate my pursuer
144 In the presence of the warrior Nuska.

The witches (that is, their remains) are again burned (V 145–148 // RT 87′):

145 Melt, dissolve, and drip ever away!
146 May your smoke rise ever heavenward,
147 May the Sun extinguish your embers,
148 May Ea's son, the exorcist, cut off the terror that emanates from you.

And in "May the mountain cover you" (V 149–157 // RT 88′–89′) the wish is expressed that a mountain confine and pulverize them. Finally, in "Be off, be off" (V 158–175// RT 90′–91′), the last incantation of Tablet V, the dead witches are expelled and commanded never to return. (For V 149–157 and 158–175, see above, the discussion of the short version.)

In the **second division**, fumigation is performed to counteract and disperse attacks of witchcraft. Alongside fumigation, objects are set up for the protection of the patient, and he himself is massaged with oil.

Prominent among the fumigants are the *kukru*-plant, sulphur, and salt. Examples of addresses to these fumigants are the incantations VI 25–33 (*kukru*), 78–84 (Sulphur), and 119″–126″ (Salt).

KUKRU

24 [*kukru*, *kukru*],
25 [*kukru,* dweller in the pure ho]l[y mountains],
26 [the small *terhu*-vessels of the] *en*-prieste[sses],
27 [the small cones o]f the *qadištu*-votaries:
28 [Come hither] and [b]reak the [strong] bond of my warlock and witch,
29 [Turn] her [wit]chcraft into a storm, her words into a wind.

16. For these two incantations, see the discussion of the short version, above.

30 [May] her witchcraft [be] blown away like chaff,
31 [May it bla]cken her like ashes,
32 May her witchcraft crumble l[ike the plast]er of a wall,
33 May m[y witch's] anger be undone.

SULPHUR

78 Sulphur, Sulphur, Sulphur, daughter of River, Sulphur, daughter-in-law of River,
79 Whose witches are seven and seven, whose enemies are seven and seven.
80 They performed sorcery against her, but she is not ensorcelled,
81 They bewit[ched her], but she is not bewitched.
82 Who is it that can perform witchcraft against Sulphur?
83 May Sulphur rele[ase] the sorcery that the seven and seven have performed against me.
84 May Sulphur [...] ... release the sorcery that the seven and seven have performed against me so that I may live.

SALT

119″ You, Salt, who were created in a pure place,
120″ For food of the great gods did Enlil destine you.
121″ Without you a meal would not be set out in Ekur,
122″ Without you god, king, noble, and prince would not smell incense.
123″ I am so-and-so, the son of so-and-so, whom witchcraft holds captive,
124″ Whom machinations hold in (the form of a skin) disease.
125″ Release my witchcraft, O Salt, dispel my spittle,
126″ Take over from me the machinations, then will I constantly praise you as (I praise) my creator god.

An example of an incantation to accompany a ritual involving both a fumigant (asafetida) and an object set up for protection (twine around the bed) is VI 127″–134″. This incantation follows immediately upon the completion of the address to salt and introduces a group of four incantations that are variations of each other. (I shall discuss this group below, as an example of the history of incantations).

127″ Ha! my witch, my inseminatrix,
128″ Who has lit a fire (against me) at a distance of one league,

129″ Who has repeatedly sent her messengers towards me at a distance of two leagues.
130″ I know and have gained full confidence (in my abilities to hold you off).
131″ I have installed a watch on my roof, a protective emblem at my gate.
132″ I have surrounded my bed with (colored) twine,
133″ I have scattered asafœtida (upon a censer) at the head of my bed—
134″ Asafoetida is especially strong, it will cause all your witchcraft to wither.

The last three incantations of the second division (VII 22–28, 29–46, and 47–54) focus on the healing and protection of the patient by the application of oil to his body. This is developed most clearly in VII 29–46, a well-known *Kultmittelbeschwörung* that was imported into Maqlû.

29 Pure oil, clear oil, bright oil,
30 Oil that purifies the body of the gods,
31 Oil that soothes the sinews of mankind,
32 Oil of the incantation of Ea, oil of the incantation of Asalluḫi.
33 I coat you with soothing oil
34 That Ea granted for soothing,
35 I anoint you with the oil of healing,
36 I cast upon you the incantation of Ea, lord of Eridu, Ninšiku.
37 I expel Asakku, *aḫḫāzu*-jaundice, chills of your body,
38 I remove dumbness, torpor, and misery of your body,
39 I soothe the sick sinews of your limbs.
40 By the command of Ea, king of the apsû,
41 By the spell of Ea, by the incantation of Asalluḫi,
42 By the soft bandage of Gula,
43 By the soothing hands of Nintinugga
44 And Ningirima, mistress of incantation.
45 On so-and-so, Ea cast the incantation of the word of healing
46 That the seven sages of Eridu soothe his body.

This incantation is a good example of a *Kultmittelbeschwörung*, that is, an incantation addressed to objects used in rituals in order to enhance and elicit their qualities. What is striking about this incantation is its development from a typical *Kultmittelbeschwörung* into a composition in which there is an overlapping of an address to enhance and activate material and an address that emphasizes the independent force of speech.[17]

We are now approaching the end of the night and of the second division. But before taking leave of them, we should take note of the fact that both the introductory and the concluding incantations of the second division (VI 1–15 and VII 47–54) begin with the words "Enlil is my head" and that in both the speaker identifies himself with several nocturnal heavenly bodies. The introductory incantation (VI 1–15) reads:

1 Enlil is my head, my face is *ū*[*mu*],
2 Uraš, the perfect god, is the pupil(s) of my face,[18]
3 My neck is the necklace of Gula,
4 My arms are the crook of Sin (and) Amurru,
5 My fingers are tamarisk, the divine bone—
6 They shall not allow spittle to reach my body,
7 Lugaledinna and Latarak are my chest,
8 My knees are Muhra, my pacin[g] feet are the whole (heavenly) flock.
9 Whoever you are, O evil god whom the warlock and witch have sent here to kill me:
10 Even if you are awake, do not come here,
11 Even if you are asleep, do not rise up (to come) here.
12 May your words be (bad) apples, before god and king may [they cr]umble.
13 At my doorway, I have set Lugalirra, the stro[ng(est)] god, and the vizier of the gods, Papsukkal.
14 "Strik[e the cheek of] my warlock and witch,
15 Tu[rn her word back] into her mouth."

The concluding incantation (VII 47–54) reads:

47 Enlil is my head, Sirius is my form,

17. For a discussion of *Kultmittelbeschwörungen* see Tzvi Abusch, "Blessing and Praise in Ancient Mesopotamian Incantations," in *Literatur, Politik und Recht in Mesopotamien: Festschrift für Claus Wilcke,* ed. Walther Sallaberger, Konrad Volk, and Annette Zgoll (Wiesbaden: Harrassowitz, 2003), 1–14; for a detailed analysis of the incantation *šamnu ellu*, see ibid., 4–6, and part 2 of my "Notes on the History of Composition of Two Incantations," in *From Source to History: Studies on Ancient Near Eastern Worlds and Beyond Dedicated to Giovanni Battista Lanfranchi on the Occasion of His 65th Birthday on June 23, 2014*, AOAT 412, ed. Salvatore Gaspa et al. (Münster: Ugarit-Verlag, 2014), 1–10.

18. Emendation yields: Uraš and Gula are the pupils of my eyes.

48 My forehead is the rising sun,
49 My arms are the Crook[19] at the gate of Marduk,
50 My ears are Bull,[20] my feet are the *laḫmu*-monsters trampling on the flesh of *laḫmu*-monsters.
51 You, O great gods, shine forth in the sky <like> Šamaš.
52 As tin(?) (and) ir[on](?), sorcery, rebellion, an evil word,
52a Witchcraft, spittle, enchainment, [evil] mach[inations]
53 Cannot approach you, cannot draw near to you,
54 So sorcery, rebellion, an evil word,
54a Wi[tchcraft, spittle, enchainment], evil [machina]tions
54 (cont.) shall not approach me, shall not draw near to me myself.

The speaker identifies with the gods of the night sky, the stars and planets, the powers that were present or visible in the night sky. This identification has several purposes. Most of all, it allows the ritual actor to take on the quality of wakefulness or sleeplessness associated with the heavenly bodies of the night. By not sleeping he is able to avoid attacks by the witch and by witchcraft that come in the form of evil dreams. The witch—especially the demonic witch—has the power to send a dream or such associated forms as clouds, and she is readily thought of as a wind (see, e.g., V 76–82; cf. VII 1–7). Perhaps the witch appears in the dream; perhaps a dead human that the witch has enlisted appears in it. Evil dreams, themselves demonic powers or beings, assume increased importance in our text during the course of its development. But not only dreams, also sleep—which allows one to dream—becomes a matter of concern. For sleep may lead to or turn into death. These evils can be warded off—even prevented—by assuming the quality of wakefulness of the gods of the night.

With the coming of dawn, a new day has arrived; the orientation of the ceremony now changes from nighttime to morning. Washing is the primary rite in the **third division**, the concluding division of the ceremony. The ritual now centers on water rather than fire, as in the earlier divisions. The patient welcomes the day and repeatedly washes himself, often over representations of the witch (frequently made of flour). Of course, washing is a typical morning activity, but here it serves the dual purposes of causing the witchcraft to return to and seize the witch (reversion) and of cleansing the patient of evil.

The themes of retribution and reversion are especially evident in the very first incantation in the last division, "Whoever you are, O witch, who

19. That is, the constellation Auriga.
20. Perhaps *lē'û* here is a play on *is lê* = α Tauri + Hyades.

has made my figurine" (VII 55–79). This incantation describes the process quite clearly, for it presents in detail the witch's actions and the parallel actions of her victim and describes how he rinses off her evil witchcraft and makes it come back upon her.

55 Whoever you are, O witch, who has made a figurine of me—
56 Who has looked at my form and created my image,
57 Who has seen my bearing and given rich detail to my physical build,
58 Who has comprehended my appearance
59 And reproduced my features,
60 Who has bound my body,
61 Who has tied my limbs together, who has twisted my sinews.
62 As for me, Ea, exorcist of the gods, has sent me,
63 And before Šamaš I draw your likeness—
64 I look at your form and create your image, I see your bearing
65 And give rich detail to your physical build, I comprehend your appearance
66 And reproduce your features with pure flour,
67 I bind your body, I tie your limbs together,
68 I twist your sinews.
69 The sorcery that you have performed against me I perform against you,
70 The (ominous) encounter that you have caused me to encounter I make you take over,
71 The vengeance that you have wreaked on me I wreak back on you.
72 Your witchcraft, your spittle, your enchainment, your evil manipulations,
73 Your hostile machinations,
74 Your messages of evil,
75 Your love (-magic), your hate(-magic), your perversion of justice, your *Zikurrudâ*-magic,
76 Your muteness, (and) your madness—may they attend to you (rather than to me).
77 With the water of my bo[dy] and the washing of my hands may it rinse off
78 And come upon your head and body so that I may live.
79 May a (female) substitute stand in for me, may one who encounters (me) take (it) over from me,
79a I have encountered an ominous encounter; may they take (it) over from me.

In this incantation the victim addresses a witch. He first describes how the witch had formed a detailed replica of his person and has twisted and bound its limbs. He then states that he has gone before Šamaš at the behest of Ea, drawn a flour representation of the witch, and created a form of the witch by performing the same actions of formation that she had performed against him. He then states that he has caused her to experience the witchcraft that she had performed against him. He expresses the wish that her acts of witchcraft stand ready to overwhelm her and then asks that it—the evil—be rinsed off his body with his wash water and flow onto the person of his addressee. He concludes with the wish that a substitute stand in for him and receive the evil consequences of an unlucky encounter.

In its present form, the incantation is intended to counter evil signs that were sent by the witch and encountered by her victim. But it was originally not a standard witchcraft incantation. It is rooted in and has features of the *namburbi* type (an incantation type intended to counter all sorts of evil signs) and is the result of earlier transformations of a text in *namburbi* garb into one that is more like a witchcraft text. The incantation originally emphasized the use of a substitute as the recipient of the evil, but eventually conflated the witch and the substitute, thereby also punishing the witch and causing her to suffer the harm that she had initiated against her victim.

The cleansing from evil itself comes to expression very clearly in the incantation "At dawn my hands are washed" (VII 162–169). This incantation is recited at the coming of morning.

162 At dawn my hands are washed.
163 May a propitious beginning begin for me,
164 May happiness (and) good health ever accompany me,
165 Whatsoever I seek, may I attain it,
166 May [the dre]am I dreamt be made favorable for me,
167 May anything evil, anything unfavorable,
168 The spittle of warlock and witch, [not rea]ch me, not touch me—
169 [By] the command of Ea, Šamaš, Marduk, and the princess Bēlet-ilī.

Thus, the patient cleanses himself from evil, specifically the evil of witchcraft augured by, or incorporated in, dreams of the night.

Finally, representations of the witch in an edible form are thrown to dogs. Protective amulets are then prepared, and concluding rites are performed.

History of Incantations

I have alluded more than once to the fact that some of the incantations of the standard version have undergone change. We know of this both from the existence of variant forms of an incantation and through critical internal analysis. I need hardly emphasize how important knowledge of the history and development of a text is for its understanding. There are many examples of literary and textual adaptation, revision, and development in Mesopotamian incantations generally, and in the incantations of Maqlû specifically. But I should preface my examination of several Maqlû incantations with a preliminary remark.

While many of the incantations in Maqlû were composed specifically for inclusion in it, others were taken over from different, often simpler, magical ceremonies. Some of these incantations already dealt with witchcraft, but others were originally composed for purposes other than combating witchcraft and were only afterwards adapted for that use. Their incorporation into Maqlû, a ceremony against witchcraft, involved a change that adapted the incantation to its new function; of the texts quoted thus far, I would cite I 135–143, VII 29–46, and VII 162–169 as examples of this. But it is not only the adaptation of a text for a new purpose that resulted in change. Revision of an incantation and/or incorporation therein of new materials could also result from other factors, such as: the need to adapt an incantation to a change in ritual usage; the integration of a simple text into a new, more complex, framework; the adaptation of a text to new religious beliefs or cognitive/intellectual norms.

Here I will discuss in some detail three examples from Maqlû for which there is some manuscript evidence of change. I will proceed from the example that requires the least amount of analysis and interpretation to the one that requires the most.

1) The incantations found in the fragmentary Nimrud tablet CTN 4, nos. 92 + 145 + 147 are—with one possible exception—variants of incantations found in Maqlû V–VIII.[21] CTN 4, 92 + seems to reflect some form of proto- or deviant version of canonical Maqlû.[22] The three Nimrud incantations,

21. For an edition and discussion of this tablet, see Schwemer, *Abwehrzauber und Behexung*, 44–53.

22. Cf. Schwemer's comment that, "der Text von einem jungen *āšipu* als Teil seiner Ausbildung geschrieben wurde. Dabei kopierte er nicht einfach eine kanonische Maqlû-Tafel, sondern schrieb—wohl aus dem Gedächtnis—Maqlû-Beschwörungen und notierte dazu ihre Verwendung in Stichworten.... Insgesamt sind die Varienten aber zu zahlreich, um allein als Erinnerungsschwächen erklärt werden zu können. Vielmehr wird man den Text als

col. iii lines 19′–27′, 35′–46′, and 48′–56′,[23] are clear variants or parallels to the four incantations Maqlû VI 127″–134″, 135″–142″, 143″–151″, and 152″–158″ (the ending of this last incantation is still missing).[24]

Col. iii lines 19′–27′ makes use of a variant of the opening lines in Maqlû VI 127″–134″ and VI 135″–142″, but contains the ritual of Maqlû VI 143″–151″.

Col. iii lines 35′–46′ makes use of a variant of the opening lines in Maqlû VI 143″–151″ and VI 152″–158″, but contains in combination the first ritual of VI 127″–134″ (=VI 132″) and the ritual of VI 135″–142″.

Col. iii lines 48′–56′ makes use of a variant of the opening lines in Maqlû VI 143″–151″ and VI 152″–158″, but contains the second ritual of VI 127″–134″ (=VI 133″–134″).[25]

The texts read:

CTN 4, nos. 92 + 145 + 147, iii[26]		**Maqlû VI**	
19′	ÉN *attī kaššāptī ša ana ištēn bēri*	127″	ÉN *ē kaššāptiya lū raḫḫātiya*
	ippuḫu išāta	128″	*ša ana ištēn bēri ippuḫu išāta*
20′	*ana šinā bērī ištappara mār šipriša*	129″	*ana šinā bērī ištappara mār šipriša*
21′	*anāku īdēma attakal nikla*	130″	*anāku īdēma attakil takālu*
22′	*ina ūriya maṣṣartu ina bābiya azaqqap kidinnu*	131″	*ina ūriya maṣṣartu ina bābiya azzaqap kidinnu*[27]
23′	*ina imitti bābiya u šumēl bābiya*	148″	*ina imitti bābiya u šumēl bābiya*
24′	*ultezziz ilī ša maṣṣarte*	149″	*ultezziz* ^{d}*Lugalirra u* ^{d}*Meslamtaea*
25′	^{d}*Lugalirra u* ^{d}*Meslamtaea nāsiḫ libbi*	150″	*ilū ša maṣṣarte nāsiḫ libbi*
26′	*muštēmidū kalīte*		*muštēmidū kalâti*
27′	*kaššāpta lidūkūma anāku lubluṭ*	151″	*kaššāpta lidūkūma anāku lubluṭ*

Zeugnis einer gewissen Variabilität der in *Maqlû* verwendeten Beschwörungen ausserhalb ihres serialisierten Kontextes werten müssen" (*Abwehrzauber und Behexung*, 52–53).

23. The three incantations are composed of the joining pieces: no. 145 iii 19′ff, no. 147 iii side A (=rev.) 1′ff, and no. 92 iii 1′ff; more precisely, 145 iii 19′ff + 147 side A 1′ff; 147 side A 9′ + 92 iii 1′ff.

24. It is possible that col. iii lines 8′–18′, the preceding incantation in CTN 4, 92+, should be included as the fourth parallel to this group of four Maqlû incantations because of its proximity to the other three and because its opening lines (8′–9′) seem, like those of the following incantation (iii 19′–27′), to contain opening lines parallel to Maqlû VI 127″–129″ // VI 135″–137″. However, the later lines in col. iii lines 8′–18′ are similar to lines in Maqlû VII 153–61 and do not seem to resume the ritual of any of the four incantations in Maqlû VI.

Werner R. Mayer in his review of CTN 4 in *Or*NS 67 (1998): 269 has already noted the Maqlû parallels for the incantations found on CTN 4, no. 92.

25. The three CTN 4, 92+ incantations and the four Maqlû incantations all have the same middle lines (= Maqlû VI 130″–131″, etc.).

26. For ease of comparison, I have eliminated all square brackets in both texts.

35′	ÉN *ē kaššāptiya eliyānītu*	143″	ÉN *ē kaššāptiya elēnītiya*
36′	*ša tattallaku kal mātāti*	144″	*ša tattanallakī kal mātāti*
37′	*tartappuda kal šadâni*	145″	*tattanablakkatī kal šadâni*
38′	*anāku īdēma attakal nikla*	146″	*anāku īdēma attakil*[28] *takālu*
39′	*ina ūriya maṣṣartu*	147″	*ina ūriya maṣṣartu*
40′	*ina bābiya azaqqap kidinnu*		*ina bābiya azzaqap kidinnu*[29]
41′	*eršī altami ulinna*	132″	*eršī altame ulinna*
42′	*ina rēš eršiya aštakan*	140″	*ina rēš eršiya aštakan*
43′	... *ša'errī*		*šinšeret ša'errī*
44′	*kurummat eṭemmi*? <*riḫīt*>	141″	*kurummat eṭemmi riḫīt* ^{d}*Girra*
	^{d}*Girra qāmê*		*qāmîki*
45′	^{d}*Nisaba rabīti*	142″	*u* ^{d}*Nisaba šarratu*
46′	*mukassisat ubānātīša*		*mugaṣṣiṣat ubānātīki*

48′	ÉN *ē kaššāptī eliyānītu*	143″	ÉN *ē kaššāptiya elēnītiya*
49′	*ša tattallaku kal mātāti*	144″	*ša tattanallakī kal mātāti*
50′	*tartappuda kal šadâni*	145″	*tattanablakkatī kal šadâni*
51′	*anāku īdēma attakal nikla*	146″	*anāku īdēma attakil*[30] *takālu*
52′	*ina ūriya maṣṣartu*	147″	*ina ūriya maṣṣartu*
53′	*ina bābiya azaqqap kidinnu*		*ina bābiya azzaqap kidinnu*[31]
54′	*ina rēš eršiya assaraq nuḫurta*	133″	*ina rēš eršiya assaraq nuḫurta*
55′	*dannat nuḫurtumma*	134″	*dannat nuḫurtumma*
56′	*unaḫḫara kal kišpīša*		*unaḫḫara kal kišpīki*

The comparison indicates the existence of a textual fluidity in the text of this group of incantations. It is difficult to know whether the four found in the standard version of Maqlû or the parallels from Nimrud are the more original, but I should guess that the Nimrud tablet contains an earlier or more original version of these incantations. This conclusion is suggested by the grammatical forms in CTN 4, 92+ iii 37 and 50. These lines have *tartappuda* (*t*[*a*]*r-tap-pu-da*) instead of *tattanablakkatī* (*ta-at-ta-nab-lak-ka-ti*) in Maqlû (VI 145 and 154). *tartappuda* here is a Gtn preterite of *rapādu*, while the parallel in Maqlû is a Ntn durative. The openings of the first two incantations in the Maqlû sequence (Maqlû VI 128–129 and 136–137)—as well as in the parallel to these two in CTN 4, 92+ iii 19′–20′—have the preterites *ip-pu-ḫu* (G preterite of *napāḫu*)[32] and *iš-tap-pa-ra* (Gtn preterite of *šapāru*). These

27. CTN 4, 92+ iii 19′–22′ duplicates both Maqlû VI 127″–131″ and 135″–139″.
28. Var.: ⸢*attakal*⸣.
29. CTN 4, 92+ iii 35′–40′ duplicates both Maqlû VI 143″–147″ and 152″–156″.
30. Var.: ⸢*attakal*⸣.
31. CTN 4, 92+ iii 48′–53′ duplicates both Maqlû VI 143″–147″ and 152″–156″.
32. But note that the form in CTN 4, 92+ iii 19′ is not explicit because the word there is written logographically.

preterite forms suggest that the preterite forms of *rapādu* in CTN 4, 92+ iii 37′ and 50′ are the correct forms. Accordingly, we should expect preterite forms in all the opening lines of these incantations. But while we do find this expectation met in the Nimrud version, we do not find it met in Maqlû VI 144″–145″ and 153″–154″. The preterite forms of *rapādu* in CTN 4, 92+ iii 37′ and 50′ suggest that the Nimrud text contains the more original versions of these incantations.

2) For our second text we turn to the incantation *amsi qātīya* (Maqlû VII 114–140), which provides an excellent example of expansion and adaptation. In the Standard Version, this incantation reads:

114 I wash my hands, I cleanse my body
115 In the pure spring water that was formed in Eridu.
116 Anything evil, anything unfavorable
117 That is in my body, flesh, and sinews,
118 The evil of (i.e., portended by) evil, unfavorable dreams, signs, and portents,
119 The evil of defective, frightening, evil, unfavorable entrails
120 (observed) in the ritual act (of extispicy), in the killing of the she[ep], in the offering of the sacrifice, or in the exercise (var.: + of any sort) of divination,
121 That which I have looked at daily,
122 Have stepped on in the street, or have repeatedly seen in the outskirts,
123 An evil *šēdu*-spirit, an evil *utukku*-demon,
124 Illness, he[ad]ache, sleeplessness,
125 dumbness, torpor, misery, grief, losses, moaning,
126 (Cries of) woe (and) alas, depression,
127 Terror, fear, apprehension,
128 (The evil consequences of) a curse by the gods, an appeal to the gods, a complaint to the [gods, an o]ath by the god, the raising of hands, curse,
129 The evil(s) of witchcraft, spittle, enchainment, evil machinations of mankind—
130 With the water of my body and the washing of my hands
131 May it (the various evils) rinse off and come [up]on a figurine of a substitute,
132 May the figurine of the sub[stitute] bear my sin as a replacement,
133 May street and way undo my sins,
134 May a (female) substitute stand in for me, may one who encounters (me) take (it) over from me,

135 I have encountered an ominous encounter; may they take (it) over from me.
136 May the day bring well being, the month joy, the year its prosperity.
137 O Ea, Šamaš, and Marduk, help me so that
138 Witchcraft, spittle, enchainment,
139 Evil machinations of mankind be released,
140 And curse go forth from my body.

This version of *amsi qātīya* contains some twenty-seven lines. I would summarize it as follows: The speaker first states that he is washing himself in the pure water of Eridu. He then expresses the wish that all evils, which are enumerated in a list that culminates in a standard enumeration of witchcraft evils, be rinsed off his body and flow onto a figurine of a substitute, a *nigsagilâ*. The incantation ends with a series of wishes: that the street release his sin, that a substitute stand in for him and receive the evil consequences of an unlucky encounter, that the day, month, and year bring goodness, that Ea, Šamaš, and Marduk assist him, and finally, that the witchcraft be released and the *māmītu* take leave of his body.

There is an inner tension in the text created by the fact that whereas the list of evils (VII 118–129) suggests that the incantation was used against many different kinds of evil and had a universal character, the incantation, in actuality, was used to combat witchcraft. The text has a disjointed appearance and contains both secondary elaborations and alien motifs. A detailed internal analysis of the incantation would allow us to solve these problems and to reconstruct the development of this text from a simpler and shorter incantation. But such an analysis proves unnecessary because we actually find an earlier shorter version preserved in a Neo-Babylonian recension of Maqlû Tablet VII. That version reads:

[Incantation. I wash my hands, I clean]se my body
[In the pure spring water that] was formed [in Eridu].
May [everything evil, everything unfavorable that i]s [in] my [bo]dy, my flesh,
[and my sinews] rinse off with the water of my body
[and the washin]g of my hands
and come [upon your head and] upon your body.
[May a substitute s]tand in for me, may one who encounters (me) take (it) over from me,
[I have encountered an ominous encounter; may] they [t]ake (it) over from me.

In this version, the speaker begins by stating that he is washing himself in the pure water of Eridu; he then expresses the wish that unspecified evil (*mimma lemnu*)—not a list of evils—be rinsed off onto the person of an unspecified addressee, presumably the substitute mentioned in the last two lines.

This Neo-Babylonian Version is a form of text from which we would derive the long text found in the Standard Version. It contains a base text that could have served as the kernel for the much-expanded Standard text. The incantation was expanded by the insertion of a standard general list of evils of the *namburbi*-type. In addition, the witchcraft entry—"The evil(s) of witchcraft, spittle, enchainment, evil machinations of mankind"—that originally occurred much earlier in that list was moved to the end of the list. The concluding section presently found in the Neo-Babylonian Version of *attīmannu kaššāptu* (VII 55–79)—an ending associated primarily with the *namburbi*'s—was transferred to our incantation; and the original ending—"May a (female) substitute stand in for me, may one who encounters (me) take (it) over from me, I have encountered an ominous encounter; may they take (it) over from me"—was incorporated into the new ending.[33]

3) The third text that I have chosen is Maqlû I 73–121. You will recall that in the earlier short version this incantation opened with a call to Šamaš (*Šamaš annûtu ṣalmū ēpišiya).* When this portion of the ceremony was moved from morning to night, Nuska took over Šamaš's role in this incantation. Changes were introduced into the text as part of the process or dynamic of adaptation. Traces of these revisions are still visible and point to the direction of change. It is unfortunate that we possess only the first line of the earlier version and do not (yet) possess a verbatim version of this earlier incantation. Yet knowing that the incantation was once addressed to Šamaš allows us not only to resolve some of the difficulties in the extant standard version of the incantation but also to prove that the version addressed to Šamaš was the more original text.

Textual variants in the extant manuscripts support this reconstruction, but I limit my remarks here to a point of major confusion introduced into the main text by the changeover. This incantation belongs to a common type of incantation in which Šamaš is addressed in the capacity of judge and asked

33. For a detailed analysis of the two incantations and their versions and a reconstruction of the development and relationship of the two, see Tzvi Abusch, *Babylonian Witchcraft Literature*, 13–44, and "A Neo-Babylonian Recension of *Maqlû*: Some Observations on the Redaction of *Maqlû* Tablet VII and on the Development of Two of Its Incantations," in *Festschrift für Gernot Wilhelm anläßlich seines 65. Geburtstages am 28. Januar 2010*, ed. Jeanette C. Fincke (Dresden: Islet, 2010), 1–16.

to give a judgment. Once Šamaš has been asked to sentence the witch to death by fire, the plaintiff calls on the fire-god to carry out the execution; this fire god is usually Girra. In our incantation, however, the first part—lines 73–109—is addressed to Nuska who, having replaced Šamaš, now functions in his stead as a judge. The concluding part of the text (lines 110–121) is given throughout in second person form and calls upon the god addressed in the second person to function both as a fire executioner and a judge. Since this concluding part is introduced by an invocation to the fire-god Girra in the second person (line 110), it appears as if this part of the text is addressed only to Girra and that Girra is being asked to take over and to play both the role of judge and of executioner.

But what has happened to Nuska? There seems to be a complete confusion regarding the identity of the actual judge. Indeed, the text itself seems uncertain as to which of the two gods mentioned is in fact the judge and leaves the reader with the uncomfortable feeling that Nuska and Girra may perhaps be taking turns as judge; for whereas Nuska is treated as judge in the first part of the incantation (73–109), the second part (110–121) seems to be addressed only to Girra and to no other god, addressing him as if he were both judge and executioner. So while the judge is not Šamaš, neither is it clear which of the two fire-gods[34] is to be treated as the judge.[35]

Of course, when this incantation type follows its normal pattern and is addressed to Šamaš, there are no such difficulties because it is clear that Šamaš is the judge throughout the incantation and that Girra is invoked as the hypostatization of the sun's killing rays. Accordingly, we must posit the originality of the Šamaš version known from the short version used in the morning *Bīt rimki* ceremony in order to arrive at a reasonable explanation of the text and its history.

Originally, then, our incantation was addressed to Šamaš. It would have opened with an appeal to Šamaš in his capacity of judge, then turned to Girra with the request that he burn the witches (lines 110–112, 115–116), and finally ended with a request to Šamaš that the execution be carried out in accordance with his unalterable verdict. When, at a later stage, the ceremony was moved to nighttime and the text was adapted for a new ritual use, Šamaš was eliminated and Nuska was introduced in his place. Some further changes in the text were required and were introduced as part of this initial adaptation. But these changes gave the text an even more confused appearance, a confusion that was only exacerbated by the increasing association and over-

34. For the character of Girra and Nuska and their relationship, see Abusch, "An Early Form," 32–33.

35. The characterization of Maqlû 73–121 as an incantation originally addressed to a composite fire-god is an unsatisfactory solution.

lapping of the images of Nuska and Girra. Further attempts, documented in the manuscripts, were then made to rectify the text. But, overall, the text still reveals the multiple disturbances to which it had been subjected.

Our reconstruction explains and resolves many of the difficulties in our text—most notably, the occurance of Nuska and Girra together and the subsequent confusion of their roles.[36]

The Text of Maqlû

All manuscripts (i.e., clay tablets and fragments) containing the standard text of Maqlû are from the first millennium, the single-most important source being Assurbanipal's library. A full listing of all manuscripts will appear in my edition of Maqlû in the series Ancient Magic and Divination (AMD), where all manuscripts are presented in a synoptic fashion. The manuscripts come from the following sites:

- northern Mesopotamia: Nineveh (Neo-Assyrian script), Nineveh (Neo-Babylonian script), Assur, Nimrud (Kalah), Sultantepe;
- southern Mesopotamia: Sippar, Babylon, Babylonia (without specific provenance), Kish, Nippur, Uruk, Ur.

A few notes are in order: The manuscripts from Nineveh are usually written in Assyrian script, but a significant number are in Babylonian script. As for manuscripts from the south (all in Babylonian script), it is not always possible to specify the site from which they derive; hence some of them are characterized simply as "Babylonian." I expect that the list of sites from which Maqlû manuscripts derive is not significantly different from the lists of manuscript provenance for most important canonical (better: standard) religious (i.e., magical, medical, divinatory) or literary texts.

The text of Maqlû is attested in different tablet formats. Most Maqlû manuscripts have four columns of text, though two-column versions are known for all Tablets with the exception of Tablet VIII[37] and even form the majority of manuscripts of Tablet I. Almost all manuscripts follow the standard division into eight tablets of incantations and a ritual tablet, but there are several notable exceptions: a Babylonian text containing at least parts of Tablets I–II; two Assur texts—one containing a version of III–IV, the other

36. For a detailed analysis of the history of Maqlû I 73–121, see Abusch, "An Early Form," 27–39.

37. This is probably due to the fact that Tablet VIII is the least well documented of the Tablets.

containing parts of IV–V;[38] and, finally, a Neo-Assyrian (non-Nineveh) text written microscopically and containing the whole composition on one tablet.

Most of the witnesses to Maqlû are manuscripts that carry the standard version of the composition (more rarely a deviant version). But, in addition, there are also tablets that contain extracts[39] and two commentaries that quote individual lines and then comment on them.

This Edition

I should say a few words about the method used to create the **transcription** (or, as some call it, normalization)[40] and translation of the standard text of Maqlû given here. Usually the **transcription** follows the main Nineveh Assyrian text(s), that is, the Nineveh Assyrian manuscript(s) on which the text is most fully preserved, though occasionally I will choose to follow a different but "better" Nineveh (Assyrian) reading. When Nineveh (Assyrian) is broken, I have restored from other manuscripts, usually first from Assyrian manuscripts and then from Babylonian ones. The readings presented in the transcription are, therefore, not always those that I deem to be the best or the most original. But, here and there, even when Nineveh (Assyrian) is preserved, I have made minor adjustments based upon other traditions; furthermore, when I regard all Nineveh (Assyrian) manuscripts as wrong, I have sometimes followed other manuscripts or emended the text.

As already noted, our texts are often not well preserved. Since the standard text presented here does not and cannot follow only one manuscript, the text is drawn from several manuscripts. Brackets indicate that a sign is broken or missing, and the use of brackets in the transcription is loose. To avoid an overloaded presentation, I have tried to keep the use of quarter-

38. These Assur texts may preserve a somewhat deviant version.

39. Usually the extract consists of part of an incantation, though occasionally the extract may contain a complete incantation. Most extracts include only one Maqlû incantation; sometimes several may appear together.

40. I should note that I have usually rendered *i* preceding syllable-final *r* or *ḫ* as *e*. However, I have kept *i* with nouns when I was concerned that the reader might have some difficulty identifying the dictionary entry, with verbs when *i* appears as the third person prefix vowel (e.g., *liḫmuṭ*, not *leḫmuṭ*), and with readings when I found a vocalization with *e* to be very peculiar.

While I generally do not lengthen short vowels before suffixes, I do lengthen the case ending of feminine plural nouns and plural adjectives before suffixes on the grounds that this length is due to analogy (the long vowel being an allomorph) and not to a change of stress (the lengthened vowel being an allophone)—see *GAG* §65k and especially Borger BAL[2] vol. II 163: §65k–l. I also indicate the length of the final vowel of third weak verbs before a suffix/enclitic.

brackets to a minimum, especially within words, and therefore have mainly used them only for long stretches of text or for full words. Generally, within words I have used full square brackets, sometimes even when quarter-brackets around a larger segment would have been more accurate. Not infrequently, when the text is only very slightly damaged, this has not been indicated. For purposes of a transcription, brackets are meant to point the reader to the fact that the text is not fully preserved. But usually the text is certain even when brackets have been used; when the restored text is not certain, I have indicated so by means of a note, a question mark, or a parentheses around the word in question. In the transcription, a question mark in parentheses, viz. (?), indicates that a reading or restoration is uncertain.

Scribes will often write KI.MIN as a "ditto" mark. Unless there is some uncertainty, I have simply given the text that KI.MIN represents. The degree to which KI.MIN is preserved may determine the degree to which the text, even when certain, is represented as broken. KI.MIN is usually not included among the variant readings.

Some variants have been included in the notes. Those cited represent lexical and semantic differences as well as additions, omissions, transpositions, and some scribal errors; normally, orthographic, phonological, or grammatical variations are not indicated, except where these variants are or might be semantically significant. I have tried to include only significant variants.[41] Variations in the forms of pronominal suffixes are normally not included in these notes.

I would encourage the reader who is interested in issues such as orthography, degree of preservation, variation between, among, and within manuscripts, etc., to consult my synoptic edition of Maqlû in the series Ancient Magic and Divination (AMD) published by Brill.

Case endings are often not "correct," nor are they consistent. The absence of consistency may give a barbaric impression, but I ask the reader to remember that this is due in no small part to the nature of the sources and their state of preservation: the ancient manuscripts themselves are not always consistent in their usage of case endings; logographic writing often renders the case ending uncertain; I have often given precedence to a fully preserved occurrence of a case ending, even if it is incorrect, over one that is partially or not at all preserved. I understand that this modus operandi creates a "mixed" text, but the reader has only to consult the score in my synoptic edition in AMD to see whence the readings come.

41. A fuller set of variants are given alongside the transcription in the edition in AMD.

Square brackets in the **translation** (and translation notes) will not necessarily match those found in the transcription. They will usually be limited to words that have been fully or almost fully restored; moreover, quarter-brackets are not used in the translation (and translation notes). In the translation, I make use of round brackets to indicate some connotation of the Akkadian that is not conveyed directly in its translation. However, when round brackets are set within square brackets, I usually mean to indicate that if there is sufficient room within a break, the word(s) in round brackets should probably, but not certainly, be restored. In the translation, a question mark in parentheses on the line, viz. (?), indicates that the reading or restoration is uncertain, a superscript question mark in parentheses, viz. $^{(?)}$, indicates that the meaning is uncertain.

Notes explaining the translation or providing alternative translation are only occasionally given. The notes accompanying the translation treat select translation issues; they also provide translations for materials given in the notes to the transcription but otherwise not translated: additions, significant variants, etc. Omissions, deletions, and transpositions of whole lines that are cited in the notes to the transcription are normally not taken up in the notes to the translation.

I should make clear my understanding of the use of Akkadian tenses in incantations and my choice of translation. My rendering is based upon my understanding of the ritual context of the utterance. I have been guided by the following principles:

1. When the speaker states that he is speaking or praying, I understand the preterite form as expressing an act in the present, and I convey this with an English simple present ("I pray").[42]
2. When the speaker describes an act that he is ritually (or otherwise) performing (usually against the witch), I usually understand the preterite form as expressing an act in the present, and I convey this with an English simple present ("I burn"). To maintain a distinction between the Akkadian preterite and durative, I have often translated the durative by means of an English progressive present ("I am burning").
3. But when the speaker describes acts that the witch has performed, I usually translate the preterite form by means of an English present perfect ("she has made").

42. This coincidence of speech and act may perhaps be compared with the epistolary perfect in Akkadian and Hebrew and may perhaps be a form of performativity.

I should also mention that many different terms are used to designate various types of witches and witchcraft in Maqlû as well as in other Mesopotamian antiwitchcraft incantations and rituals. Our understanding of the differences is still primitive. I should therefore note that the translations in this volume for words denoting witches and witchcraft are often no more than conventional renderings.

Finally, I have tried to craft a translation that makes sense of the original text and creates a meaningful modern rendition. At the same time, I have tried to be true to the Akkadian original, to its word order and semantics. It has not always been easy to find the right balance between these two, sometimes conflicting, concerns.

MAQLÛ TRANSCRIPTION AND TRANSLITERATION

MAQLÛ I. TRANSCRIPTION

1 ÉN *alsīkunūši ilū mušīti*
2 *ittikunu alsi mušītu kallatu kuttumtu*
3 *alsi barārītu qablītu u namārītu*
4 *aššu kaššāptu ukaššipanni*
5 *elēnītu ubbiranni*
6 *ilī u* ^{d}*ištarī ušessû eliya*

7 *eli āmeriya amruṣu*[a] *anāku*
8 *emdēku lā ṣalālu mūša u urra*
9 *qû imtanallû pīya*
10 *upunti pîya iprusu*
11 *mê maštītiya umaṭṭû*

12 *elēlī nubû ḫidûtī sipdi*

13 *izizzānimma ilū rabûtu šimâ dabābī*
14 *dīnī dīnā alaktī limdā*
15 *ēpuš ṣalam kaššāpiya u kaššāptiya*
16 *ša ēpišiya u muštēpištiya*
17 *aškun ina šaplikunuma adabbub dīnī*
18 *aššu īpuša lemnēti išteʾʾâ lā banâti*

19 *šī limūtma anāku lubluṭ*
20 *kišpūša ruḫûša rusûša lū pašrū*
21 *bīnu lillilanni ša qimmatu šarû*
22 *gišimmaru lipšuranni māḫirat kalû šāri*
23 [a]-*maštakal libbibanni ša erṣeta malâta*-[a]
24 *terinnatu*[a] *lipšuranni ša šeʾa malâta*
25 *ina maḫrikunu ētelil kīma sassati*
26 *ētebib azzaku kīma lardi*

MAQLÛ I. TRANSLATION

1 Incantation. I call upon you, Gods of the Night,
2 With you I call upon Night, the veiled bride,
3 I call upon Twilight, Midnight, and Dawn.
4 Because[1] a witch has bewitched me,
5 A deceitful woman has accused me,
6 (Because) she has (thereby) caused my god and goddess to be estranged from me
7 (And) I have become sickening in the sight of anyone who beholds me
8 (And consequently) I am unable to rest day or night,
9 (Because) a gag that is continually filling my mouth
10 Has kept food distant from my mouth
11 (And) has diminished the water which passes through my drinking organ,
12 (Because) my song of joy has become wailing and my rejoicing mourning—
13 Stand by me, O great gods, and give heed to my suit,
14 Judge my case and grant me an (oracular) decision![2]
15 I have made a figurine of my warlock and witch,
16 Of my sorcerer and the woman who instigates sorcery against me,
17 I set (it) at your feet and am now pleading my case:
18 Because she has performed evil against me and has constantly conjured up baseless charges against me,
19 May she die, but I live.
20 May her witchcraft, her spittle, her enchainment be released.[3]
21 May the tamarisk that is copious of crown clear me,
22 May the date palm that withstands all winds release me,
23 May the soapwort that fills the earth cleanse me,
24 May the cone[4] that is full of seeds release me.
25 In your presence I have (now) become pure like grass,
26 Clean and innocent like nard.

27 *tûša ša kaššāpti lemutte*
28 *turrat amāssa ana pîša lišānša kaṣrat*

29 *ina muḫḫi kišpīša limḫaṣūši ilū mušīti*
30 *šalāš maṣṣarātu ša mūši lipšurā*! *ruḫêša*[a] *lemnūti*
31 *pûša lū lipû lišānša lū ṭābtu*
32 *ša iqbû amāt lemuttiya kīma lipî littattuk*

33 *ša īpušu kišpī kīma ṭābti*[a] *lišḫarmiṭ*[b]
34 *kiṣrūša puṭṭurū epšētūša ḫulluqā*
35 *kal amâtūša malâ*[a] *ṣēra*
36 *ina qibīt iqbû ilū mušīti* TU$_6$ ÉN[a]

---

37 ÉN *erṣetu erṣetu erṣetumma*
38 ^{d}*Gilgameš bēl māmītikunu*
39 *mimmû attunu tēpušā*[a] *anāku īde*
40 *mimmû anāku eppušu attunu ul tīdâ*
41 *mimmû kaššāpātūya ippušā ēgâ pāṭira pāšira* [a-]*ul irašši*[-a] TU$_6$ ÉN[b]

---

42 ÉN *ālī Zabban*[a] *ālī Zabban*
43 *ša āliya Zabban šittā abullātūšu*
44 [a]*ištēt ana* ^{d}*utu-è šanītu ana* ^{d}*utu-šú-a*
45 *ištēt ana ṣīt* ^{d}*Šamši šanītu ana ereb* ^{d}*Šamši*
46 *anāku era ḫaṣba maštakal našâku*
47 *ana ilī ša šamê mê anamdin*
48 *kīma anāku ana kâšunu ullalukunūši*
49 *attunu yâši ullilāʾinni* TU$_6$ ÉN

---

50 ÉN *akla nēberu aktali kāru*
51 *akli ipšīšina ša kalîšina mātāti*
52 ^{d}*Anu u Antu išpurūʾinni*
53 *mannu lušpur ana* ^{d}*Bēlet-ṣēri*
54 *ana pī kaššāpiya u kaššāptiya idî ḫargullī*
55 *idî šipassu ša apkal ilī* ^{d}*Marduk*
56 *lilsâkima lā tappalīšināti*
57 *liqbânikkimma lā tašemmîšināti*
58 *lulsīkima apulīnni*
59 *luqbâkkimma šimînni yâši*

27 Her spell being that of an evil witch,
28 Her word has been turned back into her mouth and her tongue constricted.
29 On a(c)count of her witchcraft, may the Gods of the Night strike her,
30 May the three Watches of the Night release her evil spell.[5]
31 Her mouth be tallow, her tongue be salt:
32 May that[6] which uttered an evil word against me drip ever away like tallow,
33 May that[7] which performed witchcraft against me dissolve like salt.[8]
34 Her bonds are broken, her deeds nullified;
35 All of her words fill[9] the steppe[10]—
36 By the command pronounced by the Gods of the Night. TU$_6$ ÉN[11]

---

37 [12]Incantation. Netherworld, netherworld, yea netherworld,
38 Gilgameš is the enforcer of your oath.
39 Whatever you have done,[13] I know,
40 Whatever I do, you do not know.
41 Whatever my witches do will not secure anyone who will overlook, undo, release (it).[14, 15] TU$_6$ ÉN[16]

---

42 Incantation. My city is Zabban; my city is Zabban.
43 Of my city Zabban, two are its gates.
44 One for sunrise, the second for sunset.[17]
45 One for the rising of the sun, the second for the setting of the sun.
46 Raising up a broken palm frond and *maštakal* plant,
47 I offer water to the gods of the sky (and say):
48 "As I purify you yourselves,
49 May you (in turn) purify me myself." TU$_6$ ÉN

---

50 Incantation. I have enclosed the ford, I have enclosed the quay;
51 I have enclosed the witchcraft of all the lands.
52 Anu and Antu have sent me, (saying:)
53 "whom shall we (lit., I) send to Bēlet-ṣēri?"
54 Place the lock on the mouth of my warlock and witch,
55 Place the sealing[18] of the sage of the gods, Marduk,
56 When they call to you, do not answer them,
57 When they speak to you, do not listen to them,
58 When I call to you, answer me.
59 When I speak to you, listen to me—

60 *ina qibīt iqbû* [d]*Anu Antu u* [d]*Bēlet-ṣēri* TU$_6$ ÉN

---

61 ÉN *šaprāku allak u'' urāku adabbu[b]*

62 *ana lēt kaššāpiya u kaššāptiya* [d]*Asalluḫi bēl āšipūti išpuranni*
63 *ša šamê qūlā ša erṣeti*[a] *šimâ*
64 *ša nāri qūlāni ša nābali šimâ* ⸢*pīya*⸣

65 *šāru nāziqu turruk ē tallik*
66 *ša ḫaṭṭi u martê turruk lā tallak*
67 *lizziz ḫarrānu mārat ilī rabûti*
68 *adi amāt kaššāpiya u kaššāptiya aqabbû*
69 *alpu ipaššar immeru ipaššar*

70 *amāssunu lippašerma amātī lā ippaššar*
71 *adi amātī aqabbû amāssunu ana pān amātiya ul ipparrik*

72 *ina qibīt* <*iq*>*bû* [d]*Asalluḫi bēl āšipūti* TU$_6$ ÉN

---

73 ÉN [d]*Nuska annûtu ṣalmū ēpišiya*
74 *annûtu ṣalmū ēpištiya*
75 [a-]*ṣalmū kaššāpiya u kaššāptiya*[-a]
76 *ṣalmū ēpišiya u muštēpištiya*

77 *ṣalmū sāḫiriya u sāḫertiya*
78 *ṣalmū rāḫîya u rāḫītiya*
79 [a-]*ṣalmū bēl ikkiya u bēlet ikkiya*[-a]
80 *ṣalmū bēl ṣerriya u bēlet ṣerriya*
81 [a]*ṣalm[ū] bēl rīdiya u bēlet rīdiya*
82 *ṣalmū bēl dīniya u bēlet dīniya*
83 [a]*ṣalm[ū] bēl amātiya u bēlet amātiya*
84 *ṣalmū bēl dabābiya u bēlet dabābiya*
85 *ṣalm[ū] bēl egerrêya u bēlet egerrêya*
86 *ṣalmū bēl lemuttiya u bēlet lemuttiya*
87 [a-]*ša attā* [d]*Nuska dayyānu tīdēšunūtima anāku lā īdēšunūti*[-a]
88 *ša kišpī ruḫê rusî upšāšê lemnūti*[a]
89 *ipšu bārtu amāt lemutti râmu zīru*
90 *dibalâ zikurrudâ kadabbedâ šurḫungâ*
91 *šabalbalê ṣūd pānī u šanê ṭēmu*

60 By the command pronounced by Anu, Antu, and Bēlet-ṣēri. TU$_6$ ÉN

---

61 Incantation. I have been sent and I will go; I have been commissioned and I will speak.
62 Asalluḫi, lord of exorcism, has sent me against my warlock and witch.
63 You of the heavens, pay heed, you of the netherworld, listen,
64 You of the river, pay heed to me, you of the dry land, listen to my speech!
65 The howling wind is stilled—do not blow!
66 The bearer of the staff and pole is stilled—you shall not blow!
67 May the road, the daughter of the great gods, stand still.
68 While I present the testimony against my warlock and witch,
69 The ox shall set (the judge) at ease;[19] the sheep shall set (the judge) at ease.
70 May their testimony be undone, but let my testimony not be undone.[20]
71 While I present my testimony, let their testimony not stand in the way of my testimony[21]—
72 By the command pronounced by Asalluḫi, lord of exorcism. TU$_6$ ÉN

---

73 Incantation. O Nuska, these are the figurines of my sorcerer,
74 These are the figurines of my sorceress,
75 The figurines of my warlock and my witch,
76 The figurines of my sorcerer and the woman who instigates sorcery against me,
77 The figurines of my enchanter and my enchantress,
78 The figurines of my male and female inseminators,[22]
79 The figurines of the male and female who are enraged at me,
80 The figurines of my male and female enemies,
81 The figurines of my male and female persecutors,
82 The figurines of my male and female litigants,
83 The figurines of my male and female accusers,
84 The figurines of my male and female adversaries,
85 The figurines of my male and female slanderers,
86 The figurines of my male and female evildoers,
87 Whom, you, Nuska, the judge, know, but I do not know,
88 Who witchcraft, spittle, enchainment, evil machinations,[23]
89 Sorcery, rebellion, evil word, love (-magic), hate (-magic),
90 Perversion of justice, *Zikurrudâ*-magic, muteness,[24] pacification,[25]
91 Mood swings, vertigo, and madness

92 *ēpušū[ni] uštēpišūni isḫurūni usasḫirūni*

93 *annûti šunu annûti ṣalmūšunu*
94 *kīma šunu lā izzazzū ṣalmīšunu našâku*
95 *attā* ^{d}*Nuska dayyānu* [a-]*kāšid lemni u ayyābi*[-a] *kušussunūtima anāku lā aḫḫabbil*
96 *ša ṣalmīya ibnû bunnannīya umaššilū*
97 *pīya uṣabbitū kišādī utarrirū*
98 *irtī*[a] *idʾipū eṣenṣērī ikpupū*
99 *libbī unnišū nīš libbiya iṣbatū*
100 *libbī itti[ya] uzannû emūqī unnišū*
101 *aḫīya išpukū birkīya iksû*[a]
102 *ummu mangu u luʾtu umallûʾinni*
103 *aklī kaššāpūti ušākilūʾinni*
104 ⸢*mê*⸣ *kaššāpūti išqûʾinni*
105 *rimk[ī l]uʾûti urammekūʾinni*
106 *napšalti šammē lemnūti ipšušūʾinni*
107 *ana mīti iḫīrūʾinni*
108 *mê napištiya ina qabri ušnillū*
109 [a-]*ila šarra kabta u rubâ ittiya uzannû*[-a]
110 *attā* ^{d}*Girra qāmû kaššāpi u kaššāpti*
111 *muḫalliq raggī zēr kaššāpi u kaššāpti*
112 *muʾabbit lemnūti attāma*
113 *anāku alsīka kīma* ^{d}*Šamaš dayyāni*[a|b]
114 *dīnī dīni purussâya purus*
115 *qumu kaššāpī*[a] *u kaššāptī*
116 *akul ayyābīya aruḫ lemnūtīya*
117 [a-]*ūmka ezzu likšussunūti*[-a]
118 *kīma mê nādi ina tīki liqtû*
119 *kīma tirik abnī ubānātīšunu liktaṣṣiṣū*
120 *ina qibītika ṣīrti ša lā uttakkaru*
121 *u annika kīni ša lā innennû* TU$_{6}$ ÉN

---

122 ÉN ^{d}*Nuska šurbû ilitti* ^{d}*Ani*
123 *tamšīl abi*[a] *bukur* ^{d}*Enlil*
124 *tarbīt apsî binût* ^{d}*Enanki*[a]
125 *ašši gizillâ unammerka kâša*
126 *kaššāpu ikšipanni kišpī ikšipanni kišipšu*

92 Against me have performed, have had performed, have sought, have had sought.
93 These are they, these are their figurines.
94 Since they are not present, I bear aloft their figurines (and say):
95 You, Nuska, the judge, vanquisher of the wicked and the enemy, vanquish them so I not be wronged,
96 (Those) who have made my figurines, reproduced my facial features,
97 Seized my mouth, made my neck tremble,
98 Pressed against my chest,[26] bent my spine,
99 Weakened my heart, taken away my sexual drive,
100 Made me turn my anger against myself,[27] sapped my strength,
101 Caused my arms to fall limp, bound my knees,[28]
102 Filled me with fever, stiffness, and debility,
103 Fed me bewitched food,
104 Given me bewitched water to drink,
105 Bathed me in dirty wash water,
106 Rubbed me with a salve of harmful herbs,
107 Betrothed me to a dead person,
108 Laid the water of my life[29] in a grave,
109 Caused god, king, noble, and prince to be angry with me.
110 You, O Girra, it is you who are the burner of warlocks and witches,
111 The annihilator of the wicked, seed of warlock and witch,
112 The destroyer of the evildoers.
113 I call upon you in the stead of Šamaš, the judge.[30] [31]
114 Judge my case, render my verdict.
115 Burn my warlock and my witch,
116 Devour my enemies, consume the ones who would do evil to me!
117 Let your raging (fire-)storm[32] vanquish them.
118 May they come to an end in a trickle like water from a waterskin.
119 May their fingers be cut back as if smashed by stones.[33]
120 By your preeminent command that cannot be altered
121 And your affirmative assent that cannot be changed. TU$_6$ ÉN

---

122 Incantation. O Grand Nuska, offspring of Anu,
123 Likeness of the father,[34] scion of Enlil,
124 Reared in the *apsû*, creation of Enanki.[35]
125 I raise up a reed torch and set you yourself alight.
126 A warlock has bewitched me; bewitch him with the witchcraft with which he bewitched me,

127 *kaššāptu takšipanni kišpī takšipanni kišipši*

128 *ēpišu īpušanni ipšū īpušanni epussu*

129 *ēpištu tēpušanni ipšū tēpušanni epussi*

130 [a-]*muštēpištu tēpušanni ipšū tēpušanni epussi*[-a]

131 *ša ṣalmī ana pī ṣalmīya ibnû bunnannīya umaššilū*

132 *ru'tī ilqû* [a-]*šārtī imlusū*[-a]
133 *sissiktī ibtuqū etequ eper šēpīya išbušū*

134 ^{d}*Girra qardu šipassunu lipaššer* TU$_6$ ÉN

---

135 ÉN *anašši dipāru ṣalmīšunu aqallu*
136 *ša utukku šēdu rābiṣu eṭemmu*

137 ^{d}*Lamašti* ^{d}*labāṣi aḫḫāzu*
138 *lilû lilītu ardat-lilî*
139 *u mimma lemnu muṣabbitu amēlūti*[a]
140 *ḫūlā zūbā u itattukā*
141 *quturkunu lītelli šamê*
142 *la'mīkunu liballi* ^{d}*Šamši*
143 *liprus ḫayyattakunu mār* ^{d}*Ea mašmaššu* TU$_6$ ÉN

---

144 ÉN ^{d}*Nuska šurbû mālik ilī rabûti*
145 DUB 1.KAM* *Maqlû*[a]

127 A witch has bewitched me; bewitch her with the witchcraft with which she bewitched me,
128 A sorcerer has ensorcelled me; ensorcell him with the sorcery with which he ensorcelled me,
129 A sorceress has ensorcelled me; ensorcell her with the sorcery with which she ensorcelled me,
130 A woman who instigates sorcery has ensorcelled me; ensorcell her with the sorcery with which she ensorcelled me.
131 (Those) who have made figurines corresponding to my figurines, reproduced my facial features,
132 Taken my spittle, plucked out my hair,
133 Cut off my hem, collected a clump of dirt (over which) my feet (had passed),
134 May Girra, the warrior, release their incantation. TU$_6$ ÉN

---

135 Incantation. I am raising the torch and burning their statues,
136 (Those) of the *utukku*-demon, the *šēdu*-spirit, the lurker-demon, the ghost,
137 Lamaštu, *labāṣu* (disease), *ahhāzu*-jaundice,
138 *lilû*, *lilītu*, *ardat-lilî*,[36]
139 And any evil that seizes mankind,[37]
140 Melt, dissolve, drip ever away!
141 May your smoke rise ever heavenward,
142 May the sun extinguish your embers,
143 May Ea's son, the exorcist, cut off the terror that emanates from you. TU$_6$ ÉN

---

144 Incantation. O Grand Nuska, counselor of the great gods.
145 The first tablet of Maqlû.[38]

MAQLÛ II. TRANSCRIPTION

1 ÉN ^{d}*Nuska šurbû mālik ilī rabû[ti]*
2 *pāqid nindab[ê] ša kala* ^{d}*Igig[ī]*
3 *mukīn māḫāzī muddišu parakkī*
4 *ūmu namru ša qibīssu ṣīrat*
5 *sukkal* ^{d}*Ani šēmû pirišti* ^{d}*Enlil*
6 *šēmû* ^{d}*Enlil māliku šadû* ^{d}*Igigī*

7 *gašru tāḫāzu ša tību šu dannu*
8 ^{d}*Nuska āriru mušabriq zayyāri*
9 *ina balika ul iššakkan naptanu ina Ekur*
10 *ina balika ilū rabûtu ul iṣṣinū qutrinnu*
11 *ina balika* ^{d}*Šamaš dayyānu ul idâni dīnu*
12 *ḫāsis šumeka teṭṭer ina dannati tagammil ina pušqi*

13 *anāku aradka annanna mār annanna ša ilšu annanna* ^{d}*ištaršu annannītu*

14 *asḫurka ešēka bašâka*^{a} *uznāya šapalka akmis*
15 *qumi kaššāpī u kaššāptī*
16 *ša kaššāpiya u kaššāptiya [a]rḫiš ḫanṭiš napištašunu liblēma*

17 *yâši bulliṭannima narbîka lušāpi dalīlīka ludlul*^{a}

---

18 $^{a-}$KA.INIM.MA U[Š$_{11}$.BÚR.R]U.DA *ṣalam lipî*-KAM^{*-a}

---

19 ÉN ^{d}*Girra* ⸢*bēlu*⸣ *[g]itmāl[u]* ^{d}*[na]nnārāta nabi šumka*

20 *[t]ušnammar bīt[ā]t ilī kalāma*
21 *[tu]šnammar g[im]er kal(î)šina mātāti*

Maqlû II. Translation

1 Incantation. O Grand Nuska, counselor of the great gods,
2 Provider of cereal offerings to all the Igigi,
3 Establisher of sanctuaries, renewer of shrines,
4 Radiant light, whose command is preeminent,
5 Minister of Anu, confidant of Enlil,[39]
6 The one who listens to Enlil, (who is) the counselor, (and) the mountain of the Igigi,[40]
7 Powerful battle, whose onslaught is overwhelming,
8 Blazing Nuska, who strikes down the enemy with lighting.
9 Without you a meal would not be set out in Ekur,
10 Without you the great gods would not smell incense,
11 Without you Šamaš, the judge, would not render judgment.
12 He who mentions[41] your name you rescue from hardship, you save from distress.
13 I, your servant, so-and-so, the son of so-and-so, whose god is so-and-so, whose goddess is so-and-so,
14 I turn to you, I seek you, I hearken to you, I kneel at your feet.
15 Burn my warlock and my witch,
16 May the lives of my warlock and my witch quickly and speedily be extinguished,
17 Thereby save me myself so that I may declare your great deeds and sing your praises.

---

18 It is the wording (of the incantation) to [undo] wit[chcraft]: a figurine of tallow.

---

19 [42]Incantation. O Girra, perfect lord, "You are the light," (thus) your name is invoked,
20 You illumine the houses of all the gods,
21 You illumine the to[tal]ity of all the lands.

22 [*a*]*ššu attā* [*ana yâš*]*i tazzazzuma*
23 *kīma* ^{d}*Sîn u* ^{d}*Šamaš tadinnu dīnu*
24 *dēnī dīni purussâya purus*
25 *ana nūrika namri nišū kalîšina upaqqāka*
26 *ana elleti dipārika asḫurka ešēka*
27 *bēlu sissiktaka aṣbat*
28 *sissikti ilūtik*[*a rabīt*]*i aṣbat*
29 ⸢*sissikti*⸣ *i*[*liya u* ^{d}*ištariya*] *aṣbat*
30 [*sissikti il ā*]*liya u* ^{d}*ištar āliya aṣbat*
31 [x (x)]-x-*ma r*[*ē*]*manni bēlu kaššāptu kīma lilissi iltasi eliya*

32 *iṣbat qaqqadī kišādī u muḫḫī*
33 *iṣbat īnīya nāṭilāti*
34 *iṣbat šēpīya allakāti*
35 *iṣbat birkīya ebberēti*
36 *iṣbat aḫīya muttabbilāti*
37 *enenna ina maḫar ilūtika rabīti*
38 *šinā ṣalmī siparri etgurūti*
39 *ša kaššāpiya u kaššāptiya*
40 *ša ēpišiya u muštēpištiya*
41 *ša sāḫiriya u sāḫertiya*
42 *ša rāḫîya u rāḫītiya*
43 *ša bēl ikkiya u bēlet ikkiya*
44 *ša bēl ṣerriya u bēlet ṣerriya*
45 *ša bēl rīdiya u bēlet rīdiya*
46 *ša bēl dīniya u bēlet dīniya*
47 *ša bēl amātiya u bēlet amātiya*
48 *ša bēl dabābiya u bēlet dabābiya*
49 *ša bēl egerrêya u bēlet egerrêya*
50 *ša bēl lemuttiya u bēlet lemuttiya*
51 *ša ana mīti puqqudūʾinni namrāṣa kullumūʾinni*

52 *lū utukku lemnu lu alû lemnu*
53 *lū eṭemmu lemnu lū gallû lemnu*
54 *lū ilu lemnu lū rābiṣu lemnu*
55 *lū* ^{d}*Lamaštu lū* ^{d}*labāṣu lū* ^{d}*aḫḫāzu*
56 *lū lilû lū lilītu lū ardat-lilî*
57 *lū liʾbu ṣibit šadî*
58 *lū bennu riḫû*[*t*] ⸢^{d}*Šulpaeʾa*⸣

22 Because you are present [for m]e
23 And decide lawsuits in the stead of Sîn and Šamaš,
24 Judge my case, render my verdict.
25 For your bright light, all the people await you,
26 For your pure torch, I turn to you, I seek you.
27 Lord, I seize your hem,
28 I seize the hem of you[r grea]t divinity,
29 I seize the hem of [my] go[d and my goddess],
30 I seize [the hem of] my ci[ty god] and my city goddess.
31 [. . .] . . . have pity on me, O lord. The witch has (now) roared at me like a drum.
32 She has seized my head, my neck, and my skull,
33 She has seized my seeing eyes,
34 She has seized my walking feet,
35 She has seized my crossing knees,
36 She has seized my (load) bearing arms.
37 Now in the presence of your great divinity,
38 Two crisscrossed bronze figurines
39 Of my warlock and my witch,
40 Of my sorcerer and the woman who instigates sorcery against me,
41 Of my enchanter and my enchantress,
42 Of my male and female inseminators,[43]
43 Of the male and female who are enraged at me,
44 Of my male and female enemies,
45 Of my male and female persecutors,
46 Of my male and female litigants,
47 Of my male and female accusers,
48 Of my male and female adversaries,
49 Of my male and female slanderers,
50 Of my male and female evildoers,
51 Who have given me over to a dead man, who have made me experience hardship—
52 Be it an evil *utukku*-demon, be it an evil *alû*-demon,
53 Be it an evil ghost, be it an evil (demonic) constable,
54 Be it an evil god, be it an evil lurker-demon,
55 Be it Lamaštu, be it *labāṣu* (disease), be it *ahhāzu*-jaundice,
56 Be it *lilû*, be it *lilītu*, be it *ardat-lilî*,
57 Be it *liʾbu*-illness, the seizure of the mountain,
58 Be it *bennu*-epilepsy, the spawn of Šulpaeʾa,

59 *lū antašubbû lū* ⌜^{d}⌝[*Lugalurra*]
60 ^{a}*lū šudingirrakku lū š*[*uʾinannakku*]
61 *lū šugidimmakku* $^{a-}$*lū šu*[*namerimmakku*]$^{-a}$
62 *lū šunamlullukku lū lamaštu ṣeḫertu mārat* ^{d}*Ani*

63 *lū sangḫulḫazû mukīl rēš lemutti*
64 *lū dikiš šīrī šimmatu rimûtu*
65 *lū* [*mimm*]*a lemnu ša šuma lā nabû*
66 *lū* [*mimm*]*a ēpiš lemutti ša amēlūti*
67 *ša ṣabtannima mūša u urra irteneddânni*
68 *uḫattû šīrīya kal ūmi ṣabtannima*
69 *kal mūši lā umaššaranni*
70 *enenna ina maḫar ilūtika rabīti*
71 *ina kibrīti elleti aqallīšunūti ašarrapšunūti*
72 *naplisannima bēlu usuḫšunūti ina zumriya*
73 *pušur kišpīšunu lemnūti*
74 *attā* ^{d}*Girra bēlu ālik idīya*
75 *bulliṭannima narbîka lušāpi dalīlīka ludlul*

---

76 $^{a-}$KA.INIM.M UŠ$_{11}$.BÚR.RU.DA *ṣalam siparri kibrīti*-KÁM^{-a}

---

77 ÉN ^{d}*Girra āriru bukur* ^{d}*Ani*
78 *dāʾin dīni atmê pirišti attāma*
79 *eklēti tušnammar*
80 *ešâti dalḫāti tušteššer*
81 *ana ilī rabûti purussâ tanamdin*
82 *ša lā kâta ilu mamman purussâ ul iparras*
83 *attāma nādin ûrti u ṭēme*
84 *ēpiš lumni attāma arḫiš takammu*
85 *lemnu u* ⌜*ayyāba*⌝ *takaššad arḫ*[*iš*]^{a}
86 $^{a-}$*anāku* [*annanna mār annan*]*na ša ilšu annanna* ^{d}*ištaršu annannītu*$^{-a}$

87 *ina kišp*[*ī l*]*upputākuma maḫarka azziz*
88 *ina maḫar ili* [*š*]*arri bēl*[*u*]^{a} *šuzzurākuma allika ana maḫrika*

89 *eli ām*[*eriy*]*a murruṣākuma šapalka akmis*

90 ^{d}[*G*]*irra šurbû ilu ellu*

59 Be it *antašubba*[44]-epilepsy, be it [*Lugalurra*-epilepsy],
60 Be it Hand-of-a-god-disease, be it Han[d-of-a-goddess-dise]ase,[45]
61 Be it Hand-of-a-ghost-disease, be it Hand-[of-a-curse]-disease,[46]
62 Be it Hand-of-mankind-disease, be it young Lamaštu, the daughter of Anu,
63 Be it *Sanghulhaza*-demon, the attendant who provides evil,
64 Be it swelling, paralysis, numbness,
65 Be it [anythi]ng evil that has not been named,
66 Be it [anythi]ng that causes harm to humanity,
67 That seizes me and constantly persecutes me night and day,
68 Afflicts [47] my flesh, seizes me all day,
69 And does not let go of me all night.
70 Now in the presence of your great divinity,
71 With pure sulfur, I am burning them, I am scorching them,
72 Look at me, O lord, and uproot them from my body,
73 Release their evil witchcraft.
74 You, Girra, are the lord, the one who goes at my side,
75 Keep me well that I may declare your great deeds and sing your praises.

---

76 It is the wording (of the incantation) to undo witchcraft: a figurine of bronze (with) sulphur.[48]

---

77 Incantation. O blazing Girra, scion of Anu,
78 It is you who renders judgment, the secret speech,
79 You illumine darkness,
80 You set straight confusion and disorder,
81 You grant decisions for the great gods,
82 Were it not for you, no god would deliver a verdict,
83 It is you who gives instruction and direction.
84 You alone speedily capture the evildoer
85 (And) speedily[49] overcome the wicked and the enemy.
86 I, [so-and-so, the son of so-and]-so, whose god is so-and-so, whose goddess is so-and-so[50]—
87 I have been attacked by witchcraft, and so I enter into your presence,[51]
88 I have been made detestable in the presence of god, king, and lord,[52] and so I come toward you,
89 I have been made sickening in the [sight of anyone who b]eholds me, and so I bow down before you.
90 Grand Girra, pure god,

91 *enenna ina maḫar ilūtika rabīti*
92 *šinā ṣalmī kaššāpi u kaššāpti ša siparri ēpuš qātukka*

93 *maḫarka uggeršunūtima kâša apqidk*[*a*]
94 *šunu limūtūma anāku lubluṭ*
95 *šunu lītebbirūma*[a] *anāku lūšir*
96 *šunu liqtûma anāku lumīd*
97 [a-]*šunu līnišūma anāku ludnin*[-a]
98 ^{d}*Girra šarḫu ṣīru ša ilī*
99 *kāšid lemni u ayyābi kušussunūtima anāku*[a] *lā aḫḫabbil*

100 *anāku aradka lubluṭ lušlimma maḫarka luzziz*

101 *attāma ilī attāma bēlī*
102 *attāma dayyānī attāma rēṣuya*
103 *attāma muterru ša gimilliya* TU$_6$ ÉN

---

104 [a-]KA.INIM.MA UŠ$_{11}$.BÚR.RU.DA *ṣalam siparri*-KÁM[-a]

---

105 ÉN ^{d}*Girra āriru mār* ^{d}*Ani qardu*
106 *ezzu aḫḫīšu attā*
107 *ša kīma* ^{d}*Sîn u* ^{d}*Šamaš tadannu*[a] *dīnu*
108 *dīnī dīni purussâya purus*
109 *qumi kaššāpī u kaššāptī*
110 [a-]^{d}*Girra qumu kaššāpī u kaššāptī*[-a]
111 ^{d}*Girra quli kaššāpī u kaššāptī*
112 ^{d}*Girra qumīšunūti*
113 ^{d}*Girra qulīšunū*[*t*]*i*
114 ^{d}*Girra kušussunūti*
115 ^{d}*Girra aruḫšunūti*
116 ^{d}*Girra šutābilšunūti*
117 [a]*ēpiš kišpī lemnūti u ruḫê lā ṭābūti*
118 *ša ana lemutti ikpudūni yâši*
119 *dannu makkūršunu šulqi*
120 *šutbil būšašunu ekkēma*
121 *eli manāḫātīšunu ḫabbāta šurbiṣ*
122 ^{d}*Girra ezzu gitmālu rašubbu*

91 Now in the presence of your great godhead
92 Two bronze figurines of the warlock and the witch I have fashioned with your power.
93 In your presence I cross them, and to you I hand them over.
94 May they die, but I live,
95 May they be bound,[53] but I be acquitted,[54]
96 May they come to an end, but I increase,
97 May they weaken, but I become strong.
98 O splendid Girra, preeminent one of the gods,
99 Vanquisher of the wicked and the enemy, vanquish them so I not be wronged.
100 May I, your servant, live and be well so that I may stand before you (and declare):
101 You alone are my god, you alone are my lord,
102 You alone are my judge, you alone are my aid,
103 You alone are my avenger! TU$_6$ ÉN

---

104 It is the wording (of the incantation) to undo witchcraft: a figurine of bronze.[55]

---

105 Incantation. O blazing Girra, warlike son of Anu,
106 Indeed you are the fiercest among your brothers.
107 As[56] you decide lawsuits in the stead of Sîn and Šamaš,
108 Judge my case, hand down my verdict.
109 Burn my warlock and my witch,
110 Girra, burn my warlock and my witch,
111 Girra, scorch my warlock and my witch,
112 Girra, burn them,
113 Girra, scorch them,
114 Girra, vanquish them,
115 Girra, consume them,
116 Girra, confound them!
117 The doers of evil witchcraft and not good spittle,
118 Who plotted evil against me myself:
119 Cause a strong one to take away their furnishings,[57]
120 Cause a robber to carry off their goods,
121 Cause a plunderer to lie in wait at their resting place.
122 Raging Girra, perfect, awe inspiring,

123 *ina Ekur ašar tallaktika ē t*[*u*]*šapšeḫšunūti adi surriš*

124 *ina amāt* ^{d}*Ea bānîka* ^{d}*Šamaš ilu namru*
125 *sebet apkallū šūt Eridu likpudūšunūti ana* ⸢*lemutti*⸣ [a-]TU$_{6}$ ÉN[-a]

---

126 [a-][KA.INI]M.MA UŠ$_{11}$.BÚR.RU.DA *ṣalam līši*-KÁM[-a]

---

127 ÉN ^{d}*Girra gašru ūmu nanduru*
128 *tušteššer ilī u malkī*
129 *tadâni dēn ḫabli u habilti*
130 *ina dīniya izizzamma kīma* ^{d}*Šamaš qurādu*
131 *dīnī dīni purussâya purus*
132 *qumi kaššāpī u kaššāptī*
133 *akul ayyābīya aruḫ lemnūtīya*
134 *ūmka ezzu likšussunūti* TU$_{6}$[a] ÉN

---

135 [a-]KA.INIM.MA UŠ$_{11}$.BÚR.RU.DA *ṣalam ṭīṭi*-KÁ[M][-a]

---

136 ÉN ^{d}*Girra šarḫu bukur* ^{d}*Ani*
137 *ilitti elleti šaqūtu* ^{d}*Šalaš*[a]
138 *šarḫu eddēšû nūr*[a] *ilī kayyānu*
139 *nādin nindabê*[a] *ana ilī* ^{d}*Igigī*
140 *šākin namerti ana* ^{d}*Anunnakkī ilī rabûti*
141 *ezzu* ^{d}*Girra mušḫarmiṭ api*[a]
142 ^{d}*Girra allallû* [a-]*mu*ʾ*abbit iṣṣī u abnī*[-a]
143 *qāmû lemnūti zēr kaššāpi u kaššāpti*
144 *muḫalliq raggī zēr kaššāpi u kaššāpti*[a]
145 *ina ūmi annî ina dīniya izizzamma*
146 *ēpiš bārti tēnânâ kušud lemnu*
147 *kīma ṣalmū annûti iḫūlū izūbū u ittattukū*
148 [a-]*kaššāpu u kaššāptu*[-a] *liḫūlū lizūbū u littattukū*[b]

---

149 [a-]KA.INIM.MA UŠ$_{11}$.BÚR.RU.DA *ṣalam iṭṭî*-KÁM[-a]

---

150 ÉN *keš libiš kedeš*
151 *arabbeš nadreš*

123 In the (netherworld) Ekur, the place of your travel, speedily cause them not to have rest.[58]
124 By the word of Ea, your creator, (and) Šamaš, the radiant god,
125 May the seven Sages of Eridu plot evil against them.[59] TU$_6$ ÉN

---

126 It is the [word]ing (of the incantation) to undo witchcraft: a figurine of dough.

---

127 Incantation. O powerful Girra, wild (fire-)storm,
128 You give correct decisions to gods and rulers,
129 You provide justice for the oppressed man and woman.
130 Stand by me in my judgement like Šamaš, the warrior,
131 Judge my case, render my verdict.
132 Burn my warlock and my witch,
133 Devour my enemies, consume the ones who would do evil to me!
134 Let your raging (fire-)storm vanquish them. TU$_6$ ÉN

---

135 It [i]s the wording (of the incantation) to undo witchcraft: a figurine of clay.[60]

---

136 Incantation. O splendid Girra, scion of Anu,
137 Offspring of the pure one, the exalted Šalaš,[61, 62]
138 Splendid, ever-renewing, constant light[63] of the gods,
139 Dispenser of cereal offerings[64] to the gods, the Igigi,
140 Provider of illumination to the Anunakki, the great gods.
141 Raging Girra, obliterator of reed marsh,[65]
142 Mighty Girra, destroyer of (buildings of) wood and stones,[66]
143 Burner of the evildoers, seed of warlock and witch,
144 Annihilator of the wicked, seed of warlock and witch,[67]
145 On this day, stand by me at my trial,
146 And vanquish the rebel, the one who changes,[68] the evil one!
147 As these figurines dissolve, melt, and drip ever away,
148 So may my! warlock and witch dissolve, melt, and drip ever away.

---

149 It is the wording (of the incantation) to undo witchcraft: a figurine of bitumen.[69]

---

150 Incantation. *keš libiš kedeš*
151 *arabbeš nadreš*

152 *ša dipāri rākib šāri*
153 *Lirun<di Na>ḫundi*
154 *kaṣāṣu izannun*
155 *kīma šam[ām]ī elkun*
156 $^{a-}$*kīma ṣerri*$^{-a}$ *līterrubāma iṣâ*
157 *liktumkunūši šiptu ezzetu rabītu ša* ^{d}*Ea mašmašši*
158 ⸢*u tuduqqû*⸣ *ša* ^{d}*Ningirima*
159 *lilappit bunnannīkunu* TU$_{6}$ ÉN

---

160 $^{a-}$KA.INIM.MA U[Š$_{11}$.BÚR.RU.DA] *ṣalam kupsi*-[KÁM]$^{-a}$

---

161 [É]N *eppušūni ēteneppušūni*

162 ⸢*kīma*⸣ *kīti ana kapāliya*
163 *kīma ḫuḫāri ana saḫāpiya*

164 *kīma kāpi ana abātiya*
165 *kīma šēti ana katāmeya*
166 *kīma pitilti ana patāliya*
167 *kīma pitiqti ana nabalkutiya*
168 *kīma mê musâti asurrâ ana mullîya*
169 *kīma šūšurāt bīti ana bābi ana nasākiya*

170 *anāku*^{a} *ina qibīt* ^{d}*Marduk bēl nubatti*

171 *u* ^{d}*Asalluḫi bēl āšipūti*
172 *ēpišī u ēpištī*
173 *kīma kīti akappilšunūti*
174 *kīma ḫuḫāri asaḫḫapšunūti*

175 *kīma kāpi abbassunūti*
176 *kīma šēti akattamšunūti*
177 *kīma pitilti apattilšunūti*
178 *kīma pitiqti abbalakkissunūti*
179 *kīma mê musâti asurrâ umallāšunūti*
180 *kīma šūšurāt bīti ana bābi anassukšunūti*

152 The (carrier) of the torch, the rider of the wind,
153 Lirun<di Na>ḫundi[70]
154 *Kaṣāṣu*-rain will rain
155 On you like (the rain of) heaven,
156 May they enter and come out(?) like a snake.
157 May the raging, great incantation of Ea, the exorcist, cover you
158 And may the spell of Ningirima
159 destroy your features. TU$_6$ ÉN

---

160 [It is] the wording (of the incantation) [to undo] witc[hcraft]: a figurine of sesame pomace.[71]

---

161 Incantation. They perform sorcery against me, they keep on performing sorcery against me
162 In order to wrap me up as a reed mat (would wrap me up),
163 In order to clamp down on me as a bird trap (would clamp down on me),
164 In order to crush me as a (falling) rock wall (would crush me),
165 In order to cover me as a net (would cover me),
166 In order to twist me as (one twists) a string,
167 In order to cross over me as (over) a brick course,
168 In order to fill the sewer with me as (is done with) wash water,
169 In order to cast me out through the door as sweepings of a house (are cast out).
170 (But) I[72]—by the command of Marduk, lord of the evening ceremonies,
171 And Asalluḫi, lord of exorcism—
172 My sorcerer and my sorceress:
173 I am wrapping them up as a reed mat (would wrap them up),
174 I am clamping down on them as a bird trap (would clamp down on them),
175 I am crushing them as a (falling) rock wall (would crush them),
176 I am covering them as a net (would cover them),
177 I am twisting them as (one twists) a string,
178 I am crossing over them as (over) a brick course,
179 I am filling the sewer with them as (is done with) wash water,
180 I am casting them out through the door as sweepings of a house (are cast out).

181 ^{d}*Gir*[*ra ina ša*]*plika ṣalam kaššāpi u kaššāpti a*[*d*]*dinka* [a]-T[U$_6$ ÉN]-[a]

---

182 [a]-KA.IN[IM.MA U]Š$_{11}$.BÚR.RU.DA *ṣalam iṭṭî ša gaṣṣa ballu*-KÁM-[a]

---

183 ÉN *attīmannu kaššāptu ša ina nāri imluʾu ṭīṭaya*

184 *ina bīti eṭî utammeru ṣalmīya*
185 *ina qabri itmeru mêya*
186 *ina tubkinnāti ulaqqitu ḫuṣābēya*
187 *ina bīt ašlāki ibtuqu sissikt*[*ī*]
188 *ina askuppati išbušu eper šē*[*pīya*]
189 *ašpur ana bāb kāri išāmūni lipâki*

190 *ašpur ana ḫirīt āli ikriṣūni ṭīṭaki*

191 *ašapparakkimma āliku tinūru* ^{d}*Girra munnaḫzu*
192 ^{d}[*Gi*]*rra eddēšû nūr ilī kayyānu*
193 ^{d}[*Sîn*] *ina Uri* ^{d}*Šamaš ina Larsa*
194 [^{d}*N*]*ergal adi ummānātīšu*
195 ^{d}*Ištar Akkadê adi kummiša*
196 *ana laqāt zēr ša kaššāpiya u kaššāptiya mala bašû*
197 *kaššāpta lidūkūma anāku lubluṭ*
198 *aššu lā ēpušaššimma*![a] *īpuša*

199 *aššu*[a] *lā asḫuraššimma isḫura*

200 *šī taklat ana kišpīša kitpudūt*[*i*]
201 *u anāku ana kay*[*yāni*] *nūr* <*ilī*> ^{d}*Girra dayyān*[*u*]
202 ^{d}*Girra qum*[*īši* ^{d}*Gi*]*rra qulīš*[*i*]
203 ^{d}*Girra* ⸢*kušussi*⸣ TU$_6$ ÉN

---

204 [a]-KA.INIM.MA UŠ$_{11}$.BÚR.RU.DA *ṣalam ṭīṭi ša lipâ ballu*-[K]ÁM-[a]

---

205 ÉN *attīmannu kaššāptu ša tubtanaʾʾînni*
206 *ana lemutti teštenеʾʾînni*
207 *ana lā ṭābti tassanahhurīnni*

181 Girr[a, at] your [fe]et I give you a figurine[73] of the warlock and the witch. T[U$_6$ ÉN]

---

182 It is the word[ing] (of the incantation) to undo [witc]hcraft: a figurine of bitumen mixed with gypsum.[74]

---

183 Incantation. Whoever you are, O witch, who has taken out clay (for a figurine) of me from the river,
184 Buried my figurines in a dark house,[75]
185 Buried my (funerary) water in a grave,
186 Collected my leavings from a garbage pit,
187 Cut off my hem in the house of a launderer,
188 Collected the dust from [my fe]et at the threshold.
189 I have sent to the gate of the quay—they have bought me tallow (for) your (figurine),
190 I have sent to the city ditch—they have pinched off for me the clay (for) your (figurine).
191 I am sending against you a burning oven, flaring Girra,
192 Ever-renewing Girra, constant light of the gods,
193 [Sîn] from Ur, Šamaš from Larsa,
194 Nergal with his troops,
195 Ishtar of Agade together with her sanctuary,
196 To collect the seed of my warlock and my witch, as much as there is.
197 May they kill the witch, but may I live,
198 Because I![76] have not performed sorcery against her, but she has performed sorcery against me,
199 Because I have not sought (to perform witchcraft against) her, but she has sought (to perform witchcraft against) me.
200 She relies on her scheming witchcraft,
201 But I (rely) on the con[stant] light <of the gods>, Girra, the Judge.
202 Girra, bur[n her, Gi]rra, scorch her,
203 Girra, vanquish her. TU$_6$ ÉN

---

204 It is the wording (of the incantation) to undo witchcraft: a figurine of clay mixed with tallow.

---

205 Incantation. Whoever you are, O witch, who keeps on seeking me,
206 Who keeps on searching for me with evil intent,
207 Who keeps on looking for me to no good purpose.

208 *ālki ul īde bītki ul īde šumki ul īde šubatki ul īde*

209 *šēdū liba’’ûki*
210 *utukkū lište’’ûki*
211 *eṭemmū lissahrūki*
212 *bennu lā ṭābu eliki limqut*
213 *rābiṣū lemutti likillū rēški*
214 ^{d}*Lu*[*gal*]*i*[*rra u* ^{d}*Meslamta*]*’ea linārūki*
215 [a]-[^{d}x] x-[a] *bēl šīm*[*āti*(?) *šumk*]*i*(?) *lipšiṭ*
216 ^{d}[*N*]*in*[*u*]*rta lā pādû* [*lišānk*]*i*(?) *lissuḫ*
217 [^{d}*G*]*ula azugallatu rabītu l*[*ē*]*tki*(?) *limḫaṣ*
218 ^{d}*Girr*[*a*] *ezzu zumurki liḫmuṭ*
219 *ut*[*ū*]*nu elletu mārat* ^{d}*Ani rabītu*
220 *ša ina lib*[*b*]*iša nanḫuzat išāt qabri*
221 [*ina lib*]*biša* ^{d}*Girra qardu irmâ* [*šub*]*assu*
222 [*ina*(?)] *n*[*apāḫiš*]*a*(?) *šamāmī ikšudū nabl*[*ūša*]
223 *ka*[*ššāpt*]*ī qumî qulî ḫumm*[*iṭī*]
224 [a]-*arḫiš ḫanṭiš ša kaššāpiya u ka*[*ššāptiya*]-[a] *napištašunu li*[*blēma*]

225 *yâši bulliṭannima narbîka lušāpi* [*d*]*alīlīka ludlul* [T]U$_{6}$ ÉN

---

226 [a]-[KA].INIM.MA UŠ$_{11}$.BÚR.R[U.DA *ṣalam bīni ṣalam erēni*-KÁ]M-[a]

---

227 ÉN *kaššāptu muttalikt*[*u ša sū*]*qāti*
228 DUB 2.KÁM *Ma*[*ql*]*û*[a]

208 I do not know your city, I do not know your house, I do not know your name, I do not know your dwelling.
209 May *šēdu*-spirits seek you,
210 May *utukku*-demons search for you,
211 May ghosts look for you,
212 May not good *bennu*-epilepsy befall you,
213 May evil lurker-demons attend to you,
214 May Lu[gal]i[rra and Meslamta]ʾea kill you,
215 May [Enli]l(?), lord of dest[inies(?)], erase you[r name],
216 May merciless Ninurta tear out you[r tongue(?)],
217 May Gula, the great doctor, strike your ch[ee]k(?),
218 May raging Girra inflame your body.
219 O pure oven, great daughter of Anu,
220 In whose inside the fire of the grave flares,
221 [In] whose [ins]ide Girra, the warrior, set down his [dwel]ling,
222 [Whose f]lame [when] ig[nited(?)] reaches heaven,
223 Burn, scorch, bur[n up] my w[itch].
224 Quickly and speedily, may the lives of my warlock and [my wit]ch be [extinguished],
225 Thereby save me myself so that I may declare your great deeds and sing your praises. TU$_6$ ÉN

---

226 I[t is] the [word]ing (of the incantation) [to] undo witchcraft: [a figurine of tamarisk, a figurine of cedar].

---

227 Incantation. The witch, she who roams [the stre]ets.
228 The second tablet of Maqlû.[77]

MAQLÛ III. TRANSCRIPTION

1 ÉN *kaššāptu muttalliktu ša sūqāti*
2 *mūterribtu ša bītāti*
3 *dayyālītu ša birêti*
4 *ḫayyāṭītu ša rebâti*
5 [a]*ana pāniša u arkiša issanaḫḫur*
6 *izzaz ina sūqimma* [a]-*usaḫḫar šēpī*-[a]
7 *ina rebīti ip-ta-ra-as*[a] *alaktu*
8 [a]*ša eṭli damqi dūssu īkim*
9 *ša ardati damiqti inibša itbal*
10 *ina nekelmêša kuzubša ilqe*
11 *eṭla ippalisma* ^{d}*lamassašu īki*[*m*]
12 *ardata ippalisma inibša itbal*

13 *īmurannima kaššāptu illika arkiya*
14 *ina imtiša ip-ta-ra-as*[a] *alaktu*
15 *ina ruhêša išdiḫī iprus*
16 *ušassi ilī u* ^{d}*ištarī ina zumriya*
17 *ša kaššāpti*<*ya*>[a] *ina kullati agdariṣ ṭīṭaša*
18 *ša ēpištiya abtani ṣalamša*
19 *aškun ina libbiki lipâ ḫābilki*
20 *usanniš ina kalâtīki ēra qāmâki*
21 *ēra qāmâki imatki*[a] *liprus*
22 *eli āli attapaḫ išātu*
23 *ina šupāl āli attadi tumurtu*
24 *ana bīt terrubī attadi išātu*
25 *tēpušīmma* ^{d}*Girra līkulki*
26 *tušēpišīmma* ^{d}*Girra likšudki*

27 *takpudīmma* ^{d}*Girra lidūkki*
28 *tušakpidīmma* ^{d}*Girra liqmīki*

MAQLÛ III. TRANSLATION

1 [78]Incantation. The witch, she who roams the streets,
2 Who continually intrudes into houses,
3 Who prowls in alleys,
4 Who spies about the broad ways—
5 She[79] keeps turning around from front to back,
6 Standing, in the street she turns foot (progress) around,[80]
7 (And) in the broad way she cuts off (commercial) traffic.
8 She robbed the fine young man of his virility,
9 She carried off the attractiveness of the fine young woman,
10 With her malignant stare she took away her charms.
11 She looked at the young man and (thereby) robbed his vitality,
12 She looked at the young woman and (thereby) carried off her attractiveness.
13 The witch has seen me and has come after me,
14 With her venom, she *has* cut off (commercial) traffic,
15 With her spittle, she has cut off my trading,
16 She has driven away my god and goddess from my person.
17 From the clay pit I have (now) pinched off clay for <my> witch,
18 I have (now) formed the figurine of my sorceress.
19 "I set in your abdomen tallow, which destroys you,
20 I implant in your kidneys cornel, which burns you.
21 May the cornel, which burns you, cut off your venom.[81]
22 Above the city, I have (now) set a fire,
23 Underneath the city, I have (now) cast embers.
24 To the house that you enter, I have (now) cast a fire.
25 You have performed sorcery against me, so may Girra consume you,
26 You have had sorcery performed against me, so may Girra vanquish you,
27 You have plotted against me, so may Girra kill you,
28 You have had others plot against me, so may Girra burn you.

29 *ḫarrān lā târi lišaṣbitki* ^{d}*Girra ḫābilki*
30 ^{d}*Girra ezzu zumurki liḫmuṭ* TU$_{6}$ ÉN

30a [a]-[KA].INIM.MA UŠ$_{11}$$^{!}$.BÚR.RU.DA.KÁM *ṣalam ṭīṭi lipâ ina libbi u ē[ra ina kalâti]*-[a]

---

31 ÉN *šittā šina mārāt* ^{d}*Ani ša šamê*
32 *šalāš šina mārāt* ^{d}*Ani ša šamê*
33 *ṭurra ṣabtānimma ultu šamê urradāni*
34 *ēkīam tebâtina ēkīam tallakā*
35 *ana ēpiši u ēpišti ša annanna mār annanna ana saḫāri nillika*

36 *ana luqquti ša ḫuṣābīšina*
37 *ana ḫummumi ša ḫumāmātīšina*
38 *ša līlâti ḫuluppaqqa ana šarāpi nillika*[a]

38a [a]-KA.INIM.MA <UŠ$_{11}$.BÚR.RU.DA.(KÁM)> *ṣalam lipî ḫimmāti*-[a]

---

39 ÉN *kaššāptu nērtānītu*
40 *elēnītu naršimdatu*
41 *āšiptu eššebūti*
42 *mušlaḫḫatu agugiltu*
43 *qadištu nadītu*
44 *ištarītu kulmašītu*
45 *bayyārtu*[a] *ša mūši*
46 *ḫayyāṭītu ša kal ūme*
47 *mulaʾʾītu ša šamê*
48 *mulappitu ša erṣeti*
49 *kāmītu ša pī ilī*
50 *kāsītu ša birkī*[a] ^{d}*ištarāti*
51 *dayyiktu ša eṭlūti*
52 *lā pādītu ša sinnišāti*
53 *šaḫḫuṭītu ṣabburītu*
54 *ša ana ipšīša u ruḫêša lā ušarru mamma*
55 *enennama ītamrūki*[a] *iṣṣabtūki*
56 *uštēnûki uštabalkitūki*
57 *uštapēlū amāt ipšīki*
58 ^{d}*Ea u* ^{d}*Marduk iddinūki ana* ^{d}*Girra qurādi*

29 May Girra, your destroyer, cause you to take the road of no-return,
30 May raging Girra inflame your body." TU$_6$ ÉN

30a It is the [wo]rding (of the incantation) to undo witchcraft: a figurine of clay—tallow in the epigastrium, *ēr*[*u*-wood in the kidneys].

---

31 Incantation. Two are they, the heavenly Daughters of Anu,
32 Three are they, the heavenly Daughters of Anu.
33 Holding the rope, they descend to me from heaven.
34 (I ask them:) "For what have you arisen, whither do you go?"
35 "We have come to seek out the sorcerer and sorceress of so-and-so, the son of so-and-so;
36 In order to collect their leavings,
37 In order to gather their refuse,
38 In order to light the brazier at night have we come."

38a <It is> the wording (of the incantation) <to undo witchcraft>: a figurine of tallow (and) sweepings.

---

39 Incantation. Witch,[82] murderess,
40 Denouncer, *naršimdatu*.
41 Exorcist, ecstatic,
42 Snake charmer, *agugiltu*.
43 *qadištu*-votary, *nadītu*-priestess,
44 Ishtar-votary, *kulmašītu*-votary.
45 Huntress[83] of the night,
46 Espier of the daytime.
47 Defiler of the heavens,
48 Besmircher of the netherworld.
49 Seizer of the mouth of the gods,
50 Binder of the knees of the goddesses.
51 Killer of young men,
52 The one who shows no mercy to women.
53 Attacker, mutterer,
54 Into whose sorcery and spell no one can penetrate.[84]
55 Now then, having seen[85] you, seized you,
56 Changed you, turned you around,
57 Reversed your words of sorcery,
58 Ea and Marduk give you over to Girra, the warrior.

59 ^{d}*Girra qurādu rikiski liḫpe*
60 *u mimma mala tēpušī* [a-]*lišamḫerki kâši*[-a] T[U$_6$][b] ÉN

60a [a-][KA.INIM.M]A UŠ$_{11}$.BÚR.RU.DA *ṣalam išk[ū]ri*[-a]

---

61 ÉN ^{d}*id*[a] *ellu namru quddušu anāku*
62 *ēpišūʾa apkallū ša apsî*
63 *ēpišētūʾa mārāt* ^{d}*Ani ša šamê*
64 *eppušūni īteneppušūni*[a]

65 *eppušūnimma ul ileʾʾû zumrī*
66 *ēteneppušūnimma ul ileʾʾû ana ṣabātiya*

67 *anāku ēpušma elišunu azziz*

68 *ētelil kīma* ^{d}*id ina šadîya*[a]
69 *ētebib*[a] *kīma namri ina bīt*[b] *purussêya*
70 *ša kaššāpiya u kaššāptiya*
71 ^{d}*id u namru nabalkattašunu liškunūma*
72 *kišpīšunu libbalkitūma*
73 *ana muḫḫišunu u lānišunu lillikū*
74 [a-]*kīm[a i]ṭṭî liṣlimū pānīšunu*[-a]
75 *liḫūlū lizūbū u littattukū*
76 *u anāku kīma* ^{d}*id ina šadîya*[a] *lū ellēku* [b]ÉN

---

77 ÉN *lamânni sutû elamû redânni*
78 *katmanni agû edû saḫpanni*
79 *kaššāptu sutāte dāni ṣibissa*
80 *elēnītu elamāta ṣibissa mūtu*
81 ^{d}*Girra tappê* ^{d}*Šamaš izizzamma*
82 *kīma šadî ina kibrīti inuḫḫu*[a]
83 *kišpī*[a] *ruḫê*[b] *rusê*[c] *ša kaššāptiya*
84 *elēnītiya* ^{d}*Girra liqmi*
85 ^{d}*id ellu libbaša liḫpe*
86 *mû nāri ellūtu lipšurū kišpīša*
87 *u anāku kīma* ^{d}*id ina šadîya*[a] *lū ellēku* [b]ÉN

---

59 May Girra, the warrior, break your bond,
60 And cause whatever sorcery you have performed to confront you yourself.[86] TU$_6$ ÉN

60a It is [the wordin]g (of the incantation) to undo witchcraft: a figurine of w[a]x.

---

61 [87]Incantation. Pure River (and) holy Sun am I.
62 My sorcerers are the Sages of the *apsû*,[88]
63 My sorceresses are the heavenly Daughters of Anu.
64 They perform sorcery against me, they keep on performing sorcery against me,
65 They perform sorcery against me, but they cannot overpower my body,
66 They keep on performing sorcery against me, but they (still) are unable to seize me.
67 I have performed sorcery (against them) and stand victorious over them.
68 Like River, I have (now) become pure[89] in my mountain,[90]
69 Like Sun, I have (now) become bright[91] in the place of my judgment.
70 Of my warlock and witch,
71 May River and Sun establish their retreat,
72 And (thus) may their witchcraft turn back
73 And go onto their head and body.
74 Lik[e bi]tumen may their faces become black,[92]
75 May they dissolve, melt, drip ever away.
76 And may I, like River, become pure in my mountain.[93] ÉN

---

77 Incantation. The Sutean surrounds me, the Elamite pursues me,
78 The wave covers me, the current overwhelms me.
79 The witch, the Sutean[94]—strong is her hold,
80 The denouncer, the Elamite—her hold is death.
81 Girra, companion of Šamaš, stand by me (at the judgment) and
82 —as the mountain is made quiet by sulphur[95]—
83 The witchcraft, the spittle, (and) the enchainment[96] of my witch
84 (And) of my denouncer may Girra burn.
85 May pure River smash her heart,
86 May the pure waters of the river release her witchcraft.
87 And may I, like River, become pure in my mountain.[97] ÉN

87a [a-][K]A.INIM.MA UŠ$_{11}$.BÚR.RU.DA *ṣalam iṭṭî ša kibrīta ballu*[-a]

---

88 ÉN *attīmannu kaššāptu ša iqbû*[a] *amāt lemuttiya* [b-]*ina libbiša*[-b]

89 *ina libbiša ibbanû ruḫûʾa*
90 *ina šaptīša ibbanû*[a] *rusûʾa*
91 *ina kibis takbusī izzaz mūtu*
92 *kaššāptu aṣbat pâki aṣbat lišānki*
93 *aṣbat īnīki nāṭilāti*
94 *aṣbat šēpīki allakāti*
95 *aṣbat birkīki ebberēti*
96 *aṣbat aḫīki muttabbilāti*
97 *aktasi idīki ana arki[k]i*
98 ^{d}*Sîn ellammê liqattâ pagarki*
99 *ana miqit mê u išāti liddīkima*
100 *kaššāptu kīma seḫer kunukki annê*
101 *liṣūdū līriqū pānūki*

101a [a-]<KA.INIM.MA UŠ$_{11}$.BÚR.RU.DA> *ṣalam ṭīṭi* <*ina*> *ku[nukki arqi p]âšu tabarram*[-a]

---

102 ÉN *attīʾē ša tēpušīnni*
103 *attīʾē ša tušēpišīnni*
104 [a]*attīʾē ša tukaššipīnni*
105 *attīʾē ša tuḫappipīnni*
106 *attīʾē ša tuṣabbitīnni*
107 *attīʾē ša tukannikīnni*
108 *attīʾē ša tuʾabbitīnni*
109 *attīʾē ša tubbirīnni*
110 *attīʾē ša tukassînni*[a]
111 *attīʾē ša tulaʾʾînni*
112 *taprusī ittiya ilī u* ^{d}*ištarī*
113 *taprusī ittiya* [a-]*šēʾu*[b] *šeʾītu*[-a|c] *aḫu aḫatu ibru tappû u kinattu*

114 *aleqqâkkimma ḫaḫâ ša utūni diḫmennu*[a] *ša diqāri*
115 *amaḫḫaḫ atabbak ana*[a] *qaqqad raggati*[b] *šīmtiki*[c]

87a It is the [wo]rding (of the incantation) to undo witchcraft: a figurine of bitumen mixed with sulphur.

* * *

88 Incantation. Whoever you are, O witch who has spoken[98] an evil word against me in her heart,
89 In whose insides was formed spittle against me,
90 On whose lips was formed[99] enchainment against me.
91 In your footsteps stands death.
92 O witch, I have seized your mouth, I have seized your tongue,
93 I have seized your seeing eyes,
94 I have seized your walking feet,
95 I have seized your crossing knees,
96 I have seized your (load) bearing arms.
97 I have (now) tied your arms behind your back.
98 May Sin, pure of rites, bring your body to an end,
99 May he cast you into a fall of water and fire,
100 So that, O witch, like the rim of this seal
101 May your face melt (and glow) and become yellow.[100, 101] TU$_6$ ÉN

* * *

101a <It is the wording (of the incantation) to undo witchcraft>: a figurine of clay—you seal its [mo]uth <with> [a yellow] sea[l].

* * *

102 Incantation. O you who have performed sorcery against me,
103 O you who have had sorcery performed against me,
104 O you who have bewitched me,
105 O you who have shattered me,
106 O you who have seized me,
107 O you who have sealed me,
108 O you who have destroyed me,
109 O you who have bound me,
110 O you who have tied[102] me,
111 O you who have defiled me.
112 (Thereby) you have estranged from me my god and my goddess,
113 You have estranged from me male neighbor (and) female neighbor,[103] brother (and) sister, friend, companion, and peer.
114 I am taking against you slag from a kiln, soot from a pot,
115 And am moistening and pouring (it) on the head of your evil[104] character$^{(?)}$.

* * *

115a [a]KA.INIM.MA UŠ$_{11}$.BÚR.RU.DA ^{d}*ištar kubši* ⸢*kinṣi ša ṭīṭi teppuš ḫaḫâ*⸣ *ša utū[ni]*

115b *diḫmenni ša diqāri t[amaḫḫaḫma t]a*<*tab*>*bak ana* ⸢*qaqqadiša*⸣

---

116 ÉN *ša ēpušanni uštēpišanni*[a]

117 *ina mīli nāri ēpušanni*
118 *ina mīṭi nāri ēpušanni*
119 *ana ēpišti epšīma iqbû*
120 *ana sāḫerti suḫrīma iqbû*
121 *annīta lū makurraša*
122 *kīma makurru annīta ibbalakkitu*[a]
123 *kišpūša libbalkitūma ana*[a] *muḫḫiša u lāniša lillikū*
124 *dīnša lissaḫipma*[a] *dēnī līšir* [b]ÉN[c]

124a [a-]KA.INIM.MA UŠ$_{11}$.BÚR.RU.DA *makur ṭīṭi šinā ṣalmī ṭī[ṭi] ina* ⸢*libbiša*⸣[-a]

---

125 ÉN[a] *makurraya*[b] ^{d}*Sîn ušēpiš*
126 [a]*ina birīt qarnīša našât pišertu*
127 *ašbū ina libbiša* [a-]*kaššāpu u kaššāptu*[-a]
128 *ašbū ina libbiša* [a-]*ēpiš(u) u ēpištu*[-a]
129 *ašbū ina libbiša* [a-]*sāḫiru u sāḫertu*[-a]
130 *ša makurrišunu libbatiq ašalša*
131 *markassa lippaṭerma*[a] *tarkullaša linnaseḫ*
132 *edû*[a] *ana*[b] *tâmti lišēṣīšunūti*
133 *šamrūti agû elišunu lītellû*[a]
134 *šāršunu ayy-izīqamma ayy-iḫīṭanni*
135 *ina qibīt* ^{d}*Nuska u* ^{d}*Girra ilī dayyānī* [a]ÉN

135a [a-]K[A.INIM.MA UŠ$_{11}$.BÚR.RU.DA *m]akur līši šinā ṣalmī l[īši (ina libbiša)]*[-a]

---

136 ÉN *ḫaṣabtu*[a] *sūqāti ammēni tugdanarrênni*

137 *ammēni našparātūki ittanallakāni*[a]
138 *kaššāptu qaqdâ(?) amât[ī]ki*
139 *ammēni ittanakšadā ana ṣabātiya*

115a It is the wording (of the incantation) to undo witchcraft: You make (a figurine of) a goddess from head to toe(?)[105] out of clay. Slag from a ki[ln]
115b (And) soot from a pot yo[u moisten and] p<o>ur on [her] head.

---

116 Incantation. She who has performed sorcery against me, has had sorcery performed[106] against me,
117 Has performed sorcery against me when the river was at its fullest,
118 Has performed sorcery against me when the river was at its lowest,
119 Has said "perform sorcery" to a sorceress,
120 Has said "enchant" to an enchantress[107]—
121 This be her boat:
122 Just as this boat turns over/back,[108]
123 So may her witchcraft turn over/back and go onto her head and body.
124 May her case be overturned,[109] but may my case go straight.[110] ÉN

124a It is the wording (of the incantation) to undo witchcraft: a boat of clay—two figurines of cl[ay] insi[de i]t.

---

125 Incantation. I have had Sîn make my boat.[111]
126 Between its horns[112] it carries release (from witchcraft).
127 In its hold sit the[113] warlock and witch,
128 In its hold sit the sorcerer and sorceress,
129 In its hold sit the enchanter and enchantress.
130 May the tow rope of their boat be cut,
131 May its cable come loose, may its mooring post be uprooted,
132 May the flood drive them out to the[114] ocean,
133 May raging waves surge over them.
134 May their wind not blow toward me and locate me—
135 By the command of Nuska and Girra, the divine judges. ÉN

135a [It is] the w[ording (of the incantation) to undo witchcraft: a b]oat of dough—two figurines of d[ough (inside it)].

---

136 Incantation. O sherd of the streets, why are you constantly hostile to me?
137 Why do your messages keep coming to me?
138 O witch, *constantly*(?) your words,
139 Why do they reach me again and again so as to seize me?[115]

140 *elli ana ūri aptaki aka[ttam]*
141 *urrad ana qaqqarimma uṣabbat kibsī[ki]*
142 *ina kibsīki rābiṣu ušeššeb*
143 [a-]*eṭem ridâti*[-a] *ḫarrānki ušaṣbat*
144 *amaḫḫaṣ muḫḫaki ušanna ṭēnki*
145 *adallaḫ libbaki tamaššî šīrīki*
146 *ēpištu u muštēpištu*
147 *šamû anākuma ul tulappatīnni*[a]
148 *erṣetu anākuma ul turaḫḫînni*[a]
149 [a]*siḫil balti anākuma ul takabbasīnni*
150 *ziqit zuqaqīpi anākuma ul talappatīnni*
151 *šadû zaqru anākuma kišpūki ruḫûki*
152 *rusûki upšāšûki lemnūti*
153 *ul iṭeḫḫûni ul iqarribūni yâši* [a]ÉN

153a [a-]KA.INIM.MA UŠ$_{11}$.BÚRU *ḫaṣabti sūq erbetti lipâ tapaššaš na[bā]sa takarrik*[-a]

---

154 ÉN *rittumma rittu*
155 *rittu dannatu ša amēlūti*
156 *ša kīma nēši iṣbatu amēlu*
157 [a]*kīma ḫuḫāri isḫupu eṭlu*
158 *kīma šēti ukattimu qarrādu*
159 *kīma šuškalli ašārēdu ibāru*[!a]
160 *kīma gišparri iktumu dannu*
161 *kaššāpu u kaššāptu*[a] *rittakunu* ^{d}*Girra liqmi*
162 ^{d}*Girra līkul*[a] ^{d}*Girra lišti* ^{d}*Girra lištābil*
163 ^{d}*Girra lilsâ eli dannati rittekunu*
164 *ša rittakunu ēpušu zumurkunu*[a] *liḫmuṭ*
165 *lispuḫ*[a] *illatkunu mār* ^{d}*Ea mašmaššu*
166 *qutri* ^{d}*Girra līrim*[a]/*ā pānīkunu*
167 *kīma tinūri ina ḫiṭâtīkunu*
168 *kīma diqāri ina luḫummêkunu*[a]
169 *lispuḫkunūši* ^{d}*Girra ezzu*
170 *ayy-iṭḫûni kišpīkunu*[a] *ruḫêkunu lemnūti*[b]
171 *ētellâ kīma nūnī ina mêya*
172 *kīma šaḫî ina rušumtiya*[a]
173 *kīma maštakal ina*[a] *ušalli*
174 *kīma sassati ina aḫi atappi*

140 I ascend the roof to cover your window,
141 I descend to the ground to seize (and thereby block) [your] tracks—
142 In your tracks I set a lurker-demon,
143 I cause a pursuing ghost[116] to seize your path.
144 I smite your skull and make you go mad,
145 I disturb your mind[117] so that you forget your flesh.[118]
146 O sorceress and the woman who instigates sorcery,
147 I myself am heaven: you cannot besmirch[119] me,
148 I myself am the Netherworld: you cannot impregnate[120] me,
149 I myself am a thorn of the *baltu*-thornbush: you cannot tread on me,
150 I myself am the sting of the scorpion: you cannot take hold of me,
151 I myself am a high mountain: your witchcraft, spittle,
152 Enchainment, evil machinations
153 cannot approach me, cannot come close to me myself. ÉN

153a It is the wording (of the incantation) to undo witchcraft: a sherd from the crossroad you rub with tallow (and) wrap up with red [wo]ol.

154 Incantation. Hand, hand,
155 Strong hand of humankind,
156 Which, like a lion, seized a man,
157 Like a bird trap, clamped down on a young man,
158 Like a hunting net, covered over the warrior,
159 Like a battle net, caught the leader,
160 Like a trap, covered the strong one.
161 O warlock and witch,[121] may Girra burn your hand,
162 May Girra consume, may Girra drink, may Girra confound,
163 May Girra roar at your strong hand.
164 Because your hand performed sorcery, may he[122] inflame your body,[123]
165 May the son of Ea, the exorcist, scatter[124] your cohort.
166 May the smoke of Girra cover your face.[125]
167 Like an oven through your cracks,
168 Like a pot through your mud,
169 May raging Girra scatter you.
170 May your witchcraft (and) evil spittle not approach me.
171 I rise up like fish from my water,
172 Like a pig from my mud,[126]
173 Like soapwort from[127] the flood plain,
174 Like grass from the canal bank,

175 *kīma zēr ušî ina aḫi tâmti*
176 *ellet* ^{d}*ištar munammerat šīmti*
177 *uṣurāt balāṭi uṣṣurāku anāku*
178 *ina qibīt iqbû* ^{d}*Girra rašubbu*
179 *u* ^{d}*Girra āriru mār* ^{d}*Ani qardu*[a]

---

180 [a]ÉN *rittumma rittu*
181 *rittu dannatu ša amēlūti*
182 *kaššāptu aššu pîki dabbibu*
183 *aššu dannati rittaki*
184 *āla amātu aššâkki*
185 *bīta amātu uba*ʾʾ*âkki*
186 *kaššāpu*[a] *kaššāptu ēpiš(u) u ēpištu*
187 [a-]*bilī*[b|c] *rittakunuma*[-a] *ana išāti luddi*[d] [e]ÉN

187a [a-]KA.INIM.MA UŠ$_{11}$.BÚRU *rittu išk*[*ūri*][-a]

---

188 ÉN *bišlī bišlī qidê qidê*
189 [a-][DUB] 3.KAM[-a] *Maqlû*[b]

175 Like seed of an ebony tree[128] from the seashore.
176 (By) bright Ishtar, who illumines fate,
177 I have been designated with the design of life[129]—
178 By the command pronounced by awesome Girra
179 And blazing Girra, warlike son of Anu.

---

180 Incantation. Hand, hand,
181 Strong hand of humankind.
182 O witch, because of your slanderous mouth,
183 Because of your strong hand,
184 In (your) city, I have borne a message to you,
185 In (your) house, I have sought you out with a message:
186 "O warlock (and) witch, sorcerer and sorceress,
187 Bring[130] your hand so that I[131] may cast it into the fire." ÉN

187a It is the wording (of the incantation) to undo witchcraft: a hand of w[ax].

---

188 Incantation. Burn, burn, blaze, blaze!
189 The third [tablet] of Maqlû.[132]

Maqlû IV. Transcription

1 ÉN *bišlī bišlī qidê*[a] *qidê*
2 *raggu*[!a] *u ṣēnu ē tērub atlak*
3 *attāmannu mār manni attīmannu mārat manni*

4 *ša ašbātunuma ipšēkunu upšāšêkunu tēteneppušāni yâši*

5 *lipšur* ^{d}*Ea mašmaššu*
6 *lišbalkit kišpīkunu* ^{d}*Asalluḫi mašmaš ilī mār* ^{d}*Ea apkallu*

7 [a-]*akassīkunūši akammīkunūši*[-a] *anamdinkunūši*
8 *ana* ^{d}*Girra qāmê qālî kāsî kāšidu ša kaššāpāti*
9 ^{d}*Girra qāmû lītallal idāya*
10 *ipšu bārtu amāt lemutti râmu zīru*
11 *dibalâ zikurrudâ kadabbedâ šurḫungâ*
12 *šabalbalâ ṣūd pānī u šanê ṭēmu*
13 *tēpušāni tušēpišāni* ^{d}*Girra lipšur*

14 *ana mīti tahīrā'inni*
tē(pušāni tušēpišāni ^{d}*Girra lipšur)*

15 *ana gulgullati t*[*apqi*]*dā'i*[*nn*]*i*
⸢*tē(pušāni tušēpišāni* ^{d}*Girra lipšur)*⸣

16 *ana eṭem kimtiya tapq*[*idā'inni*]
[*tē(pušāni tušēpišāni* ^{d}*Girra lipšur)*]

17 *ana eṭemmi aḫî tapqidā'i*[*nni*]
[*tē(pušāni tušēpišāni* ^{d}*Girra lipšur)*]

Maqlû IV. Translation

1 [133]Incantation. Burn, burn, blaze, blaze!
2 Evil and wicked one, do not enter, go away!
3 Whoever you are, the son of whomever, whoever you are, the daughter of whomever,
4 Who sit and repeatedly perform[134] your sorcery and machinations against me myself:
5 May Ea, the exorcist, release.
6 May Asalluḫi, the exorcist of the gods, Ea's son, the sage, divert your witchcraft.
7 I am binding you, I am holding you captive, I am giving you over
8 To Girra, the burner, the scorcher, the binder, the vanquisher of witches.
9 May Girra, the burner, be joined to my side.
10 Sorcery, rebellion, evil word, love (-magic), hate (-magic),
11 Perversion of justice, *Zikurrudâ*-magic, muteness, pacification,
12 Mood swings, vertigo, and madness
13 You have performed against me, have had performed against me: may Girra release.
14 You have betrothed me to a dead person,
You (have performed (sorcery) against me, have had (sorcery) performed against me: may Girra release).
15 You have h[anded m]e over to a skull,
You (have performed against me, have had performed against me: may Girra release).
16 You have han[ded me] over to a ghost of (a member of) my family,
[You (have performed against me, have had performed against me: may Girra release)].
17 You have handed me over to the ghost of a stranger,
[You (have performed against me, have had performed against me: may Girra release)].

18 *ana eṭemmi murtappidu ša pāqida lā īšû tapqid*[*āʾinni*]
[*tē(pušāni tušēpišāni* ^{d}*Girra lipšur)*]

19 *ana eṭem ḫarbī nadûti tapqidāʾinni*
⸢*tē(pušāni tušēpišāni* ^{d}*Girra lipšur)*⸣

20 *ana ṣēri kīdi u namê tapqidāʾinni*
⸢*tē(pušāni tušēpišāni* ^{d}*Girra lipšur)*⸣

21 ⸢*ana*⸣ *dūri u samēti tapqidāʾinni*
tē(pušāni tušēpišāni ^{d}*Girra lipšur)*

22 *ana* ^{d}*Bēlet ṣēri u bamâti tapqidāʾinni*
tē(pušāni tušēpišāni ^{d}*Girra lipšur)*

23 *ana utūni lapti tinūri kinūni* KI.UD.BA *u nappaḫāti tapqidāʾinni*
tē(pušāni tušēpišāni ^{d}*Girra lipšur)*

24 *ṣalmīya ana mīti tapqidā*
tē(pušāni tušēpišāni ^{d}*Girra lipšur)*

25 *ṣalmīya ana mīti taḫīrā*
tē(pušāni tušēpišāni ^{d}*Girra lipšur)*

26 *ṣalmīya itti mīti t*[*ušn*]*illā*
tē(pušāni tušēpišāni ^{d}*Girra lipšur)*

27 *ṣalmīya ina sūn mī*[*ti tušni*]*llā*
tē(pušāni tušēpišāni ^{d}*Girra lipšur)*

28 *ṣalmīya ina kimaḫ mī*[*ti ta*]*qbirā*
tē(pušāni tušēpišāni ^{d}*Girra lipšur)*

29 *ṣalmīya ana gulgullati tapqidā*
tē(pušāni tušēpišāni ^{d}*Girra lipšur)*

18 You have hand[ed me] over to a roaming ghost who has no one to take care of it,
[You (have performed against me, have had performed against me: may Girra release)].

19 You have handed me over to a ghost in the uninhabited wastelands,
You (have performed against me, have had performed against me: may Girra release).

20 You have handed me over to the steppe, open country, and desert,
You (have performed against me, have had performed against me: may Girra release).

21 You have handed me over to a wall and battlement,
You (have performed against me, have had performed against me: may Girra release).

22 You have handed me over to the (divine) mistress of the steppe and open country,
You (have performed against me, have had performed against me: may Girra release).

23 You have handed me over to a kiln, a roasting oven, a baking oven, a brazier, a . . .-oven, and bellows,
You (have performed against me, have had performed against me: may Girra release).

24 You have handed over figurines of me to a dead man,
You (have performed against me, have had performed against me: may Girra release).

25 You have betrothed figurines of me to a dead man,
You (have performed against me, have had performed against me: may Girra release).

26 You have l[ai]d figurines of me with a dead man,
You (have performed against me, have had performed against me: may Girra release).

27 You have [la]id figurines of me in the lap of a dead [man],
You (have performed against me, have had performed against me: may Girra release).

28 You have buried figurines of me in the grave of a dead [man],
You (have performed against me, have had performed against me: may Girra release).

29 You have handed over figurines of me to a skull,
You (have performed against me, have had performed against me: may Girra release).

30 *ṣalmīya ina igāri tapḫâ*
tē(pušāni tušēpišāni ^{d}*Girra lipšur)*

31 *ṣalmīya ina askuppati tušnillā*
tē(pušāni tušēpišāni ^{d}*Girra lipšur)*

32 *ṣalmīya ina biʾi ša dūri tapḫâ*
tē(pušāni tušēpišāni ^{d}*Girra lipšur)*

33 *ṣalmīya ina titurri taqbirāma ummānu ukabbisū*
[a]-*tē(pušāni tušēpišāni* ^{d}*Girra lipšur)*-[a]

34 *ṣalmīya ina burê ša ašlāki būrta taptâ taqbirā*
tē(pušāni tušēpišāni ^{d}*Girra lipšur)*

35 *ṣalmīya ina rāṭi ša nukaribbi būrta taptâ taqbirā*
tē(pušāni tušēpišāni ^{d}*Girra lipšur)*

36 *ṣalmīya lū ša bīni lū ša erēni lū ša lipî*
37 *lū ša iškūri lū ša kupsi*
38 *lū ša iṭ*[*ṭî lū*] *ša ṭīṭi lū ša līši*
39 *ṣalmī muš*[*šulāti š*]*a pānīya u lāniya tēpušāma*
40 [*k*]*alba t*[*u*]*šākilā šaḫâ tušākilā*
41 *iṣṣū*[*ra t*]*ušākilā ana nāri taddâ*
42 *ṣalmīya ana Lamašti mārat* ^{d}*Ani tapqidā*
tē(pušāni tušēpišāni ^{d}*Girra lipšur)*

43 *ṣalmīya ana* ^{d}*Girra tapqidā*
tē(pušāni tušēpišāni ^{d}*Girra lipšur)*

44 *mêya itti mīti tušnillā*
tē(pušāni tušēpišāni ^{d}*Girra lipšur)*

45 *mêya ina sūn mīti tušnillā*
tē(pušāni tušēpišāni ^{d}*Girra lipšur)*

30 You have immured figurines of me in a wall,
You (have performed against me, have had performed against me: may Girra release).
31 You have laid figurines of me under a threshold,
You (have performed against me, have had performed against me: may Girra release).
32 You have immured figurines of me in the drainage opening of a wall,
You (have performed against me, have had performed against me: may Girra release).
33 You have buried figurines of me on a bridge so that crowds would trample over them,
You (have performed against me, have had performed against me: may Girra release).
34 You have made a hole in a fuller's mat[135] and (therein) buried figurines of me,
You (have performed against me, have had performed against me: may Girra release).
35 You have made a hole in a gardener's channel[136] and (therein) buried figurines of me,
You (have performed against me, have had performed against me: may Girra release).
36 Figurines of me—whether of tamarisk, or of cedar, or of tallow,
37 Or of wax, or of sesame pomace,
38 Or of bit[umen, or] of clay, or of dough,
39 Figurines, repre[sentations o]f my face and my body you have made
40 And fed to dog(s), fed to pig(s),
41 Fed to bir[d(s)], cast into a river.
42 You have handed over figurines of me to Lamaštu, daughter of Anu,
You (have performed against me, have had performed against me: may Girra release).
43 You have handed over figurines of me to Girra,
You (have performed against me, have had performed against me: may Girra release).
44 You have laid my (funerary) water[137] with a dead man,
You (have performed against me, have had performed against me: may Girra release).
45 You have laid my water in the lap of a dead man,
You (have performed against me, have had performed against me: may Girra release).

46 [*mêya ina k*]*imaḫ mīti taqbirā*
tē(pušāni tušēpišāni [d]*Girra lipšur)*

47 [*ina* . . .][a] *erṣeti mêya taqbirā*
tē(pušāni tušēpišāni [d]*Girra lipšur)*

48 [*ina* . . .] *erṣeti mêya taqbirā*
tē(pušāni tušēpišāni [d]*Girra lipšur)*

49 *i*[*na*] *ma*[*ḫar ilī (ša) mūš*]*i*(?) *mêya taḫbâ*
tē(pušāni tušēpišāni [d]*Girra lipšur)*

50 [a-]x x [x x] x[-a] *ana* [d]*Gilgameš taddinā*[b]
tē(pušāni tušēpišāni [d]*Girra lipšur)*

51 [*a*]*na a*[*ral*]*lê taḫīrāʾinni*
tē(pušāni tušēpišāni [d]*Girra lipšur)*

52 *zik*[*urr*]*udâ ana pāni* [d]*Sîn*
tē(pušāni tušēpišāni [d]*Girra lipšur)*

53 *zikurrudâ ana pāni* [d]*Šulpaʾea*
[a-]*tē(pušāni tušēpišāni* [d]*Girra lipšur)*[-a]

54 *zikurrudâ ana pāni* [mul]*Nimri*
[*t*]*ē(pušāni tušēpišāni* [d]*Girra lipšur)*

55 *zikurrudâ ana pāni* [d]*Gula*[a]
[*t*]*ē(pušāni tušēpišāni* [d]*Girra lipšur)*

56 [a-][*zi*]*kurr*[*u*]*dâ ana pāni* [mul]*Urgulî*
[*t*]*ē(pušāni tušēpišāni* [d]*Girra lipšur)*[-a]

57 *zikurrudâ ana pāni* [mul]*Ereqqi*
tē(pušāni tušēpišāni [d]*Girra lipšur)*

58 [*zi*]*kurr*[*u*]*dâ ana pāni* [mul]*Zuqaqīpi*
tē(pušāni tušēpišāni [d]*Girra lipšur)*

46 You have buried [my water in the g]rave of a dead man,
You (have performed against me, have had performed against me: may Girra release).

47 You have buried my water [in . . .] of the earth/netherworld,[138]
You (have performed against me, have had performed against me: may Girra release).

48 You have buried my water [in . . .] of the earth/netherworld,[139]
You (have performed against me, have had performed against me: may Girra release).

49 You have drawn my water in the pre[sence of the gods of the nigh]t(?),
You (have performed against me, have had performed against me: may Girra release).

50 You have given over[140] m[y . . .][141] to Gilgameš,
You (have performed against me, have had performed against me: may Girra release).

51 You have betrothed me to the [nether]world,
You (have performed against me, have had performed against me: may Girra release).

52 *Zikurrudâ*-magic in the presence of the moon (*Sîn*),
You (have performed against me, have had performed against me: may Girra release),

53 *Zikurrudâ*-magic in the presence of Jupiter (*Šulpaeʾa*),
You (have performed against me, have had performed against me: may Girra release).

54 *Zikurrudâ*-magic in the presence of Cygnus (*Nimru*),[142]
You (have performed against me, have had performed against me: may Girra release).

55 *Zikurrudâ*-magic in the presence of Lyra (^{d}*Gula*),[143]
You (have performed against me, have had performed against me: may Girra release).

56 [*Zi*]*kurrudâ*-magic in the presence of Leo (*Urgulû*),
You (have performed against me, have had performed against me: may Girra release).

57 *Zikurrudâ*-magic in the presence of Ursa Major (*Ereqqu*),
You (have performed against me, have had performed against me: may Girra release).

58 [*Zi*]*kurrudâ*-magic in the presence of Scorpio (*Zuqaqīpu*),
You (have performed against me, have had performed against me: may Girra release).

59 *zikurrudâ ana pāni* ^{mul}*Šitaddari*
tē(pušāni tušēpišāni ^{d}*Girra lipšur)*

60 [*zi*]*kurrudâ ana pāni* ^{mul}*Ḫabaṣīrāni*
tē(pušāni tušēpišāni ^{d}*Girra lipšur)*

61 [*ziku*]*rrudâ ša ṣerru šikkû* ⸢*arrabu perurūtu*⸣
[*t*]*ē(pušāni tušēpišāni* ^{d}*Girra lipšur)*

62 [*ziku*]*rrudâ ša* ⸢*pagri(?)*⸣ x [x x] x ⸢*ša ruḫê*⸣
$^{\mathrm{a-}}$[*tē(pušāni tušēpišāni* ^{d}*Girra lipšur)*]$^{\mathrm{-a}}$

63 $^{\mathrm{a-}}$[*ina a*]*kalu ukultu inbu*$^{\mathrm{-a}}$ *t*[*usākilā*]*ʾinni*
[*t*]*ē(pušāni tušēpišāni* ^{d}*Girra lipšur)*

64 ⸢*ina*^{a} *mê šizbi*⸣ *šikāri k*[*a*]*rāni ta*[*šq*]*âʾinn*[*i*]
[*t*]*ē(pušāni tušēpišāni* ^{d}*Girra lipšur)*

65 *ina mê* $^{\mathrm{a-}}$*u uḫūli*$^{\mathrm{-a}}$ *turammek*[*āʾi*]*nn*[*i*]
$^{\mathrm{b-}}$[*tē(pušāni tušēpišāni* ^{d}*Girra lipšur)*]$^{\mathrm{-b}}$

66 *ina šamni tapšušāʾi*[*nni*]
[*tē(pušāni tušēpišāni* ^{d}*Girra lipšur)*]

67 *ina šūbulāti tušēbilā*[*ʾi*]*nn*[*i*]
[*tē(pušāni tušēpišāni* ^{d}*Girra lipšur)*]

68 ^{a}*ina maḫar ili*$^{\mathrm{!b}}$ *šarri kabti u rubê tušaškināʾi*[*nni*]
69 *ina maḫa*[*r t*]*īru manzazi u bāb ekalli t*[*ušaškināʾinni*]

70 *ina maḫar ibri tap*[*p*]*ê u kinatti tušaš*[*kināʾinni*]
71 *ina maḫar abi u ummi aḫ*[*i (u) a*]*ḫāti aššati māri u mārti tušaškināʾinni*

72 *ina maḫar bīti u bābi ardi u amti ṣeḫer rabi ša bīti tuša*[*škināʾinni*]

73 *eli āmeriya t*[*uša*]*mriṣāʾinni*

59 *Zikurrudâ*-magic in the presence of Orion (*Šitaddaru*),
You (have performed against me, have had performed against me: may Girra release).

60 [*Zi*]*kurrudâ*-magic in the presence of Centaurus (*Ḫabaṣīrānu*),
You (have performed against me, have had performed against me: may Girra release).

61 [*Zi*]*kurrudâ*-magic by means of a snake, a mongoose, a dormouse(?), a *perurūtu*-mouse,
You (have performed against me, have had performed against me: may Girra release).

62 [*Zi*]*kurrudâ*-magic by means of a corpse(?), [. . .], *Z*[*ikurrudâ*-magic(?)] by means of 'spittle' (*ruḫû*),
[You (have performed against me, have had performed against me: may Girra release)].

63 [You have fed] me bread, food, (and) fruit,[144]
You (have performed against me, have had performed against me: may Girra release).

64 You have given me to drink water, m[ilk], beer, and wine,
You (have performed against me, have had performed against me: may Girra release).

65 You have washed me with water and potash,[145]
[You (have performed against me, have had performed against me: may Girra release)].

66 You have salved me with oil,
[You (have performed against me, have had performed against me: may Girra release)].

67 You have sent me gifts,
[You (have performed against me, have had performed against me: may Girra release)].

68 You have caused me to be rejected by god!, king, noble, and prince.

69 You have caus[ed me to be rejected] by courtier, attendant, and (personnel at) the palace gate.

70 You have caused me to be [rejected] by friend, companion, and peer.

71 You have caused me to be rejected by father and mother, brother [(and)] sister, wife, son, and daughter.

72 You have caused me to be [rejected] by household and city quarter, male and female servants, young and old of the household.

73 You have made me sickening in the sight of one who beholds me.

74 *aktamīkunūši aktasīkunūši attadinkunūši*

75 *ana* ^{d}*Girra qāmî qāl*[*î*]^{a} *kāsî kāšidu ša kaššāpāti*
76 ^{d}*Girra qāmû lipaṭṭer riksīkunu*
77 *lipaššer kišpīkunu* [*lipaš*]*šer sirqīkunu*
78 *ina qibīt* ^{d}*Marduk mār* ^{d}*Ea apkalli*
79 *u* ^{d}*Girra āriru mār* ^{d}*Ani qardu* TU$_{6}$ ÉN^{a}

---

80 ÉN *attīmannu kaššāptu*^{a} *ša zikurrudâ ippuša*

81 *lū ibru lū tappû*
82 *lū aḫu lū itbāru*
83 *lū ubāra lū mār āli*
84 *lū mūdû lū lā mūdû*
85 [*l*]*ū kaššāpu* [*l*]*ū kaššāptu*
86 *lū zikaru lū sinništu*
87 *l*[*ū mītu l*]*ū balṭu*
88 $^{a-}$*lū* ⸢*ḫablu*⸣ *lū ḫabilti*$^{-a}$
89 *lū kurgarrû lū saḫḫiru*
90 [$^{a-}$*lū eššebû*$^{-a}$ *l*]*ū naršindû*
91 *lū mušlaḫḫu lū agug*[*illu*]
92 [*l*]*ū lišānu nakertu ša ina māti bašâtu*
93 *mušītu kallatu kuttumtu*
94 *kakkašunu lišberma* ⸢*lā ṣalālu*⸣ *līmissunūt*[*e*] TU$_{6}$ É[N]^{a}

---

95 [ÉN *nērtiya ka*]*ššāptiya* ⸢*kušāpātīya*⸣
96 [*šūquki ša š*]*amê šupulki š*[*a qaqqari*^{a}]

97 [x x x x] x kur-*ki ša sub*[*arti*]
98 [*ma*-x x x-*ki*] *ša p*[*i*-x]
99 [x x x x] x ḫar-*ki šūquki ša š*[*amê*]
100 [x x (x x)-*k*]*i*^{a} *ša qaqqa*[*ri*]
101 x [x x x x kur]-*ki ša suba*[*rti*]
102 *ma*-[x x x-*ki*] *ša* [*pi*(?)-x]
103 *ana*[*pp*]*assunūti k*[*i*(?)(-)x x x (x)]
104 *a*[*s*]*ammakšunūti k*[*i*(-)x x x (x)]
105 *ašakkanšunūti ana pī* ^{d}[*Girra qāmî*]
106 [*q*]*ālî kāsî k*[*āšid*]*u ša kaššāpāti* $^{a-}$ T[U$_{6}$ ÉN]$^{-a}$

---

74 I have (now) captured you, I have (now) bound you, I have (now) given you over
75 To Girra, the burner, the scorcher, the binder, the vanquisher of witches.
76 May Girra, the burner, undo your bindings,[146]
77 Release your witchcraft, [rele]ase your scattered-offerings—
78 By the command of Marduk, Ea's son, the sage,
79 and blazing Girra, Anu's son, the warrior. TU$_6$ ÉN[147]

---

80 Incantation. Whoever you are, O witch, who performs *Zikurrudâ* magic against me,
81 Whether friend or companion,
82 Whether brother or colleague,
83 Whether 'newcomer' or (native) citizen,
84 Whether acquaintance or stranger,
85 Whether warlock or witch,
86 Whether male or female,
87 Whe[ther dead person o]r living person,
88 Whether wronged man or wronged woman,
89 Whether cultic performer or *enchanter*,[148]
90 [Whether ecstatic o]r *naršindû*,
91 Whether snake-charmer or *agugillu*,
92 Or whatever foreign language (speaker) that is in the country—
93 May the Night, the veiled bride,
94 Break their weapon and impose sleeplessness upon them. TU$_6$ ÉN[149]

---

95 [Incantation. My murderess, my w]itch, my sorceress(?).
96 [Your height is that of] the heavens, your depth is th[at of the netherworld],
97 [. . .] your [. . .] . . . is that of Sub[artu],
98 [Your . . .] is that of a . . . [. . .],
99 [. . .] your [. . .] . . ., your height is that of the hea[vens],
100 [Yo]ur [. . .][150] is that of the netherworld,
101 [. . .] your [. . .] is that of Suba[rtu],
102 [Your] . . . [. . .] is that of a [. . .]!
103 I am smashing them li[ke . . .],
104 I am driving(?) them away li[ke . . .]
105 I am placing them in the mouth of [Girra, the burner],
106 The scorcher, the binder, the va[nquish]er of witches. T[U$_6$ ÉN]

---

107 ÉN *ša* ^{d}*Šamši mannu abušu ma*[*nnu ummašu*]
108 *mannu aḫāssuma šū dayyā*[*nu*]
109 *ša* ^{d}*Š*[*amš*]*i* ^{d}*Sîn abuš*[*u* ^{d}*Ni*]*kkal umma*[*šu*]
110 ^{d}*Ma*[*nzâ*]*t aḫāssuma*[a] *šū dayyā*[*nu*]
111 ^{d}*Šamaš k*[*išpī uḫallaq r*]*uḫê upaš*[*šar*]
112 *u šī* ^{d}*M*[*anz*]*ât uḫappe rik*[*sī*]
113 *kišpī uḫallaq ruḫê upa*[*ššar*]
114 *ipšu bārt*[*u amā*]*t lemutti ušabbal* $^{a-}$<<*ana*>> *šāra*$^{!-a}$ *te* É[N]

---

115 ÉN *ippušāni īteneppušān*[*i*]

116 *gutêti elamâtu ḫabigalbatâtu*[a]
117 *mārāt māti irakkasāni riksī*
118 *šeššet riksūšina sebet piṭrūʾa*
119 *ša mūši ippušānimma ša kal ūmu apaššaršināti*

120 *ša kal ūmu ippušānimma ša mūši apaššaršināti*

121 *ašakkanšināti ana pī* ^{d}*Girra qāmî*[a]
122 *qālî*[a] *kāsî kāšidu ša kaššāpāti* TU$_6$[b] ÉN

---

123 ÉN *ruʾuʾa kaššāpat anāku pāširāk*
124 *kaššāptu kaššāpat anāku pāširāk*
125 *kaššāptu elamâti anāku pāširāk*
126 *kaššāptu qutâti anāku pāširāk*
127 *kaššāptu sutâti anāku pāširāk*
128 *kaššāptu lullubâti anāku pāširāk*
129 *kaššāptu ḫabigalbatâti anāku pāširā*[*k*]
130 *kaššāptu agugillat anāku pāširā*[*k*]
131 *kaššāptu naršindat anāku pāširā*[*k*]
132 *kaššāptu mušlaḫḫat anāku pāširāk*
133 *kaššāptu eššebâti anāku pāširāk*
134 *kaššāptu qurqurrati anāku pāširāk*
135 *kaššāptu ši-i-mat* a-ši[a] *bābiya anāku pāširāk*
136 *kaššāptu mārat āliya anāku pāširāk*
137 *ašpur ana ereb* ^{d}*Šamši ṣalmīšina ilqutūni*
138 *ša sebe u sebe kaššāpāti ṣalmīšina ana* ^{d}*Girra apqid*
139 *ana utūni ālikti ašarrapšināti*[a]
140 $^{a-d}$*Girra qumi kaššāpī u kaššāptī*$^{-a|b}$

107 Incantation. Of the Sun, who is his father, wh[o is his mother],
108 Who is his sister? He is the judge.
109 Of the S[u]n, Sîn is his father, [Nik]kal is [his] mother,
110 Ma[nzâ]t is his sister: He is the judge.
111 Šamaš [destroys] the w[itchcraft], releas[es] the spittle,[151]
112 And she, M[anz]ât, breaks the bon[ds].
113 (So) I destroy the witchcraft, I rele[ase] the spittle,
114 I cause the wind! to carry off sorcery, rebellion, evil [wor]d.[152] *te* ÉN

---

115 Incantation. They perform sorcery against me, they keep on performing sorcery against me.
116 The Gutean women, the Elamite women, the Hanigalbatean women,
117 The native women[153] are securing bindings against me.
118 Six are their bindings, seven are my undoings.
119 Should they be performing sorcery against me at night, I will be releasing them[154] all day (long),
120 Should they be performing sorcery against me all day (long), I will be releasing them at night.
121 I am placing them in the mouth of Girra, the burner,[155]
122 the scorcher,[156] the binder, the vanquisher of witches. TU$_6$ ÉN

---

123 Incantation. My friend is a witch; (but) I am a releaser,
124 The witch is a witch;[157] (but) I am a releaser,
125 The witch is an Elamite; (but) I am a releaser,
126 The witch is a Gutean; (but) I am a releaser,
127 The witch is a Sutean; (but) I am a releaser,
128 The witch is a Lullubean; (but) I am a releaser,
129 The witch is a Hanigalbatean; (but) I am a releaser,
130 The witch is an *agugiltu*; (but) I am a releaser,
131 The witch is a *naršindatu*; (but) I am a releaser,
132 The witch is a snake-charmer; (but) I am a releaser,
133 The witch is an ecstatic; (but) I am a releaser,
134 The witch is a metal-worker; (but) I am a releaser,
135 The witch is a . . . of my gate;[158] (but) I am a releaser,
136 The witch is a native of my city; (but) I am a releaser,
137 I have sent to the west—they have gathered their figurines for me.
138 I hand over figurines of the seven and seven witches to Girra,
139 I am burning[159] them in a burning stove.
140 Girra, burn my warlock and witch,

141 ^{d}*Girra quli kaššāpī u kaššāptī*
142 ^{d}*Girra qumīšināti*
143 ^{d}*Girra qulīšināti*
144 ^{d}*Girra kušussināti*
145 ^{d}*Girra aruḫšināti*
146 ^{d}*Girra šutābilši[n]āti*
147 *ezzu* ^{d}*Girra linēḫkināši*
148 ^{d}*Girra lulīmu l[i*-x-x-*kin]āši*
149 *kaššāpu u kaššāptu ēpiš(u) u ēpištu*
150 *šunu lū* ⸢*ana*⸣ [*bī*ʾ]*ima*
151 ⸢*anāku kīma*⸣ *mê mīlima lubāʾšināti* TU$_6$ ÉN

---

152 [ÉN] *ēpištu u muštēpištu*

153 [D]UB 4.KAM* *Maqlû*

141 Girra, scorch my warlock and witch!
142 Girra, burn them,
143 Girra, scorch them,
144 Girra, vanquish them,
145 Girra, consume them,
146 Girra, confound them!
147 May raging Girra calm you,
148 May Girra, the red stag, . . . you.
149 Warlock and witch, sorcerer and sorceress—
150 May they be (meant) for the drainage opening,
151 But may I like flood water sweep over them. TU$_6$ ÉN

152 [Incantation]. My sorceress and the woman who instigates sorcery against me.
153 The fourth [ta]blet of Maqlû.

MAQLÛ V. TRANSCRIPTION

1 ÉN *ēpištī u muštēpištī*

2 *ašbat ina ṣilli amari ša libitti*
3 *ašbatma ipšīya ippuša ib[a]nnâ ṣalmīya*
4 *ašapparakkimma ḫašê u šamaššammī*
5 *usappaḫ kišpīki utār amâtīki ana pîki*

6 *ipšī tēpušī lū ša attūki*
7 *ṣalmū tabnî lū ša ṭēmeki*
8 *mû taḫbî lū ša ram[ān]iki*
9 *šipatki ayy-iqriba amâtūki ayy-ikšud[āʾi]nni*

10 *ina qibīt* ^{d}*Ea* ^{d}*Šamaš u* ^{d}*Marduk u rubāti* ^{d}*Bēlet-ilī* ⌜TU$_6$ ÉN⌝

---

11 ÉN *mannu pâ iptil uṭṭata ukaṣṣer*
12 *ana*$^{!}$[a] *šamê kišpī ana erṣeti bārta īpuš*

13 *ana errî mārat ilī rabûti ipša bārta amāt lemutt[i] mannu uqarrib*

14 *kīma pû lā ippattil<u> uṭṭ[a]tu lā uk[t]aṣṣaru*$^{!}$[a]

15 *ana šamê kišpī ana erṣeti bārtu lā inneppušū*

16 *ana errî mā[rat] ilī rabûti*
17 *ipša bārtu amāt lemutt[i l]ā* ⌜*iṭeḫḫû*⌝ *lā iqarrubu*[a]
18 *ipša bārtu amāt lemutt[i] lā iṭeḫḫâ*[a] *lā iqarrub[a y]âši* TU$_6$ ÉN[b]

Maqlû V. Translation

1 Incantation. My sorceress and the woman who instigates sorcery against me,
2 She sits in the shade of a pile of bricks.
3 She sits and performs my sorcery against me, forms figurines of me.
4 I am sending against you thyme and sesame,
5 And (thereby) I am scattering your witchcraft (and) turning back your words to your mouth.
6 May the sorcery that you have performed be against you yourself,
7 May the figurines that you have formed be of your own features,
8 May the water that you have drawn be your own.
9 May your incantation not draw near to me, may your words not reach me—
10 By the command of Ea, Šamaš, and Marduk, and the princess Bēlet-ilī. TU$_6$ ÉN

---

11 Incantation. Who has twined chaff together, knotted barley (together),
12 Performed witchcraft against the Heavens, rebellion against the Netherworld,
13 Made sorcery, rebellion, an evil word draw near to Colocynth, daughter of the great gods?
14 As chaff cannot be twined together, (as) barley cannot be knotted (together),
15 (As) witchcraft cannot be performed against the Heavens, (nor) rebellion against the Netherworld,
17 (As) sorcery, rebellion, an evil word cannot approach, cannot draw near
16 To Colocynth, daughter of the great gods,
18 So may sorcery, rebellion, an evil word not approach me, not draw near to me myself. TU$_6$ ÉN[160]

---

19 ÉN *dunnānu du[nn]ānu pāris purussêni*

20 *ina maḫar* ^{d}*Nuska u* ^{d}*Girra šupêltī*(?)[a] *šaknat*
21 *alkī nabalkattu šumrī nabalkattu*
22 *ina nasāḫ šēpī ša kaššāpiya u kaššāptiya šēpīki šuknī*
23 *lillu lībilma kaššāpta ana dayyāniša*
24 *dayyānša kīma nēši lissâ eliša*
25 *limḫaṣ lēssa litēr amāssa ana pîša*
26 [a|b]-*ēpištī u muštēpištī*-[b]
27 *kīma nīnî linūšū*[a] *kišpūša*
28 *kīma azupīri liṣappirūši kišpūša*
29 *kīma saḫlê lisḫulūši kišpūša*
30 *kīma samīdi lisammûši kišpūša*
31 *kīma kasî liksûši kišpūša*
32 *kīma ḫašê liḫaššûši kišpūša*
33 *kīma qitmi liktumūši kišpūša*
34 [a]-*kīma errê līrurūši kišpūša*-[a]
35 *kīma nuḫurti* [a]-*littaḫḫirā šaptāša*-[a|b]
36 [a]-*ēpištī u muštēpištī*-[a]
37 *libbalkissi sūqu u sulû*
38 *libbalkissi ibratu u nēmedīša*
39 *libbalkitūšima ilū ša ṣēri u āli*
40 *kaššāptu kīma kalbi ina ḫaṭṭi kīma anduḫallat ina kirbanni*
41 *kīma kibsi immeri lisammekūšima lītiqūši*

42 *kīma kursinni imēri ina sūqi ētequ*[a] *likkelmēši*
43 [a]-*ēpištī u muštēpištī*-[a]
44 *ina birīt kalbī lisūrū kulūlūša*
45 *ina birīt kulūlūša lisūrū kalbū*
46 *eliša qulmû lisūrū*
47 *kīma piqan ṣabīti quturša lible* TU$_{6}$[a] ÉN

---

48 ÉN *attīmannu kaššāptu ša īteneppuša*[a] *šalāšat arḫī ešret ūmē mišil ūme*

49 *anāku anaššâkkimma kukra takur*[a] *šadî ḫašê ti'ût māt*[*i*]

50 *pitiltu pitiltu ša qašdāti terinnatu terinnatu ša še'a malâti*[a]
51 *annû ša kaššāpiya u kaššāptiya ḫepâ rikissun*
52 *terrā kišpūša ana meḫê amâtīša ana šāri*

19 Incantation. Strong one(?), strong one(?), the one who decides our verdict,
20 Before Nuska and Girra my exchange(?)[161] is established.
21 Come, Uprising, rage, Uprising,
22 Set your feet down (by) uprooting the feet of my warlock and witch![162]
23 May an idiot bring the witch to her judge,
24 And[163] may her judge roar at her like a lion,
25 Strike her cheek, (and) turn her word back into her mouth.
26 My[164] sorceress and the woman who instigates sorcery against me,
27 Like ammi may her witchcraft give way,[165]
28 Like saffron may her witchcraft cut her down,
29 Like cress may her witchcraft pierce her,
30 Like *samīdu*-plant may her witchcraft hamper her,
31 Like mustard may her witchcraft bind her,
32 Like thyme may her witchcraft chop her up,
33 Like black paste may her witchcraft cover her,
34 Like colocynth may her witchcraft curse her,
35 Like asafoetida may her lips be made to shrivel?.[166]
36 My[167] sorceress and the woman who instigates sorcery against me,
37 May street and way turn against her,
38 May cult niche and its socle turn against her,
39 May the gods of the steppe and the city turn against her.
40 The witch—like a dog with a stick, like a lizard with a clod,
41 like a footprint of a sheep[168]—may they knock her away and pass her by,
42 Like a fetlock of an ass, in the street may the passerby frown at her.
43 My[169] sorceress and the woman who instigates sorcery against me,
44 May her headbands whirl among the dogs,
45 May the dogs whirl between her headbands,
46 May an ax whirl over her.
47 Like the droppings of a gazelle may her smoke come to an end. TU$_6$ ÉN

---

48 Incantation. Whoever you are, O witch, who keeps on performing[170] sorcery against me for three months, ten days, and half a day:
49 I am lifting up against you *kukru,*[171] the offspring[172] of the mountain, (and) thyme, the nourishment of the land.
50 Cord, cord of the *qadištu*-votary, cone, cone that is full of seeds,
51 Break the bond—this one—of my warlock and witch,
52 Turn her witchcraft into a storm, her words into a wind!

53 *linnašpū kišpūša kīma pê liqqalpū kīma šūmī*

54 *liššaḫṭū kīma suluppī lippašrū kīma pitilti*
55 *ina qibīt* ^{d}*Ištar* ^{d}*Dumuzi* ^{d}*Nanaya bēlet râmi*
56 *u* ^{d}*Kanisurra bēlet kaššāpāti* ÉN

---

57 ÉN *zīru ša tēpušāni tušēpišāni ana muḫḫikun*[*u ēpuš*]*a*

58 *zikurrudâ ša tēpušāni tušēpišāni ana muḫḫikunu ēpuša*
dibalâ ša tēpušāni tušēpišāni ana muḫḫikunu ēpuša
kadabbeda [*ša tēpušāni tušēpišāni ana muḫḫikunu ēpuša*]

59 *šurḫungâ ša tēpušāni tušēpišāni ana muḫḫikunu ēpuša*
dimmakurrâ [*ša tēpušāni tušēpišāni ana muḫḫikunu ēpuša*]

60 [a]*utukku lemnu tušaṣbitāʾinni utukku lemnu liṣbatku*[*nūši*]

61 *alû lemnu tušaṣbitāʾinni alû lemnu* [*liṣbatkunūši*]

62 *eṭemmu lemnu tušaṣbitāʾinni eṭemmu lemnu* [*liṣbatkunūši*]

63 *gallû lemnu tušaṣbitāʾinni gallû lemnu* [*liṣbatkunūši*]

64 *ilu lemnu tušaṣbitāʾinni ilu lemnu liṣbatkunū*[*ši*]
65 *rābiṣu lemnu tušaṣbitāʾinni rābiṣu lemnu liṣbatkunūši*

66 [a]^{d}*Lamaštu* ^{d}*labāṣu* ^{d}*aḫḫāzu tušaṣbitāʾinni*
^{d}*Lamaštu* ^{d}*labāṣu* ^{d}*aḫḫāzu liṣbatūkunūši*

67 *lilû lilītu ardat-lilî tušaṣbitāʾinni lilû lilītu ardat-lilî liṣbatūkunūši*

68 *ina nīši u māmīti tuqattâʾinni ina nīši u māmīti pagarkunu liqti*

69 *uzzi ili šarri kabti u rubê yâši taškunāni*

53 May her witchcraft be blown away like chaff, may it be peeled like garlic,

54 May it be torn off like dates, may it be unknotted like a cord—

55 By the command of Ishtar, Dumuzi, Nanaya, the mistress of love,

56 And Kanisurra, the mistress of witches. ÉN

---

57 Incantation. Hate(-magic) that you have performed against me, have had performed against me, [I perfor]m against you.

58 *Zikurrudâ*-magic that you have performed against me, have had performed against me, I perform against you.[173]

Perversion of justice that you have performed against me, have had performed against me, I perform against you.

Muteness [that you have performed against me, have had performed against me, I perform against you].

59 Pacification that you have performed against me, have had performed against me, I perform against you.

Madness [that you have performed against me, have had performed against me, I perform against you].

60 An evil *utukku*-demon you have caused to seize me: May an evil *utukku*-demon seize you.

61 An evil *alû*-demon you have caused to seize me: [May] an evil *alû*-demon [seize you].[174]

62 An evil ghost you have caused to seize me: [May] an evil ghost [seize you].

63 An evil (demonic) constable you have caused to seize me: [May] an evil (demonic) constable [seize you].

64 An evil god you have caused to seize me: May an evil god seize you.

65 An evil lurker-demon you have caused to seize me: May an evil lurker-demon seize you.

66 Lamaštu, *labāṣu* (disease), (and) *aḫḫāzu*-jaundice you have caused to seize me: May Lamaštu, *labāṣu* (disease), (and) *aḫḫāzu*-jaundice seize you.

67 *lilû*, *lilītu*, (and) *ardat-lilî* you have caused to seize me: May *lilû*, *lilītu*, (and) *ardat-lilî* seize you.

68 By oath and curse you have brought me to an end: By oath and curse may your body come to an end.

69 The anger of god, king, noble, and prince you have inflicted on me myself:

70 *uzzi ili šarri kabti u rubê ana kâšunu liššaknakkunūši*

71 *ašuštu arurtu ḫūṣ ḫīp libbi gilittu piritti u adirti yâši taškunāni*

72 *ašuštu arurtu ḫūṣ ḫīp libbi gilittu piritti adirtu ana kâšunu liššaknakkunūši*[(sic)a]

73 *aqmūkunūši ina kibrīti elleti u ṭābat amurri*

74 *alqut quturkunu ikkib šamê*

75 *epšētēkunu turrānikkunūši* TU$_6$ ÉN

---

76 ÉN *attīmannu kaššāptu ša kīma šūti ikkimu ḫamiššeret ūmī*

77 *tilti ūmē imbaru šanat nalši*

78 *urpata ikṣuramma izziza*[a] *yâ*[*ši*]

79 *atebbâkkimma kīma gallāb šamê il*[*tāni*]

80 *usappaḫ urpataki uḫalla*[*q ūmki*]

81 *usappaḫ kišpīki š*[*a ta*]*kk*[*imī mūša u urra*]

82 *u našparāt zik*[*ur*]*ru*[*dâ ša taltapparī yâši*]

---

83 [a]ÉN *šaruḫ* [*lānī šaruḫ zīmī*]

84 *allallû* [^{d}*Girra ezzu*]

85 *qāmû š*[*a kaššāpi u kaššāpti*]

86 *ēpišū*ʾ[*a ēpišētūʾa muštēpišētūʾa*]

87 *kaššāpū*[ʾ*a kaššāpātūʾa*]

88 *ana* ^{d}*N*[*uska u*] ⸢^{d}*Girra*⸣ [(*dayyānī*) *paqdātunu* TU$_6$ ÉN]

---

89 [a]ÉN *šerʾānī tukaṣṣir*[*ā* ^{d}*Ea uptaṭṭer*]

90 *ṣalmī tuggirā tukassâ* [^{d}*Asalluḫi uptaššer*]

91 *kiṣir takṣurāni ki*[*pid takpudāni*]

92 ^{d}*Girra āriru li*[*šābil šāra*]

93 ^{d}*Nuska dayyānu bē*[*l mašmaššūti*]

70 May the anger of god, king, noble, and prince be inflicted on you yourselves.

71 Distress, trembling, depression, terror, fear, and apprehension you have inflicted on me myself:

72 May distress, trembling, depression, terror, fear, (and) apprehension be inflicted on you yourselves.

73 I burn you with pure sulphur and the salt of Amurru,

74 I gather up your smoke, an abomination to heaven.

75 Your deeds (of sorcery) are (hereby) turned back to you! TU$_6$ ÉN

---

76 Incantation. [175] Whoever you are, O witch, who like the South wind has piled up[176] for fifteen days,

77 Nine days fog, a year dew,

78 Who[177] has formed a cloud against me and stood over me:

79 I am rising up against you like the shearer of the heavens, the North [wind],

80 I am scattering your cloud, I am annihilating [your storm],

81 I am scattering your witchcraft th[at night and day you have piled] up over me

82 And the messages of *Zikur*[*rudâ* that you have repeatedly sent against me].

---

83 Incantation. Splendid is [my appearance, splendid is my countenance].

84 Mighty, [raging Girra],

85 Burner o[f the warlock and the witch].

86 [My] sorcerers, [my sorceresses, (and) the women who instigate sorcery against me],

87 [My] warlocks [(and) my witches],

88 To N[uska and] Girra [(the judges) you are handed over! TU$_6$ ÉN]

---

89 Incantation. [Ea has (now) unbound] the sinews that you have bound up,[178]

90 [Asalluḫi has (now) released] the figurines that you have twisted and fettered.

91 The knot that you have knotted against me, the pl[ot that you have plotted against me]

92 May blazing Girra ca[use the wind to carry off],

93 May Nuska, the judge, the mas[ter of exorcism],

94 *epiš tēpušāni ana m[uḫḫikunu litēr]*

95 *pašrū kišpūʾa z[akû rusûʾa]*
96 *ina mê ša n[a]gbi ru[ḫêkunu apṭur]*
97 *anāku ētelil ēteb[ib azzaku ina maḫar* ^{d}*Nuska] u* ^{d}*Girra [(ilī) dayyānī* TU$_6$ ÉN]

---

98 [a]ÉN *attunu m[û ša tattanallakā kal mātāti]*
99 *tattanablakkatā [kal šadâni]*
100 *tuḫappâ kār[a tušabbirā eleppa(?)]*
101 *mû nāri ālik[ūt]i m[û Idiqlat] u P[uratti]*
102 *mû ayabba [tâmati rapašti]*[a]
103 [a]*iḫbûnikkunūši a[pkallū ša apsî]*
104 *sebet apkallū šūt Eridu ut[ammûkunūši]*
105 *ina têšunu elli tēlil[ā u] takṣâ [(. . .)]*
106 *kīma ina têšunu el[li tēlilā u takṣâ (. . .)]*
107 *libbi kaššāpiya ka[ššāptiya līlil u likṣi]*

108 *anāku ina qibīt* ^{d}*E[a šar apsî]*
109 *asallaḫ*[a] *libbakunu m[ê nāri]*
110 *asallaḫ laʾmēkunu quturk[unu mê tâmti]*
111 *ina qibīt* ^{d}*Ea* ^{d}*Šamaš*[a] ^{d}*[Mar]duk u rubāti* ^{d}*Bēlet-ilī* T[U$_6$ ÉN]

---

112 ÉN *ēpišūʾa ēpišēt[ūʾa]*
113 *kaššāpūʾa kaššāpātū[ʾa]*
114 *ša ikpudu libbak[un]u lemuttī*
115 *taštene*ʾʾ*â ruḫê zaprūti*
116 *ina upšāšê lā ṭābūti tuṣabbitā birkīya*
117 *anāku ana puššur kišpīya u ruḫêya ina amāt* ^{d}*Ea u* ^{d}*Asalluḫi* ^{d}*Girra assaḫri*
118 *ina mê ša nagbi libbakunu unēḫ*
119 *kabattakunu uballi*
120 *ṣereḫ libbikunu ušēṣ[i]*
121 *ṭēn[k]unu ušanni*
122 *milik[k]unu aspuḫ*
123 *kišpī[k]unu aqlu*
124 *kip[d]ī libbi[k]unu ušaddīkunūši*
125 *Idiqlat u Puratta lā tebbirāni*

94 [Turn back] up[on your head] the sorcery that you have performed against me.
95 My witchcraft is released, [my enchainment is] c[leared],
96 With spring water, [I undo your "spitt]le,"
97 I have (now) become pure, cl[ean, and innocent in the presence of Nuska] and Girra, [the (divine) judges. TU$_6$ ÉN]

---

98 Incantation. You, Wa[ter, that constantly flows over all the lands],
99 That crosses to and fro [over all mountains],
100 That shatters the quay [and breaks up the boat(?)].
101 Flowing river water, wat[er of the Tigris] and Eu[phrates],
102 Water of the Ocean, [the vast sea(s)],
103 [The] s[ages of the *apsû*] drew you,
104 The seven sages of Eridu a[djured you by oath].
105 By their pure incantation, you became pur[e and] cool [(. . .)].
106 As by their pure incantation [you became pure and cool (. . .)],
107 So may the heart of my warlock (and) my wi[tch become pure and cool].
108 At the command of E[a, king of the *apsû*],
109 I am sprinkling your heart with [river w]ater,
110 I am sprinkling your embers (and) y[our] smoke [with sea water]—
111 By the command of Ea, Šamaš, [Mar]duk, and the princess Bēlet-ilī. T[U$_6$ ÉN]

---

112 Incantation. My sorcerers, my sorceresses,
113 My warlocks, my witches,
114 You whose heart has planned evil against me,
115 You keep on seeking malicious spells against me,[179]
116 You have bound my knees with not good machinations.
117 In order to release the witchcraft and spittle against me, having (first) turned to Girra at the word of Ea and Asalluḫi,
118 (Now) with spring water, I quench your heart,
119 I extinguish your mood,
120 I remove the ardor of your heart,
121 I confound your understanding,
122 I unravel your thinking,
123 I burn your witchcraft,
124 I cause you to abandon the plots of your heart.
125 You shall not cross over the Tigris and the Euphrates to me,

126 *ika u palga lā tettiqāni*
127 *dūra u samēti lā tabbalakkitāni*
128 *abulla u nērebīša lā terrubāni*
129 *kiš[p]ūkunu ⌜ayy⌝-iṭḫûni*
130 *amâtūkunu ay[y-i]kšudāʾinni*
131 *ina qibīt* ^{d}*Ea* ^{d}*Šamaš u* ^{d}*Marduk*[a] *rubāti* ^{d}*[Bēlet]-ilī* TU$_6$ ÉN

---

132 ÉN *ezzētunu šamrātunu dannātunu gaṣṣātunu*
133 *gapšātunu ašṭātunu ayyāb[ātunu] lemnētunu*
134 *ša lā* ^{d}*Ea mannu unāḫkunūši*
135 *ša lā* ^{d}*Asalluḫi mannu ušapšaḫkunūš[i]*
136 ^{d}*Ea linēḫkunūši*
137 ^{d}*Asalluḫi lišapšeḫkunū[ši]*
138 *pīya mû pīkunu išātu*
139 *pīya pâkunu liballi*[a]
140 *tû ša pîya tâ ša pîkunu liballi*
141 [a-]*kipdī ša libbiya liballâ kipdī ša libbikunū*[-a]

---

142 ÉN *akbus gallâya āb[u]t lemnī*
143 *aṭbuḫ gērâya uḫtall[iq]a rēdânāya*
144 *ina maḫri qurādi* ^{d}*Nuska* TU$_6$ ÉN

---

145 ÉN *ḫūlā zūbā u ita[t]tukā*
146 *quturkunu lītelli šamê*
147 *laʾmēkunu liballi* ^{d}*Šamšu*
148 *liprus ḫayyattakunu mār* ^{d}*Ea mašmaššu*

---

149 ÉN *šadû liktumkunūši*
150 *šadû liklākunūši*
151 *šadû linēḫkunūši*
152 *šadû liḫsīkunūši*
153 *šadû liteʾkunūši*
154 *šadû lineʾkunūši*[a]
155 [a-]*šadû likattinkunūši*[-a|b]
156 *šadû dannu elikunu limqut*
157 *ina zumriya lū tapparrasāma* TU$_6$ ÉN

---

158 ÉN *isâ isâ rēqā rēqā*

126 You shall not pass over dyke and canal to me,
127 You shall not climb over wall and battlement to me,
128 You shall not come in through the city gate and its entranceways to me!
129 May your witchcraft not approach me,
130 May your words not reach me—
131 By the command of Ea, Šamaš, and Marduk, (and) the princess [Bēlet]-ilī. TU$_6$ ÉN

---

132 Incantation. Raging, furious, strong, cruel,
133 Overbearing, tough, hos[tile], wicked are you!
134 Who but Ea can calm you?
135 Who but Asalluḫi can soothe you?
136 May Ea calm you,
137 May Asalluḫi soothe you.
138 My mouth is water, your mouth is fire:
139 May my mouth extinguish your mouth,[180]
140 May the spell of my mouth extinguish the spell of your mouth,
141 May the plots of my heart extinguish the plots of your heart![181]

---

142 Incantation. I trample down my foe,[182] I de[str]oy my evildoer,
143 I slaughter my opponent, I repeatedly anni[hil]ate[183] my pursuer
144 In the presence of the warrior Nuska. TU$_6$ ÉN.

---

145 Incantation. Melt, dissolve, and drip ever away!
146 May your smoke rise ever heavenward,
147 May the Sun extinguish your embers,
148 May Ea's son, the exorcist, cut off the terror that emanates from you.

---

149 Incantation. May the mountain cover you,
150 May the mountain hold you back,
151 May the mountain pacify you,
152 May the mountain hide you,
153 May the mountain enshroud you,
154 May the mountain turn you back,[184]
155 May the mountain cover you over,
156 May a strong mountain fall upon you.
157 From my body you shall indeed be separated! TU$_6$ ÉN

---

158 Incantation. Be off, be off, begone, begone,

159 *bēšā bēšā ḫilqā ḫilqā*
160 *duppirā atlakā isâ u rēqā*
161 *lumunkunu kīma qutri lītelli šamê*
162 *ina zumriya isâ*
163 *ina zumriya rēqā*
164 *ina zumriya bēšā*
165 *ina zumriya ḫilqā*
166 *ina zumriya duppirā*
167 *ina zumriya atlakā*
168 *ana zumriya lā taturrā*
169 *ana zumriya lā teṭeḫḫê*[a]
170 *ana zumriya lā tasanniqā*
171 *nīš* ^{d}*Šamaš kabti lū* [*t*]*amâtunu*
172 *nīš* ^{d}*Ea bēl nagbi lū t*[*amâ*]*tunu*
173 *nīš* ^{d}*Asalluḫi mašmaš ilī lū tamâtunu*
174 *nīš* ^{d}*Girra qāmîkunu lū tamâtunu*
175 *ina zumriya lū tapparrasāma* TU$_6$ ÉN

---

176 ÉN ^{d}*Enlil qaqqadī pānūʾa ūmu*
177 DUB 5.KÁM[a] *Ma*[*ql*]*û*[b] . . .

159 Depart, depart, flee, flee,
160 Go off, go away, be off, and begone!
161 May your wickedness like smoke rise ever heavenward!
162 From my body be off,
163 From my body begone,
164 From my body depart,
165 From my body flee,
166 From my body go off,
167 From my body go away!
168 To my body turn back not,
169 To my body approach not,[185]
170 To my body reach not!
171 By the life of Šamaš, the honorable, be adjured,
172 By the life of Ea, lord of the underground springs, be [adju]red,
173 By the life of Asalluḫi, the magus of the gods, be adjured,
174 By the life of Girra, your executioner,[186] be adjured!
175 From my body you shall indeed be separated! TU_6 ÉN

---

176 Incantation. Enlil is my head, my face is *ūmu*.
177 The fifth tablet of *Ma*[*ql*]*û*.[187]

MAQLÛ VI. TRANSCRIPTION

1 ÉN ^{d}*Enlil qaqqadī pānū'a ūmu*
2 $^{a-d}$*Uraš ilu gitmālu lamassat pānīya*$^{-a}$
3 *kišādī ullu ša* ^{d}*Gula*
4 *idāya gamlu ša* ^{d}*Sîn* ^{d}*Amu*[*rri*]
5 *ubānātū'a bīnu eṣemti ilūt*[*i*]
6 *lā ušasnaqā ruḫê ana zumr*[*iya*]
7 ^{d}*Lugaledina* ^{d}*Latarak irt*[*ī*]
8 *kinṣāya* ^{d}*Muḫra šēpāya ša ittanallak*[*ā*] *kalīšina laḫr*[*ī*]
9 *attāmannu ilu lemnu ša kaššāpu u kaššāp*[*tu*] *išpurūniššu ana dâkiy*[*a*]

10 *lū ērēta lā tallak*[*a*]
11 *lū ṣallāta lā tetebbâ*
12 *amâtūka lū ḫašḫūru ina* ⸢*maḫar*⸣ *ili u šarri linū*[*šā*]

13 *ultēšib ina bābiya* ^{d}*Lugalirra ilu dan*[*nu*]^{a} *sukkal ilī* ^{d}*Papsukkal*

14 ⸢*maḫṣā*⸣ [*lēta ša*] *kaššāpiya u kaššāptiya*
15 *t*[*errā amāssa a*]*na pîša* TU$_6$ ÉN

---

16 ÉN *ēpiš*[*tī*] *qumqummatu*
17 *kaššāp*[*tī*] *kuttimmatu*
18 *ēpišt*[*ī*] *eššebūtu*
19 *ummi ēpištiya naršindatu*
20 *ammēni tubbalī napištī ana malkī*
21 [*an*]*āku ana puššur kišpīki tullal našâku*
22 *kukru ša šadî li*[*ḫt*]*eppe*(?) *rikisk*[*i*]
23 ⸢*u*⸣ *k*[*išpīki*] *u*[*tār ana šāri*(?)] T[U$_6$ ÉN]

---

24 $^{a-}$[ÉN *kukrumma kukru*]$^{-a}$
25 ^{a}[*kukru* x x^{b} *ina*(?) *šadânī ellūti qudd*]*uš*[*ūti*]

Maqlû VI. Translation

1 Incantation. Enlil is my head, my face is *ūmu*,[188]
2 Uraš, the perfect god, is the pupil(s) of my face,[189]
3 My neck is the necklace of Gula,
4 My arms are the crook of Sin (and) Amurru,
5 My fingers are tamarisk, the divine bone—
6 They shall not allow spittle to reach my body,
7 Lugaledinna and Latarak are my chest,
8 My knees are Muḫra, my pacing feet are the whole (heavenly) flock.[190]
9 Whoever you are, O evil god whom the warlock and witch have sent here to kill me:
10 Even if you are awake, do not come here,
11 Even if you are asleep, do not rise up (to come) here.
12 May your words be (bad) apples, before god and king may [they cr]umble.
13 At my doorway, I have set Lugalirra, the stro[ng][191] god, and the vizier of the gods, Papsukkal.
14 "Strik[e the cheek of] my warlock and witch,
15 Tu[rn her word back] into her mouth." TU$_6$ ÉN

---

16 Incantation. My sorceress is a *qumqummatu*,
17 My witch is a charcoal burner(?),
18 My sorceress is an ecstatic,
19 The mother of my sorceress is a *naršindatu*.
20 "Why do you carry my life off to the (infernal) 'princes'?
21 In order to release your witchcraft, I raise up *tullal*.[192]
22 May *kukru* of the mountains br[ea]k up your bond,
23 And I [will turn your] w[itchcraft into a wind(?)]." T[U$_6$ ÉN]

---

24 [Incantation. *kukru*, *kukru*],
25 [*kukru*, . . .[193] in(?) the pure ho]l[y mountains],

26 [ṣeḫrūtu terḫī ša] enēt[i]
27 [ṣeḫrētu terinnātu š]a qašdāti
28 [alkānimma ša] kaššāpiya u kaššāptiya [dannu ḫ]epâ rikissa[a]
29 [terrā ki]špīša ana meḫê amâtīša ana šāri
30 [linn]ešpū kišpīša kīma pê
31 [liṣall]imūši kīma dikmenni
32 k[īma sīr]i igāri lišḫuḫū kišpūša
33 š[a kaššāptiy]a lippaṭer kiṣer libbiša

---

34 ÉN [k]ukrumma kukru
35 kukr[u] [x x] ina(?) šadânī ellūti quddušūti
36 ṣeḫrūtu t[e]rḫī ša enēti
37 ṣeḫrētu terinnātu ša qašdāti
38 alkānimma ša kaššāpiya u kaššāptiya dannu ḫepâ rikissa
39 u [m]imma mala tēpušā nutēr ana šāri

---

40 ⸢ÉN⸣ [ē] kaššāptiya elēnītiya
41 abu lā taškunī tuquntu
42 ammēni ina bītiki iqattur qutru
43 ašapparakkimm[a kukra(?) šammi(?)] ⸢pišerti⸣
44 a[s]appaḫ kišpīki u[tār amâtīki ana pîk]i

---

45 [ÉN l]ām ^{d}Ningirsu ina māti ilsû ^{d}alāla

46 [lām e]ṭlu īlû ana nakās bīni
47 [attīmannu(?)] kaššāptu ša ana annanna mār annanna tukappatī abnī

48 [taštene]ʾʾê lemutta
49 [a][aziqqakkimm]a kīma iltāni amurri
50 [usappaḫ ur]pataki uḫallaq ūmki
51 [u mimma mala] tēpušī utār ana šāri

---

52 [ÉN undu] kaššāptu ukaššipanni
53 [raḫḫāt]u[a] ureḫḫânni
54 [ēpišt]u(?) išbušu eper šēpīya
55 [muštēpišt]u(?) ilqû ṣillī[a] ina igāri

56 [^{d}Nergal[a] b]ēl ummānāti ^{d}Ea bēl šīmāti

26 [the small *terhu*-vessels of the] *en*-prieste[sses],
27 [the small cones o]f the *qadištu*-votaries:
28 [Come hither] and break the [strong] bond of my warlock and witch,[194]
29 [Turn] her [wit]chcraft into a storm, her words into a wind.
30 [May] her witchcraft [be] blown away like chaff,
31 [May it bla]cken her as ashes (would),
32 May her witchcraft crumble l[ike the plast]er of a wall,
33 May m[y witch's] anger be undone.[195]

---

34 Incantation. *kukru*, *kukru*,
35 *kukru*, [. . .] in(?) the pure holy mountains,
36 the small *terḫu*-vessels of the *en*-priestesses,
37 the small cones of the *qadištu*-votaries:
38 Come hither and break the strong bond of my warlock and witch,
39 And whatever sorcery you have performed, we turn into a wind.

---

40 Incantation. [Ha!] my witch, my deceiver:
41 What, did you not introduce strife?
42 Why is smoke rising from your house?
43 I am sending against you [*kukru*(?), the plant of] release(?),
44 I am scattering your witchcraft, tu[rning your word back into your mouth].

---

45 [Incantation. Be]fore Ningirsu called out the '*alāla*' work-song in the land,
46 [Before the y]outh went up to cut the tamarisk,
47 [Whoever you are(?)], O witch, who gathers together (hail) stones against so-and-so, the son of so-and-so,
48 [Who keeps see]king evil:
49 [I am blowing against you] like the North (and) West winds,
50 [I am scattering your cl]oud, I am annihilating your storm,
51 [and whatever] sorcery you have performed, I am turning into a wind.

---

52 [Incantation. On the day that] the witch bewitched me,
53 [That the inseminatr]ix impregnated me,[196]
54 [That the sorcer]ess(?) collected the dust of my feet,
55 [That the woman who instigates sorce]ry(?) took my shadow from the wall,
56 [O Nergal],[197] lord of troops, Ea, lord of destinies,

57 [^{d}*Asallu*]*ḫi bēl āšipūti*
58 [*maḫṣā*] *lēssa terrā amāssa ana pîša*
59 [*ēpi*]*štu u muštēpištu*
60 ⸢*pûša*⸣ *lū lipû šaptāša lū lubārū naksūti*
61 *kīma qaqqad silit kukri*
62 *ana aḫāmeš lā iqarribū*
63 *kišpūš*[*a*] *ruḫûša rusûša upšāšûša lemnūti*
64 *lā iṭeḫḫûni lā iqarribūni yâši* TU$_6$^{a} ÉN

---

65 ÉN *attī ša tēpušī kalāma*
66 *mimmû tēpušī yâši u šīmtiya*
67 *kukru ša šadî liḫteppâ*(?) *rikiski*
68 *ša imniki u šumēliki šūtu litbal* $^{a-}$TU$_6$ É[N]$^{-a}$

---

69 ÉN *kibrītu elletu mārat šamê*^{a} *rabûti anāk*[*u*]
70 ^{d}*Anu ibnânnima*
71 ^{d}*Enlil* ^{d}*N*[*i*]*nlil ušēridūni an*[*a*] *mā*[*ti*]
72 *ēp*[*i*]*štu ēkīam tēpušīnni*

73 *r*[*ā*]*ḫītu ēkīam tureḫḫî*[*nni*]

74 *ana mala qaqqadiya šamû kašdū*^{a}

75 *ana mala šēpīya erṣetu kašda*[*t*]

76 *ina si*[*ssi*]*ktiya bītānīt*[*i*]
77 *nadât šipassu ša apkal ilī* ^{d}*Mard*[*uk*^{a} ÉN]

---

78 ÉN *k*[*i*]*brītu* ⸢*kibrītu kibrītu*⸣ *mārat* ^{d}*id kibrītu kallat* ^{d}*id*

79 *ša sebe u sebe kašš*[*ā*]*pātūša ša sebe u sebe ayyābātūša*

80 *ēpu*[*š*]*āniššī*[*m*]*ma ul inneppu*[*š*]
81 *ukaššip*[*āniššim*]*ma ul ikkaššip*
82 *mannu ša ana k*[*i*]*brīti ippuša kišpī*
83 *k*[*i*]*br*[*ī*]*tu ša sebe u sebe īpušāni lip*[*š*]*ur*

57 [Asallu]ḫi, lord of exorcism,
58 [Strike] her cheek, turn her word back into her mouth.
59 [The sorc]eress and the woman who instigates sorcery—
60 May her mouth be tallow, her lips torn rags.[198]
61 Just as the tip(s) of a cut twig of *kukru*
62 Cannot draw near to each other,[199]
63 So her witchcraft, spittle, enchainment, evil machinations
64 Shall not approach me, shall not draw near to me myself. TU$_6$ ÉN

---

65 Incantation. You who have performed all kinds of sorcery,
66 Whatever sorcery you have performed against me and my destiny—
67 May *kukru* of the mountains break up your bond,
68 May the South wind carry off what is on your right and on your left. TU$_6$ ÉN

---

69 Incantation. Pure Sulphur, daughter of the great heavens[200] am I.
70 Anu created me,
71 Then Enlil (and) Ninlil brought me down to the land.
72 O sorceress, where (on my body) have you been able to perform sorcery against me?[201]
73 O inseminatrix, where (on my body) have you been able to impregnate me?[202]
74 As much as[203] my head (can be reached, so) the heavens can be reached,[204]
75 As much as my feet (can be reached, so) the netherworld can be reached.
76 On my inner hem(?)[205]
77 Is cast the incantation[206] of the sage of the gods, Mard[uk. ÉN]

---

78 Incantation. Sulphur, Sulphur, Sulphur, daughter of River, Sulphur, daughter-in-law of River,
79 Whose witches are seven and seven, whose enemies are seven and seven.
80 They performed sorcery against her, but she is not ensorcelled,
81 They bewit[ched her], but she is not bewitched.
82 Who is it that can perform witchcraft against Sulphur?
83 May Sulphur rele[ase] the sorcery that the seven and seven have performed against me.

84 [a-]*kibrītu ša sebe u sebe īpušāni*[-a] [x] x *lipšurma anāku lubluṭ* TU$_6$ É[N]

---

85 ÉN *kibrītu elletu atāʾišu šammu quddušu anāk*[*u*]
86 *ēpi*[*š*]*ūʾa apkallū ša aps*[*î*]
87 *ēpišū*[*t*]*ūʾa*[a] *mārāt*![b] ^{d}*Ani ša šam*[*ê*]
88 *kī* [*ī*]*pušāni ul ileʾʾâʾi*[*nn*]*i*

89 [*k*]*ī ēpušušināti alteʾʾīšināti*[a]

90 *ētellâ kīma nūnī ina mêya*
91 *kīma šaḫî ina rušumdiya*
92 *kīma maštakal ina ušalli*
93 *kīma sassati ina aḫi atappi*
94 *kīma zēr ušî ina aḫi tâmti*
95 *ē*[a] *ša Balīḫē ē*[b] *ša Balīḫē*
96 *narqâni*[a] *ana qaqqari*
97 *ša tunassisāni qimmatkunu yâši*

---

98 ÉN ^{d}*id qaqqadī kibrītu padattī*
99 *šēpāya nāru ša mamma lā īdû qerebš*[*a*]
100 *anḫullû pīya ayabba* [a-]*tâmtu rapaštu*[-a|b] *rittāy*[*a*]
101 *kīma* ^{d}*id qaqqadī kīma kibrīti elleti qimm*[*atī*]
102 *kīma anḫullî*![a] *imḫurlīm šamm*[*ū*] *pišert*[*e*]
103 ⸢*mešrētūʾa*⸣ *ebbā* x x x (x) [*š*]*a*(?) *kibrī*[*ti*]
104 *ina* x x x *ša* ^{d}*E*[*a* . . .]
105 ^{d}*Iš*[*tar*(?)] x ⸢la⸣ ti x x [. . .]

---

106 ÉN ^{d}*id ākul alti app*[*aši*]*š aḫḫ*[*alip*(?)] *ātapir*(*i*)[a]

107 ^{d}*id allab*[*iš* . . .]
108 ^{d}*id akalī u mê apṭur*(?)
109 ^{d}*id dal*[*tu*(?) . . .] ⸢*sippa arkus*(?)⸣
110 ^{d}*id* x [. . .]
111 ^{d}*id paršikk*[*u*![a] . . .]
112 . . . [. . .]

break of about 5 lines between 112 and 114″, into which the incipit line 113′ is to be inserted.

[———————————————————————]

84 May Sulphur [. . .] . . . release the sorcery that the seven and seven have performed against me so that I may live. TU$_6$ É[N]

---

85 Incantation. Pure Sulphur (and) *atāʾišu*, the holy plant, am I.
86 My sorcerers are the Sages of the *aps*[*û*],[207]
87 My sorceresses are the heavenly Daughters of Anu.
88 When they performed sorcery against me, they were never able to overpower me,
89 But when I performed sorcery against them, I kept on overpowering them.
90 I rise up like fish from my water,
91 Like a pig from my mud,
92 Like soapwort from the flood plain,
93 Like grass from the canal bank,
94 Like seed of ebony[208] from the seashore.
95 Ha! you[209] of the Baliḫ, Ha! you of the Baliḫ,
96 Hide yourselves here in the ground,[210]
97 You who shook your hair[211] out at me.

---

98 Incantation. River is my head, Sulphur my physique,
99 My feet are the river whose interior no one knows,
100 *Anhullû*-plant is my mouth, Ocean—the vast sea—is my hands.
101 Like River my head (is pure), like pure Sulphur my ha[ir] (is pure),[212]
102 Like *Anhullû*[!]-plant (and) *Imḫurlīmu*, the plants that release,
103 My limbs are pure, . . . Sulp[hur].
104 By the . . . of E[a . . .]
105 . . . .

---

106 Incantation. O River, I have eaten, I have drunk, I have salved my[self], I have cl[othed myself(?)], I have donned a headdress,
107 River, I have dressed my[self, I have . . .],
108 River, food and water I have cleared away(?),
109 River, [I have . . .] the do[or(?)], I have put the doorjamb into place(?),
110 River, . . . [. . .]
111 River, turba[n[!] . . .]
112 . . . [. . .]
break of about 5 lines between 112 and 114″, into which the incipit line 113′ is to be inserted.

[---]

113′ [a][ÉN *ē kaššāptiya elēnītiya īde ul īde*]
114″ [. . .] x x [. . .]
115″ [x x x (x) *ull*]*ânukki*(?) x [x x]
116″ [*ina ilī ša š*]*amê parakk*<*ī*> *ša qaqq*[*ari*]
117″ [x x x x] *kibrītu mārat ilī rabû*[*ti*]
118″ [a][*paṭrū kišpū*]*ki ina ūm*(?) *bubbuli pašrū ruḫêki*

119″ ÉN *attī ṭābtu ša ina ašri elli ibbanû*
120″ *ana mākālê ilī rabûti išīmki* [d]*Enlil*
121″ *ina baliki ul iššakkan naptan ina Ekur*
122″ *ina baliki ilu šarru kabtu u rubû ul iṣṣinū qutrinnu*
123″ *anāku annanna mār annanna ša kišpī ṣubbutūʾinni*
124″ *upšāšê leʾbūʾinni*
125″ *pušrī kišpīya ṭābtu pušširī ruḫêʾa*
126″ *upšāšê muḫrīnnima kīma ili bānîya lultammarki*

127″ ÉN *ē kaššāptiya lū raḫḫātiya*
128″ *ša ana ištēn bēri ippuḫu išāta*
129″ *ana šinā bērī ištappara mār šipriša*

130″ *anāku īdēma attakil takālu*

131″ *ina ū*[*r*]*iya maṣṣartu ina bābiya azzaqap kidinnu*
132″ *eršī altame ulinna*
133″ *ina rēš eršiya assaraq nuḫurta*
134″ *dannat nuḫurtumma unaḫḫara kal kišpīki*

135″ ÉN *ē kaššāptiya lū raḫḫātiya*
136″ *ša ana ištēn bēri ippuḫa išāta*
137″ *ana šinā bērī ištappara mār šipri*[*š*]*a*

138″ *anāku īdēma attakal takā*[*l*]*a*

139″ *ina ūriya maṣṣartu ina bābiya azzaqap kid*[*i*]*nnu*
140″ *ina rēš eršiya aštakan šinšeret ša*[ʾ]*errī*

113′ [Incantation. Ha! my witch, my deceiver, whoever you are,]
114″ [. . .] . . . [. . .]
115″ [. . . ot]her than you . . . [. . .]
116″ [at? the gods of the h]eaven, the shrines of the ear[th],
117″ [. . .] Sulphur, the daughter of the great gods,
118″ [Undone is] your [witchcraft], on the day of the disappearance of the moon your spittle is released.[213]

119″ Incantation. You, Salt, who were created in a pure place,
120″ For food of the great gods did Enlil destine you.
121″ Without you a meal would not be set out in Ekur,
122″ Without you god, king, noble, and prince would not smell incense.
123″ I am so-and-so, the son of so-and-so, whom witchcraft holds captive,
124″ Whom machinations hold in (the form of a skin) disease.
125″ Release my witchcraft, O Salt, dispel my spittle,
126″ Take over from me the machinations, then will I constantly praise you as (I praise) my creator god.

127″ Incantation. Ha! my witch, my inseminatrix,[214]
128″ Who has lit a fire (against me) at[215] a distance of one league,
129″ Who has repeatedly sent her messengers towards me at a distance of two leagues.
130″ I know and have gained full confidence (in my abilities to hold you off).
131″ I have installed a watch on my roof, a protective emblem at my gate.
132″ I have surrounded my bed with (colored) twine,
133″ I have scattered asafoetida (upon a censer) at the head of my bed—
134″ Asafoetida is especially strong, it will cause all your witchcraft to wither.[216]

135″ Incantation. Ha! my witch, my inseminatrix,
136″ Who has lit a fire against me at a distance of one league,
137″ Who has repeatedly sent [h]er messengers towards me at a distance of two leagues.
138″ I know and have gained full confidence (in my abilities to hold you off).
139″ I have installed a watch on my roof, a protective emblem at my gate.
140″ I have placed twelve (wooden) *šaʾerru*s at the head of my bed,

141″ *kurummat*[a] *eṭemmi riḫīt* ^{d}*G*[*irra q*]*āmîki*

142″ *u* ^{d}*Nisaba šarratu mugaṣṣ*[*iṣ*]*at* [*u*]*bānātīki*

143″ ÉN *ē kaššāptiya elēnītiya*
144″ *ša tattanallakī kal mātāti*
145″ *tattanablakkatī kal šadâni*
146″ *anāku īdēma attakil takālu*

147″ *ina ū*[*r*]*iya maṣṣartu ina bābiya azzaqap kidinnu*
148″ *ina imitti bābiya u šum*[*ē*]*l bābiya*
149″ *ultezziz* ^{d}*Lugalirra u* ^{d}*Mesl*[*amt*]*aʾea*
150″ *ilū ša maṣṣ*[*a*]*rte nāsiḫ libbi mušt*[*ēmid*]*ū kalâti*

151″ *ka*[*ššā*]*pta lidūkūma anāku lu*[*b*]*luṭ*

152″ [ÉN] ⸢*ē*⸣ *kaššāptiya elēnī*[*t*]*iya*
153″ *ša tattanallakī kal mātāti*
154″ *tattanablakkatī kal šadâni*
155″ *anāku īdēma attakil takālu*

156″ [*ina ūriy*]*a m*[*aṣṣart*]*u ina bābiya azzaqap kidinnu*
157″ [-*y*]*a aštapak šad*[*â e*]*llu*
158″ traces
2–3 lines missing until end of tablet
[————————————————————]
159″ [a][ÉN *rittī manzât zuqaqīpi*]
160″ [DUB 6].KAM* *Maql*[*û*]

141″ (In which are) food offerings for ghost(s), offspring[217] of G[irra], your [b]urner,
142″ And of Nisaba,[218] the queen, who chops off your fingers.

143″ Incantation. Ha! my witch, my deceiver,
144″ You who (constantly) roam over all lands,
145″ Who cross to and fro over all mountains.
146″ I know and have gained full confidence (in my abilities to hold you off).
147″ I have installed a watch on my roof, a protective emblem at my gate.
148″ At the right of my gate and the left of my gate,
149″ I have posted Lugalirra and Mesl[amt]aʾea,
150″ May the gods of the watch, they who tear out the heart (and) sq[uee]ze together the kidneys,
151″ Kill the w[it]ch so that I may live.

152″ [Incantation]. Ha! my witch, my deceiver,
153″ You who (constantly) roam over all lands,
154″ Who cross to and fro over all mountains.
155″ I know and have gained full confidence (in my abilities to hold you off).
156″ I have installed a wa[tch on] m[y roof], a protective emblem at my gate.
157″ [At m]y [. . .] I have poured out a pur[e mo]untain.
158″ . . . .

2-3 lines missing before end of tablet

[——————————————————]

159″ [Incantation. My hand is the Rainbow, the (constellation) Scorpion].
160″ [The six]th [tablet] of Maqlû.

Maqlû VII. Transcription

1 [ÉN *ri*]*ttī Manzât* [*Z*]*uqaqī*[*pi*]
2 [*u*(?)] *šī kaššāptu unakkama k*[*išpīša*]
3 [x (x)][a] *anappaḫkimma kīma* ^{d}*Manzât ina šam*[*ê*]

4 [*az*]*iqqakkimma kīma iltāni amurri*
5 [*u*]*sappaḫ urpataki uḫallaq ūmki*
6 *usappaḫ kišpīki ša takkimī mūša u urra*

7 *u našparāt zikurrudâ ša taltapparī yâši*

8 *ṣalil nēberu ṣalil kāru*
9 *mārū malāḫi kalīšunu ṣallū*
10 *eli dalti u sikkūri nadû ḫargullū*
11 *nadât šipassun ša* ^{d}*Siris u* ^{d}*Ningišzida*
12 *ša kaššāpiya u kaššāptiya ipša bārtu amāt lemutti*
13 *ayy-iṭḫûni ayy-ibāʾūni bāba ayy-īrubūni ana bīti*
14 ^{d}*Ningišzida lissuḫšunūti*
15 *libbalkitūma epšētīšunu*[a] *libārū*
16 *ilu šarru kabtu u rubû likkelmûšunūti*
17 *ina qātī ili šarri kabti u rubê ayy-ūṣi kaššāptī*[a]

18 *anāku ina qibīt* ^{d}*Marduk bēl nubatti*

19 *u* ^{d}*Asalluḫi bēl āšipūti*
20 *mimmû ēpušu lū kušīru*
21 *ipšī tēpušāni*[a] *lišābil*[b] *šāru*[c]

---

22 ÉN *araḫḫēka ramānī araḫḫēka pagrī*

Maqlû VII. Translation

1 [Incantation]. My [ha]nd is the Rainbow, the Scorpi[on].[219]
2 [But(?)] she, the witch, piles up [her] wi[tchcraft] against me.
3 [And I(?),] I am shining forth against you like the Rainbow in the heavens,
4 [I am b]lowing against you like the North (and) West winds,
5 I am scattering your cloud, I am annihilating your storm,
6 I am scattering your witchcraft that night and day you have piled up over me
7 And the messages of *Zikurrudâ*-magic that you have repeatedly sent against me.
8 The ford is asleep, the quay is asleep,
9 The sailors, all of them, are asleep.
10 Upon the door and bolt, locks are placed,
11 Cast (thereupon) is the incantation[220] of Siris and Ningišzida.
12 May sorcery, rebellion, an evil word of my warlock and witch
13 Not approach me, not pass the door to me, not enter the house to me.
14 May Ningišzida extirpate them,[221]
15 May their sorcery[222] turn[223] (on them) and capture (them),
16 May god, king, noble, and prince glower at them,
17 And may my witch not escape from the grasp of god, king, noble, and prince.
18 As for me—by the command of Marduk, lord of the evening ceremonies,
19 And Asalluḫi, lord of exorcism,
20 May what I do be successful;
21 May the wind carry off[224] the sorcery that you (pl.)[225] have performed against me.

---

22 Incantation. I am impregnating you, my self, I am impregnating you, my body.

23 *kīma* ^{d}*Šakkan irḫû būlšu*
24 [a-]*laḫra immerša ṣabīta armâša*[b] *atāna mūrša*[-a]

25 *epinnu erṣeta irḫû erṣetu imḫuru zēraša*
26 *addi šipta ana ramāniya*
27 *lirḫe ramānīma lišēṣi lumnu*
28 *u kišpī ša zumriya lissuḫū*[a] [b-]*ilū rabûtu*[-b|c]

---

29 ÉN *šamnu ellu šamnu ebbu šamnu namru*
30 *šamnu mullil zumri ša ilī*
31 *šamnu mupaššeḫ*[a] *šerʾāna*[b] *ša amēlūti*
32 *šaman šipti ša* ^{d}*Ea šaman šipti ša* ^{d}*Asalluḫi*
33 *uṭaḫḫidka šaman tapšuḫti*
34 *ša* ^{d}*Ea iddinu ana pašḫāti*[a]
35 *apšuška šaman balāṭi*
36 *addīka šipat* ^{d}*Ea bēl Eridu* ^{d}*Ninšiku*
37 *aṭrud asakku aḫḫāzu šuruppû ša zumrika*
38 *ušatbi qūlu kūru*[a] *nissatu ša pagrika*
39 *upaššeḫ*[a] *šerʾānī minâtīka lā ṭābūti*
40 *ina qibīt* ^{d}*Ea šar apsî*
41 *ina tê ša* ^{d}*Ea ina šipti ša* ^{d}*Asalluḫi*
42 *ina* [a-]*riksi rabbati*[-a] *ša* ^{d}*Gula*
43 *ina qātī pašḫāti ša* ^{d}*Nintinugga*
44 *u* ^{d}*Ningirima bēlet šipti*
45 *ana annanna mār annanna iddīšumma*[a] ^{d}*Ea* [b-]*šipat amāti ša balāṭi*[-b]
46 *sebet apkallū šūt Eridu lipaššiḫū*[a] *zumuršu* TU$_{6}$[b] ÉN

---

47 [a][É]N ^{d}*Enlil qaqqadī* ^{mul}*Šukūdu lānī*[b]
48 *pūtī*[a] ^{d}*Šamaš napḫu*
49 [*id*]*āya Gamlu ša bāb* ^{d}*Marduk*
50 *uznāya l*^{ē}/*īʾû*(?) *šēpāya laḫmu mukabbisa šēr laḫme*

51 [*a*]*ttunu ilū rabûtu* <*kīma*>[a] ^{d}*Šamaš ina šamê napḫātunu*
52 *kīma annak*[*u*](?) *parz*[*illu*](?) *ipšu bārtu amāt lemutti*
52a [a][*k*]*išpī ruḫû rusû up*[*šāšû lemnūti*]
53 *lā iṭeḫḫûkunūši lā iqar*[*r*]*ubūkunūši*
54 *ipšu bārtu amāt lemutti*
54a *k*[*išpī ruḫû rusû upšāš*]*û lemnūti*
54 (cont.) *lā iṭeḫḫûni lā iqarrubūni yâši* ÉN

---

23 As Šakkan impregnated his herd,
24 The ewe (with) her lamb, the gazelle (with) her young, the jenny (with) her donkey foal,[226]
25 (As) the plow impregnated the earth, the earth received its seed,
26 (So) I cast the spell on my self.
27 May it impregnate my self and expel the evil,
28 And may the great gods extirpate[227] the witchcraft of my body.

---

29 [228]Incantation. Pure oil, clear oil, bright oil,
30 Oil that purifies the body of the gods,
31 Oil that soothes the sinews of mankind,
32 Oil of the incantation of Ea, oil of the incantation of Asalluḫi.
33 I coat you with soothing oil
34 That Ea granted for soothing,
35 I anoint you with the oil of healing,
36 I cast upon you the incantation of Ea, lord of Eridu, Ninšiku.
37 I expel Asakku, *ahhāzu*-jaundice, chills of your body (*zumru*),
38 I remove dumbness, torpor, (and) misery of your body (*pagru*),
39 I soothe the sick sinews of your limbs.
40 By the command of Ea, king of the *apsû*,
41 By the spell of Ea, by the incantation of Asalluḫi,
42 By the soft bandage[229] of Gula,
43 By the soothing hands of Nintinugga
44 And Ningirima, mistress of incantation.
45 On so-and-so, Ea cast[230] the incantation of the word of healing[231]
46 That the seven sages of Eridu soothe his body. TU$_6$ ÉN

---

47 [Incan]tation. Enlil is my head, Sirius is my form,
48 My forehead is the rising sun,
49 My arms are the Crook[232] at the gate of Marduk,
50 My ears are the Bull,[233] my feet are the *laḫmu*-monsters trampling on the flesh of *laḫmu*-monsters.
51 You, O great gods, shine forth in the sky <like> Šamaš.[234]
52 As tin(?) (and) ir[on](?), sorcery, rebellion, an evil word,
52a Witchcraft, spittle, enchainment, [evil] mach[inations]
53 Cannot approach you, cannot draw near to you,
54 So sorcery, rebellion, an evil word,
54a Wi[tchcraft, spittle, enchainment], evil [machina]tions
54(cont.) shall not approach me, shall not draw near to me myself. ÉN

---

55 ÉN *attīmannu kaššāptu ša īpuša ṣalmī*[a]

56 *iṭṭulu lānī ibnû* ^{d}*lamassī*[a]
57 *īm[u]ru [b]āltī ušarriḫu gattī*
58 *uṣabbû nabnīt[ī]*
59 *umaššilu bunnannīya*
60 *ubbir[u m]inâtīya*
61 *ukassû mešrêtīya ukanninu manānīya*
62 *yâši* ^{d}*Ea mašmaš ilī umaʾʾiranni*[a]
63 *maḫar* ^{d}*Šamaš ṣalamki ēṣer*
64 *lānki aṭṭul lamassaki abni bāltaki āmur*
65 *gattaki ušarreḫ nabnītki uṣabbi*

66 *ina* ^{d}*Nisaba elleti bunnannīki umaššil*
67 [a-]*minâtīki ubber mešrêtīki ukassi*[-a]
68 *manānīki ukannin*
69 *ipšu*[a] *tēpušīnni ēpuški*
70 *miḫer tušamḫirīnni ušamḫerki*

71 *gimil tagmilīnni utēr agmilki*
72 *kišpīki ruḫêki rusêki* [a-]*epšētēki lemnēte*[-a]

73 *upšāšêki ayyābūte*
74 *našparātīki ša lemutti*
75 *râmki zērki dibalûki zikurrudûki*

76 *kadabbedûki dimmakurrûki likillū rēški*

77 [a]*itti mê ša zum[riy]a u musâti ša qātīya liššaḫiṭma*

78 *ana muḫḫiki u lāniki lillikma*[a] *anāku lubluṭ*
79 *ēnīta līnânni māḫerta limḫuranni*

79a [a-]*amḫur meḫru limḫurūʾinni* TU$_6$ ÉN [-a|b]

---

80 ÉN *bāʾertu ša bāʾirāti*
81 *kaššāptu ša kaššāpāti*
82 *ša ina* [a-]*sūqāta nadâtu*[-a] *šēssa*

55 [235]Incantation. Whoever you are, O witch, who has made a figurine of me—
56 Who has looked at my form and created my image,
57 Who has seen my bearing and given rich detail to my physical build,
58 Who has comprehended [my] appearance
59 And reproduced my features,
60 Who has bound my body,
61 Who has tied my limbs together, who has twisted my sinews.
62 As for me, Ea, exorcist of the gods, has sent me,
63 And before Šamaš I draw your likeness—
64 I look at your form and create your image, I see your bearing
65 And give rich detail to your physical build, I comprehend your appearance
66 And reproduce your features with pure flour,[236]
67 I bind your body, I tie your limbs together,[237]
68 I twist your sinews.
69 The sorcery that you have performed against me I perform against you,
70 The (ominous) encounter that you have caused me to encounter I make you take over,
71 The vengeance that you have wreaked on me I wreak back on you.
72 Your witchcraft, your spittle, your enchainment, your evil manipulations,
73 Your hostile machinations,
74 Your messages of evil,
75 Your love (-magic), your hate (-magic), your perversion of justice, your *Zikurrudâ*-magic,
76 Your muteness, (and) your madness—may they attend to you (rather than to me).
77 With the water of my bo[dy] and the washing of my hands may it rinse off[238]
78 And come upon your head and body so that I may live.
79 May a (female) substitute stand in for me, may one who encounters (me) take (it) over from me,
79a I have encountered an ominous encounter; may they take (it) over from me. TU$_6$ ÉN

---

80 [239]Incantation. Huntress of huntresses,
81 Witch of witches,
82 Whose net is cast in the streets,

83 *ina rebīt āli ittanallakā īnāša*
84 *eṭlūt āli ubtanaʾʾa*
85 *itti eṭlūt āli ubtanaʾʾânni yâši*
86 *ardāt āli issanaḫḫur*
87 *itti ardāt āli issanaḫḫuranni yâši*

88 *anāku ubaʾʾâkkimma kurgarrê eššebê rikiski aḫeppe*

89 *kaššāpū līpušūki rikiski aḫeppe*
90 *kaššāpātu līpušāki rikiski aḫeppe*
91 [a|b]-*kurgarrû*[c] *līpušūki rikiski aḫeppe*-[b]
92 [a]-*eššebû līpušūki rikiski aḫeppe*-[a]
93 *naršindû līpušūki rikiski aḫeppe*
94 *mušlaḫḫū līpušūki rikiski aḫeppe*
95 [a]-*agugillū līpušūki rikiski aḫeppe*-[a]
96 *amaḫḫaṣ lētki ašallapa lišānki*
97 *umalla ruʾāta īnīki*
98 *ušallak aḫīki lillūta*
99 *u akkâši ruqbūta ušallakki*
100 *u mimma mala tēteppušī*[a] *utār ana muḫḫiki*[b]

---

101 [a][ÉN[b]] *ipšīki epšētīki epšēt ipšīki*

102 *epšēt muppišētīki*
103 ^{d}*Ea mašmaš ilī upaṭṭerma mê uštābil*
104 *pûki lemnu epera lim*[*l*]*a*
105 *lišānki ša lemutti ina*[a] *qê likkaṣ*[*er*]
106 *ina qibīt* ^{d}*Enbilulu bēl balāṭi* TU$_6$ É[N]

---

107 ÉN *kiṣrīki kuṣṣurūti*
108 *epšētīki lemnēti upšāšêki ayyābūti*
109 *našparātūki ša lemutti*
110 ^{d}*Asalluḫi mašmaš ilī upaṭṭerma* [a]-*mê uštābil*-[a]
111 *pûki lemnu epera limla*
112 *lišānki ša lemutti ina*[a] *qê likkaṣer*
113 *ina qibīt* ^{d}*Enbilulu bēl balāṭi* TU$_6$[a] ÉN

---

114 [a]ÉN *amsi qātīya ubbiba zumrī*

83 Whose eyes keep roaming the broad way of the city.
84 She keeps seeking the young men of the city,
85 Among the young men of the city she keeps seeking me myself,
86 She keeps looking around for the young women of the city,
87 Among the young women of the city she keeps looking around for me myself.
88 But I am seeking[240] against you cultic performers and ecstatics, I am breaking your bond.[241]
89 May warlocks ensorcell you, I am breaking your bond.
90 May witches ensorcell you, I am breaking your bond.
91 May cultic performers[242] ensorcell you, I am breaking your bond.
92 May ecstatics ensorcell you, I am breaking your bond.
93 May *naršindu*-sorcerers ensorcell you, I am breaking your bond.
94 May snake-charmers ensorcell you, I am breaking your bond.
95 May *agugillu*-sorcerers ensorcell you, I am breaking your bond.
96 I am striking your cheek, I am tearing out your tongue,[243]
97 I am filling your eyes with spittle,
98 I am making your arms become weak,
99 And as for you: I am making you become rotten,
100 And whatever sorcery you have constantly performed, I am turning back upon your head.

---

101 [Incantation]. Your sorcery, your manipulations, the manipulations of your sorcery,
102 The manipulations of your wizardry
103 Ea, exorcist of the gods, undoes and sweeps away with water.[244]
104 May your evil mouth be full of earth,
105 May your evil tongue be bou[nd] with[245] a gag—
106 By the command of Enbilulu, lord of life. TU$_6$ É[N]

---

107 Incantation. Your tightly knotted knots,
108 Your evil manipulations, your hostile machinations,
109 Your messages of evil
110 Asalluḫi, exorcist of the gods, undoes and sweeps away with water.[246]
111 May your evil mouth be full of earth,
112 May your evil tongue be bound with[247] a gag—
113 By the command of Enbilulu, lord of life. TU$_6$ ÉN

---

114 [248]Incantation.[249] I wash my hands, I cleanse my body

115 *ina mê nagbi ellūti ša ina Eridu ibbanû*
116 [a-]*mimma lemnu mimma lā ṭābu*[-a]
117 *ša ina zumriya šīrīya šerʾānīya bašû*
118 [a]*lumun*[b] *šunāti* [c-]*idāti ittāti*[-c] *lemnēti* [d-]*lā ṭābāti*[-d]
119 *lumun šīrī ḫaṭûti pardūti lemnūti lā ṭābūti*
120 *ša lipit qātī ḫiniq imme*[*ri*] *naqî niqî*[a] *nē*[*pe*]*šti bārûti*

121 *ša attaṭṭal*[*u*] *ūmešam*
122 *ukabbisu ina sūqi ātammaru ina aḫâti*
123 *šēd lemutti utukku lemnu*
124 *murṣu d*[*i*]*ʾu dilipta*
125 *qūlu kū*[*r*]*u nissatu niziqtu imṭû tānīḫu*
126 *ūʾa ayya ḫuṣṣu ḫīpi libbi*
127 *gilittu pir*[*i*]*ttu adirtu*
128 *arrat il*[*ī*[a] *m*]*iḫerti ilī*[b] *tazzimti* [*ilī*[c] *n*]*īš ili nīš qātī māmītu*

129 *lumnū kišpī ruḫê rusê upšāšê lemnūti ša amēlūti*

130 *itti mê* ⸢*ša*⸣ *zumriya u musâti ša qātīya*
131 *liššaḫiṭm*[*a ana mu*]*ḫḫi ṣalam nigsagilê lillik*
132 *ṣalam nigs*[*agil*]*ê arnī dinānī lizbil*
133 ⸢*sūqu u*⸣ *sulû lipaṭṭirū arnīya*
134 *ēnītu līnânni māḫertu limḫuranni*

135 *amḫur meḫru limḫurūʾinni*

136 *ūmu šulma arḫu ḫidûti šattu ḫegallaša libila*
137 ^{d}*Ea* ^{d}*Šamaš u* ^{d}*Marduk yâši rūṣānimma*
138 *lippašrū kišpī ruḫû rusû*
139 *upšāšû lemnūti ša amēlūti*
140 *u māmītu littaṣi ša zumriya*

---

141 ÉN *tebi*[a] *šēru mise qātīya*
142 *pite qaqqaru* [*m*]*uḫur arnīya*
143 [a-]*ša kaššāptu ukaššipanni*[b] *eššebû us*[*a*]*lliʾann*[*i*][-a]

144 ^{d}*Šamaš pišerta libilamma*[a] *qaqqaru*[b] *limḫuranni*[c]

---

115 In the pure spring water that was formed in Eridu.
116 Anything evil, anything unfavorable
117 That is in my body, flesh, and sinews,
118 The evil[250] of[251] evil, unfavorable dreams, signs, and portents,
119 The evil of defective, frightening, evil, unfavorable entrails
120 (observed) in the ritual act (of extispicy), in the killing of the she[ep], in the offering of the sacrifice, or in the exercise of divination,[252]
121 That (which)[253] I have looked at daily,
122 Have stepped on in the street, or have repeatedly seen in the outskirts,
123 An evil *šēdu*-spirit, an evil *utukku*-demon,
124 Illness, he[ad]ache, sleeplessness,
125 dumbness, torpor, misery, grief, losses, moaning,
126 (Cries of) woe (and) alas, depression,
127 Terror, fear, apprehension,
128 (The evil consequences of) a curse by the gods, an appeal to the gods, a complaint to the [gods,[254] an o]ath by the god, the raising of hands, curse,[255]
129 The evil(s) of witchcraft, spittle, enchainment, evil machinations of mankind—
130 With the water of my body and the washing of my hands
131 May it[256] rinse off and come [up]on a figurine of a substitute,
132 May the figurine of the sub[stitute] bear my sin as a replacement,
133 May street and way undo my sins,
134 May a (female) substitute stand in for me, may one who encounters (me) take (it) over from me,
135 I have encountered an ominous encounter; may they take (it) over from me.
136 May the day bring well-being, the month joy, the year its prosperity.
137 Ea, Šamaš, and Marduk, help me so that
138 Witchcraft, spittle, enchainment,
139 Evil machinations of mankind be released,
140 And curse go forth from my body.

---

141 Incantation. Rise up, morning, wash my hands,[257]
142 Open up, earth,[258] receive my sin.
143 Because the witch has bewitched me[259] and the ecstatic has sp[rin]kled me.[260]
144 May Šamaš bring me release[261] and may the earth receive (it) from me.

---

145 [ÉN *ittamr*]*a šēru puttâ dalātu*
146 *ālik urḫi ittaṣi abul*[*la*]
147 [*mār šipri*(?)[a] *i*]*ṣṣabat ḫarrāna*
148 *ē*[*pi*]*štu ē tēpušīnni*
149 [*rāḫītu*] *ē tureḫḫînni*
150 ⸢*ūtallil*⸣ *ina napāḫ* ^{d}*Š*[*amš*]*i*
151 [*ipšī tēpu*]*šī u tuštēpišī*

152 *lis*[*ḫ*]*urūma liṣbatūki kâši*[a]

---

153 [ÉN *š*]*ērumma šēru*
154 *annû ša kaššāpiya u kaššāptiya*
155 *i*[*tb*]*ûnimma kīma mārī nāri ulappatū*[a] *ni*ʾ*ašunu*
156 *ina* [*b*]*ābiya izzaz* ^{d}*Pālil*[a]
157 *ina* [*r*]*ēš eršiya izzaz* ^{d}*Lugaledina*
158 [a]*a*[*š*]*apparakkimma ša bābiya* ^{d}*Pālil*
159 *š*[*a*] *rēš eršiya* ^{d}*Lugaledina*
160 [*š*]*a kal ištēn*[a] *bēri dibbīki ša kal ḫarrāni amâtīki*

161 [a-]*utār*[b] *kišpīki ruḫêki uṣabbatūki kâši*[-a] [c-]TU$_6$ ÉN[-c]

---

162 ÉN *ina šēri mesâ qātāya*
163 *šurrû damqu lišarrânni*
164 *ṭūb libbi*[a] *ṭūb šīri lirteddânni*
165 *ēma uṣammaru ṣummirātīya lukšud*
166 [*šu*]*tti āmuru ana damiqti liššakna*[a]
167 [*ayy-iṭ*]*ḫâ* [a-]*ayy-isniqa*[-a] *mimma lemnu mimma lā ṭābu*
168 *ruḫê ša*[a] *kaššāpi u kaššāpti*
169 [*ina*] ⸢*qibīt*⸣ ^{d}*Ea* ^{d}*Šamaš* ^{d}*Marduk u rubāti* ^{d}*Bēlet-ilī* TU$_6$ ÉN

---

170 [É]N [*a*]*msi p*[*īy*]*a*[a] *amtesi qātīya*
171 *ina* [*ḫ*]*urḫummat mê mīli rašubbat nāri*
172 [. . . (-)*k*]*ul-li bāltaki*
173 [*m*]*û gummirāni rašubbatkunu*
174 [*k*]*īma mê annûti ipšu bārtu amāt lemutti*
175 *lā iṭeḫḫû lā iqarribu*[a]
176 *ipšu bārtu amāt lemutti lā iṭeḫḫâ*

145 [Incantation]. Dawn h[as broken], doors are (now) opened,
146 The traveler has passed through the gate,
147 [The messenger(?)[262] h]as taken to the road.
148 Ha! s[or]ceress, may you not perform sorcery against me,
149 Ha! [inseminatrix],[263] may you not impregnate me!
150 For I am cleansed by the rising of the s[un];
151 May [the sorceries that you have perfor]med or have had performed (against me during the night)
152 Tu[r]n back and seize you yourself.

---

153 [Incantation]. It is morning, yea morning.
154 This is (the morning) of my warlock and witch:
155 They a[ro]se, playing their niʾu-instrument like musicians.
156 At my door stands Pālil,
157 At the [he]ad of my bed stands Lugaledina.
158 I am sending against you the one at my door, Pālil,
159 (And) the one at the head of my bed, Lugaledina.
160 Over one whole mile[264] your speech (extends), over the whole road your word (extends)—
161 I turn back (against you) your witchcraft (and) your spittle so that they seize you yourself. TU$_6$ ÉN

---

162 Incantation. At dawn my hands are washed.
163 May a propitious beginning begin for me,
164 May happiness (and) good health ever accompany me,
165 Whatsoever I seek, may I attain it,
166 May [the dre]am I dreamt be made favorable[265] for me,
167 May anything evil, anything unfavorable,
168 The spittle of warlock and witch, [not rea]ch me, not touch me—
169 [By] the command of Ea, Šamaš, Marduk, and the princess Bēlet-ilī. TU$_6$ ÉN

---

170 [Incan]tation. I wash my mou[th],[266] I have (now) washed my hands,
171 With(?) the foam of the flood waters, the awesome power of the river,
172 [May(?)] my(?) [. . .] . . . your dignity.
173 [O wa]ter, cause your awesome power to overpower for me.[267]
174 As sorcery, rebellion, evil word
175 Cannot approach, cannot draw near to these waters,
176 So sorcery, rebellion, evil word shall not approach me,

177 *lā iqarriba yâši* TU$_6$ ÉN $^{a-}$É.NU.RU$^{-a|b}$

---

178 ÉN *adi tappuḫa uqâka bēlī* ^{d}*Šamaš*

---

179 [D]UB 7.KAM* *Maqlû*

177 Shall not draw near to me myself. TU$_6$ ÉN É.NU.RU

178 Incantation. Until you rise, I await you, my lord, Šamaš.

179 The seventh [ta]blet of Maqlû.

MAQLÛ VIII. TRANSCRIPTION

1 [a][ÉN *adi tappuḫa uqâ*]*ka bēlī* ^{d}*Šamaš*
2 [. . . *ša*]*qâ rēšāya*
3 [. . . *b*]*ēlī* ^{d}*Šamaš*
4 [. . .] *taptašar aba*[*tt*]*u*
5 [. . .] x *ittebe šikar*[*š*]*a*[a]
6 [. . . *it*]*tebû arqūša*
7 [^{d}*Ea*(?) *uma*ʾʾ*ir*]*annima bēlī* ^{d}*Šamaš*
8 [*ēpištu*] *ēpušanni*
9 [*rāḫītu*] *uraḫḫânni*
10 [. . .]-*ša aḫullâ*
11 [. . . *ina*] *aḫi Idiqlat*
12 [. . . *ina aḫ*]*i atappi*
13 [. . . *n*]*āru*(?)
14 [. . . -*t*]*i*(?)
15 [. . . -*m*]*a*(?)
16 [. . .] x[a]

break of approximately 9 lines

17′ [x x (x)] bi *ina* is(?) x [. . .]
18′ [x x] x [x x x x (x)]
19′ [x x (x)] a(?) *š*[*a* x x (x)]
20′ [*kaššāpt*]*u*(?) ⌜*lū*⌝ [x x (x)]
21′ [*ēpišt*]*u*(?) *lū* [x x (x)]
22′ [x x] x *kišpūša lū ana qidd*[*atimma*]
23′ [*anāku l*]*ū ana māḫirti* TU$_6$ [ÉN]

24′ [ÉN *itta*]*pḫa* ^{d}*Šamaš akašša*[*d*] <*šadê*>[a]
25′ [x x (x)] x u *akaššad šadê*
26′ [*uqâk*]*a*[a] *bēlī* ^{d}*Šamaš*
27′ [*qātāya*[a]] ^{d}*Šamaš šammi pišerti našâ*
28′ [*anāku lu*]*špurka ana mārti* ^{d}*Šamaš pāšertiya*

MAQLÛ VIII. TRANSLATION

1 [Incantation. Until you rise, I awai]t you, my lord, Šamaš,
2 [. . .] my head is [ra]ised,
3 [. . .] my [l]ord, Šamaš.
4 [. . .] you have released the (river) pebble(?),
5 [. . .] her beer(?)[268] has arisen,
6 [. . .] her green(?) has[269] arisen.
7 [Ea(?) has se]nt me, my lord, Šamaš:
8 [A sorceress] has performed sorcery against me,
9 [An inseminatrix] has impregnated me,[270]
10 [. . .] her [. . .] on the other bank,
11 [. . . on the] bank of the Tigris,
12 [. . . on the ba]nk of the canal,
13 [. . . r]iver(?),
14 [. . .] . . .
15 [. . .] . . .
16 [. . .] . . .
break of approximately 9 lines
17′ [. . .] . . . [. . .]
18′ [. . .] . . . [. . .]
19′ [. . .] . . . [. . .]
20′ May [the witc]h(?) [. . .]
21′ May [the sorceres]s(?) [. . .]
22′ [. . .] . . . may her witchcraft be down[stream],
23′ [But m]ay [I] be upstream. TU$_6$ [ÉN]

24′ [Incantation]. Šamaš [has r]isen, I reach <the mountains(?)>,[271]
25′ [. . .] I reach the mountains(?),
26′ [I await y]ou,[272] my lord, Šamaš,
27′ [My hands],[273] O Šamaš, bear the plant of release,
28′ [. . . let me] send you[274] to Šamaš's daughter, my releaser,

29′ *ana libbi ša iqbû tuquntu*
30′ *ana rittu ša irkusu riksu*
31′ *puṭur libbi ša iqbû tuquntu*
32′ *pušur rittu ša irkusu ri[ksu]*
33′ *pušur ša kaššāpiya u kaššāpt[iya]*
34′ *kišpīšunu r[uḫêšunu] lemnū[ti (. . .)]*

35′ ^{a}[ÉN *und]u kaššāptu ī[ber nāra]*
36′ *[ēpiš]tī išlâ* x [x x]
37′ *[mušt]ēpištī ašbat ina nēberi[mma]*
38′ *[ītaš]uš(?) kār[u]*
39′ *[ubtan]aʾʾânni yâši ana saḫāliya*
40′ *[īmurū]šima*^{a} *apkallū ša apsî*
41′ *[ina iḫz]i nēmeqi nikilti* ^{d}*Ea iqbû lapānša*
42′ [^{d}*Ea] šar apsî uṭṭâ*^{a} *pānīša*
43′ *[uša]sḫipši benna tēšâ raʾība*
44′ *[i]tter ḫurbāssa*
45′ [^{d}*i]d puluḫtaša iddâ*^{a} *eliša*
46′ *ana muḫḫi ṣalmīša mesâ qātāya*
47′ *ina kukri ša šadî burāši elli*
48′ *ina maštakal mul[lil a]mēli mesâ qātāya*
49′ *ētelil anāku-m[a(?) attazizz]u(?) ina muḫḫi kišpīša*

50′ *kišpūša l[imlû] ṣēra*
51′ *amâtīša il[tānu l]itbal*
52′ *u mimma mala t[ēpušī lišābi]l šāru*

53′ ÉN *ultu* ^{d}⸢*Uru*⸣ $^{a-}$*i[na māti ilsû]*$^{-a}$ *alāla*

54′ *ultu eṭlu īlû [ana nakās b]īni*
55′ *ašbatma umm[ašu imalli]kšu*
56′ *ašbūma imallikūšu aḫḫ[ūšu]*
57′ *attīmannu kaššāptu ša yâši u* $^{a-}$*ramān[ī īpuša]*$^{-a}$
58′ *ēpištu ēpuša kišpī[ša]*
59′ *kišpūša lū šāru kišpūša lū meḫû*
60′ *kišpūša lū pû l[i]ttap(a)raššadū eli[ša]*

61′ ÉN *annû enennam[a]*

29′ Against[275] the heart that has incited strife,
30′ Against the hand that has bound a knot.[276]
31′ Unknot the heart[277] that has incited hostility,
32′ Relax the hand that has bound a kn[ot],
33′ Release my warlock's and witch's
34′ Witchcraft (and) evil sp[ittle (. . .)].

35′ [Incantation. Wh]en the witch cro[ssed the river],
36′ My sor[ceress] plunged into . . . [. . .],
37′ [The one who instigates] sorcery against me sits in the ferry,[278] and[279]
38′ [has (now) engul]fed(?) the qua[y],
39′ [She continually se]eks me out in order to pierce me.
40′ The sages of the *apsû* [saw] her,[280]
41′ [With the] wise [lear]ning, the art of Ea, they spoke her destruction.
42′ [Ea], king of the *apsû*, darkened her face,[281]
43′ [He over]whelmed her with *bennu*-epilepsy, confusion, (and) trembling.
44′ Her terror having become excessive,
45′ [Riv]er cast her (own) fear upon her.[282]
46′ Over her figurines my hands are washed,
47′ With *kukru* of the mountain (and) pure juniper,
48′ With soapwort, purifi[er of m]ankind, my hands are washed.
49′ I have (now) become pure[283] a[nd stan]d(?) (triumphantly) upon her witchcraft.
50′ May her witchcraft f[ill] the steppe,
51′ May the Nor[th wind] carry off her words,
52′ And whatever sor[cery that you have performed may] the wind [cause to be carrie]d off.

53′ Incantation. After Uru[284] [called out] the '*alāla*' work-song i[n the land],
54′ After the youth went up [to cut the t]amarisk,
55′ Seated, [his m]other [advis]es him,
56′ Seated, [his b]rothers advise him.
57′ Whoever you are, O witch who [has bewitched] me and [my] self;[285]
58′ The sorceress has performed her witchcraft against me.
59′ May her witchcraft be a wind, may her witchcraft be a storm,
60′ May her witchcraft be chaff, and may it constantly fly(?) at her.

61′ Incantation. Now, then, this (one):

62′ *kaššāptu nakratanni*
63′ ⸢*u muštēpišti*⸣ *nabalkutatanni*
64′ x x [. . .] *ina kišpīša*
65′ [. . .] x *kaššāptu*
66′ [. . . *mê*] *kaṣûti*
67′ [. . . *rēš*(?)] *libbiša*
68′ [. . . -ʾ]*a*(?)-*ki*[a]
69′ [. . . *lemut*(?)]*tiki*
70′ [. . .] ^{d}*Ea* ⸢*mašmaššu*⸣
break of approximately 25 lines
71″ [x x x x x] ⸢*tākaltaki*⸣ [*a*]*mḫ*[*aṣ*]
72″ [x x x *uš*]*ultaki ḫašêki at*[*ruk*(?)]
73″ *unâti ša libbiki kalîšina adlu*[*ḫ*]
74″ *ušēli ina libbiki kišpīki ruḫêk*[*i*]
75″ *ēpištu eṭemmu limḫaṣk*[*i*]
76″ *gallû* ⸢*emūqki*⸣ *litb*[*al*]
77″ *linārki* [. . .] x x x [x]
78″ *litēʾ* [*ki* . . .]
79″ *aššu ana le*[*mutti* . . .]
80″ *ina kišp*[*ī*(*ki*) . . .]
81″ ^{d}*Ere*[*škigal*(?)[a] . . .]
82″ ^{d}*Nin*[a]-[. . .]
83″ za x x [. . .]
84″ [a]*ša ī*[*pušu*(?) . . .]
85″ *kal a*[*mâtīša*(?) . . .]
86″ *šarr*[*at*(?) . . .]
87″ x x x [. . .]
88″ x [. . .]
89″ ⸢*ana*(?)⸣ *a*(?)-[. . .]
90″ *kamâ*[*ti* . . . -*āti*]
91″ [a]*enât*[*i nabalkutāti*]
92″ *uštepēlūki* [^{d}*Girra u* ^{d}*Marduk*(?)]
93″ ^{d}*Ea bēl Eridu rik*[*iski liḫpe*]
94″ *u mimma ma*[*la tēpušī*]
95″ *lišamḫerki* [*kâši*]

96″ ÉN *pû idbub lemnāti*[a]
97″ *pû imtall*[*a*[a|b] *lemnāti*]
98″ *ša kaššāpāti kišpīšina*

62′ The witch is hostile to me
63′ And the woman who instigates sorcery rebels against me.
64′ . . . [. . .] with her witchcraft,
65′ [. . .] . . . the witch,
66′ [. . .] cold [water],
67′ [. . .] her heart,[286]
68′ [. . .] your . . .,[287]
69′ [. . .] your [evi]l(?),
70′ [. . .] Ea, the exorcist,
break of approximately 25 lines
71″ [. . .], your stomach I stri[ke],
72″ [I . . .] your ve[in], your lungs I b[eat(?)],
73″ All your innards I disturb,
74″ I remove your witchcraft (and) your spittle from your insides.
75″ O sorceress, may a ghost strike you,
76″ May a (demonic) constable carry o[ff] your strength,
77″ May [. . .] kill you . . . [. . .],
78″ May [. . .] cover [you] over.
79″ Because with ev[il intent you . . .]
80″ By ([your]) witchcraft [. . .]
81″ Ere[škigal(?) . . .]
82″ ^{d}Nin-[. . .]
83″ . . . [. . .]
84″ Who pe[rformed sorcery(?) . . .]
85″ All [her] w[ords(?) . . .]
86″ Que[en(?) . . .]
87″ . . . [. . .]
88″ . . . [. . .]
89″ To . . . [. . .]
90″ [Y]ou have been captured, [you have been . . .],
91″ You have been changed, [you have been turned around],
92″ [Girra and Marduk(?)] have reversed you,
93″ [May] Ea, lord of Eridu, [break your bo]nd,
94″ And cause whatev[er sorcery you have performed]
95″ to confront you [yourself].

96″ Incantation. The mouth spoke evil,
97″ The mouth was constantly ful[l[288] of evil]:
98″ The witchcraft of the witches,

99″ [a-]*ša eššebâti šip*[*ātīšina*(?)][-a]
100″ *lisap*<*pi*>*ḫū lemnāti*[a]
101″ *lišallû l*[*e*]*mnā*[*ti*]
102″ *ina šipat u*[*zz*]*i pû lišānu*
103″ *našparāt mūši u kal ū*[*mi*]
104″ *ša tē*[*tepp*]*ušāni* [a]*yâ*[*ši*]
105″ *ta*[*ltapp*]*arāni ana r*[*am*]*āni*[*ya*]
106″ [a]*kišpīkunu u kušāpīk*[*unu*]
107″ [*kīma mê mus*]*âti asurrâ l*[*imlû*]

108″ [a-][ÉN *ēpištu* (*u*) *m*]*uštēpištu muribba*[*t kišpī ruḫê*][-a]

109″ [a][*ḫābilat* x] x ri[b] *mu*[*ḫabbilat ardāti*]

110″ [x x x x *nap*]*išti tābika*[*t unnīnī*]
111″ [x x x x] x ki [x x en ni]
112″ [x x x x (x)] x *qaqqadu/i ina pî*(?) [x x x (x)]
113″ [x x x x] x kàt ti x [x x x (x)]
114″ [ ] x [ ]
break of approximately 15–20 lines
115‴ *ē*[*pištī*(?) . . .]
116‴ *ḫāmim*[*at*(?)] x x [. . .]
117‴ *ṣābitat pūt*[*i*[a] . . .]
118‴ *sēkirat nešmê* [. . .]
119‴ *ḫābilat eṭlūti* [. . .]
120‴ *limqut eliki* [. . .]
break of several lines
121⁗ [x x x *li*]*štapi*[*k*(?) x x x x]
122⁗ [x x x x (x)] ^{d}*Šamaš* x [x x x (x)]
123⁗ [^{d}*Ere*]*š*[*k*]*iga*[*l*] *ana erṣeti ayy-uš*[*ē*]*r*[*idki*]
124⁗ [*eli*[a] *p*]*agriki erû u zību linnadrū*
125⁗ *qūlu ḫurbāšu limqutū eliki*
126⁗ *kalbu u kalbatu libaṣṣirūki*
127⁗ *kalbu u kalbatu libaṣṣirū šīrīki*
128⁗ *ina qibīt* ^{d}*Ea* ^{d}*Šamaš* ^{d}*Marduk u rubāti* ^{d}*Bēlet-ilī* TU$_6$ ÉN

129⁗ ÉN *attā ṣillī attā bāštī*
130⁗ *attā* ^{d}*lamassī attā gattī*

99″ The incan[tations(?)] of the ecstatics.[289]
100″ May they sca<tt>er the evil,
101″ May they tear apart(?) the [ev]il,
102″ By means of the r[ag]ing incantation, (they) the mouth (and) tongue.[290]
103″ May the messages of the night and of the whole d[ay]
104″ That you [have constantly] performed against me mys[elf],
105″ That you [have repeatedly s]ent against me, my very person,
106″ Your witchcraft and your witchcraft materials,
107″ F[ill] the sewer [like] wa[sh water.]

108″ [Incantation. The sorceress (and) the woman who] instigates sorcery, who set[s witchcraft and spittle] in motion,
109″ [Who wrongs . . .] . . .,[291] who [commits wrongs against young women],
110″ [. . . li]fe, who pours for[th entreaty],
111″ [. . .] . . . [. . .]
112″ [. . .] . . . head in mouth(?) [. . .]
113″ [. . .] . . . [. . .]
114″ [. . .] . . . [. . .]
break of approximately 15-20 lines
115‴ [My] so[rceress(?) . . .]
116‴ Who colle[cts(?)] . . . [. . .]
117‴ Who seizes the forehea[d, . . .]
118‴ Who blocks hearing, [. . .]
119‴ Who wrongs young men, [. . .]
120‴ May [. . .] befall you [. . .]
break of several lines
121⁗ [. . .] . . . [. . .]
122⁗ [. . .] Šamaš [. . .]
123⁗ May [Ere]škigal not permit [you to go] down into the netherworld,[292]
124⁗ May eagle and vulture prey [on] your corpse,
125⁗ May stupor (and) terror befall you,
126⁗ May dog and bitch tear you apart,
127⁗ May dog and bitch tear apart your flesh—
128⁗ By the command of Ea, Šamaš, Marduk, and the princess Bēlet-ilī.
TU$_6$ ÉN

129⁗ Incantation. You are my reflection, you are my vigor,
130⁗ You are my vitality, you are my physical build,

131'''' *attā padattī attā dūt[ī]*
132'''' *a[t]t[ā ṣill]ī(?)* ⸢*rabâ(?)*⸣ *attā ṣillī eddēššû*

133'''' *[ē tamḫur k]išpī ē tamḫ[ur]* ⸢*upīšī*⸣
134'''' *[ē tamḫur šagg]aštu ē tamḫur n[akā]s napišti*
135'''' *ē tamḫur ru'utta l[ā ṭ]ābtu*
136'''' *ē tamḫur kadabbedû ē tamḫ[ur d]ibalû*[a]
137'''' *[ē] tamḫur zīru ē tamḫur lumun upīšī lemnūti ša amēlūti*

138'''' *attā yā'û anāku kû*
139'''' *mamman ayy-ilmadka mimma l[emn]u ayy-iṭḫēka*
140'''' *ina qibīt* ^{d}*Ea* ^{d}*Šama[š]* ^{d}*Marduk*
141'''' *u rubāti* ^{d}*Bēlet-ilī* [T]U$_{6}$ ÉN

142'''' DUB 8.KAM* *Maqlû* ZAG.TIL.LA.BI.ŠÈ (*ana pāṭ gimrišu*)

131'''' You are my physique, you are my virility,
132'''' Yo[u] are my great(?) [reflect]ion, you are my ever renewing reflection.
133'''' [Do not accept wi]tchcraft, Do not acce[pt] sorcerous devices,
134'''' [Do not accept mur]der, Do not accept c[utt]ing off of life,
135'''' Do not accept unhealthy saliva,
136'''' Do not accept muteness, Do not accept perversion of justice,[293]
137'''' Do [not] accept hate(-magic), Do not accept the evil of[294] evil sorcerous devices of mankind,
138'''' You are mine and I am yours.
139'''' May no one know you, may no e[vil] approach you—
140'''' By the command of Ea, Šamaš, Marduk,
141'''' And the princess Bēlet-ilī. [T]U$_6$ ÉN

142'''' The eighth tablet of Maqlû, in its totality.

Maqlû Ritual Tablet. Transcription

Instructions for Tablet I

1 [a-]*[e]nūma* ⌜*nēpeši ša maqlû*⌝ *[teppušu . . .*][-a]
break of 2–3 lines
2′ [x x] x [ca. 21 signs]
3′ *[ma]rṣa mīs pî [teppuš* ca. 16 signs]
4′ *marṣu bīna ikabbas*[!a] x [ca. 8 signs]
5′ [. . .] x
6′ ÉN *alsīkun[ūš]i šalāšīšu imannu*
7′ x [ca. 10 signs] x-*e*
8′ *ša iqbû amāt lemuttiya ikaššadamma*

9′ *[gizillâ ina išā]t(?) kibrīti t[aqâdm]a(?)* [a-]*ṣalam lipî*[-a]
10′ *ṭābta ina pîšu tašakkan ṣalma*[a] *ina appi gizillî tašakkanma*

11′ *[ina muḫḫ]i burzigalli ittanattuk*
12′ ÉN *a[ls]īkunūši tu[qatt]īma(?)* ⌜*gizillâ*⌝ *adi*

13′ *b[urz]igalli a[na bābi tušeṣṣēma tuš]kên*

Lines 14′–18′[a] are preserved in fragmentary form in three manuscripts. The three texts are not easily integrated; I therefore present them individually, in the order Nineveh (Babylonian), Sultantepe, Babylon:

Nineveh (Babylonian)
14′ [a][. . .] x x [. . .] x *riksa tarakkas*[b]
15′ [. . . *k]irra(?)*[a] *tašakkan*
16′ [. . .] x tu
17′ [. . .] *šalāšīšu imannūma*[a]

Maqlû Ritual Tablet. Translation

Instructions for Tablet I

1 When [you perform] the Maqlû ritual: [. . .]
2-3 lines missing

2′ [. . .] . . . [. . .]

3′ [You perform] the ritual of Washing-the-Mouth on [the pa]tient [. . .]

4′ The patient treads! on tamarisk . . . [. . .]

5′ [. . .] . . .

6′ He recites the Incantation "I call upon you" three times.

7′ . . . [. . .] . . .

8′ When he reaches (the passage) "May that which uttered evil against me,"[295]

9′ you k[indle a torch in burn]ing(?) sulphur, [th]en a figurine of tallow—

10′ you place salt in its mouth. You place the figurine on the tip of the torch

11′ so that it drips [upo]n the *burzigallu*-vessel.

12′ When he has [comple]ted(?) the Incantation "I c[al]l upon you," the torch

13′ together with the *b*[*urz*]*igallu*-vessel [you take out through the entrance and then prostrate] yourself.

14′–18′ . . . [296]

18′ [. . . t]uškên

Sultantepe

ana bīti [tatârma x x] x [x x x] ana(?) maḫar [. . .]
ina m[uḫḫi paš]šūri(?) DU[G. . . . gizill]â ⸢ina muḫḫi⸣ [. . .]
e [x x] x x [. . .]
É[N x] x-t[u_4(?) . . .]
É[N ^{d}Nuska(?) šu]rb[û(?) . . .]

Babylon

⸢qanê(?)⸣ k[artūti(?) . . .]
ina muḫḫi šukb[u]s[i] iz[zaz(-) . . .]
ÉN ^{d}Nuska šurbû [. . .]
BA[D](?)-a(?)-šú ÉN x [. . .]

19′ [ÉN erṣetu erṣetu er]ṣetumma mê tatta[nad]d[i]

20′ ÉN alī [Za]b[b]an a[l]ī Zabban mê ta[ttanaddi]

21′ É[N akla[a] nēb]ē[ru ina(?) g]aṣṣi u maṣḫat[i]

22′ [z]isurrâ ḫuluppaqq^{i}/ī teṣṣer
23′ ÉN šaprāk[u] a[llak ṣalam bī]ni <ṣalam> erēni

24′ ṣalam lipî ṣalam iškūr[i] ṣal[am kups]i ṣalam iṭṭî ṣalam ga[ṣṣi]

25′ ṣalam ṭīṭi ṣalam lī[š]i [ina muḫḫ]i[a] ḫuluppaqqi tasaddir[(ma)] tašakkan

26′ ÉN ^{d}Nuska annûti <ṣalmī> ēp[išiy]a ubānšu [a-]ana muḫḫi[-a] itarraṣma imannu

27′ ÉN <d>Nuska šurbû ilitti ^{d}[Ani ṣa]lam lipî ṣalam iškūri

28′ ina muḫḫi gizillî tašakkanma e[rēna šurmēna] asa ballukka
29′ qanâ ṭāba ina libbi tusanna[š x x (x)] tasallaḫ[a]
30′ ina išāt kibrīti taq[âdma ÉN ana]šši d[ipāru] ⸢imannu⸣

31′ išāta ana libbi ḫuluppa[qqi tanaddi]

19′ [Incantation. "Netherworld, netherworld], yea [ne]therworld": You spri[nkle] water.

20′ Incantation. "My city is [Za]b[b]an; my c[it]y is Zabban": You sp[rinkle] water.

21′ Incan[tation. "I have enclosed the f]o[rd": With] gypsum and roasted flour

22′ you draw a circle around the crucible.

23′ Incantation. "I have been sent and I [will go": A figurine of tama]risk, <a figurine> of cedar,

24′ a figurine of tallow, a figurine of wax, a figur[ine of sesame pom]ace, a figurine of bitumen, a figurine of gyp[sum],

25′ a figurine of clay, a figurine of dough,[297] you place in order on the crucible.

26′ Incantation. "O Nuska, these are <the figurines> of m[y sor]cerer": He points his finger toward them (i.e., the figurines) and recites (the incantation).

27′ Incantation. "O Grand Nuska, offspring of [Anu]": A fig]urine of tallow, a figurine of wax

28′ You place on a torch, and c[edar, cypress], myrtle, *ballukku*-aromatic,

29′ and sweet reed you insert into it. . . . you sprinkle (on it).

30′ You kin[dle (it/them)] in burning sulphur, and he recit[es the Incantation "I am rai]sing the to[rch]."

31′ [You put] the fire into the crucible.

INSTRUCTIONS FOR TABLET II

32′ [a]ÉN ^{d}*Nuska šurbû mālik il*[*ī rabûti ṣalam lipî*]

33′ ÉN ^{d}*Girra bēlu*[a] *gitmālu ṣalam s*[*iparri kibrīti*]

34′ ÉN ^{d}*Girra āriru b*[*ukur*] ⸢^{d}*Ani*⸣ [*ṣalam siparri*]
35′ ÉN ^{d}*Girra āriru mār* ^{d}*Ani qardu ṣalam l*[*īši*]

36′ ÉN ^{d}*Girra gašru ūmu nanduru ṣalam* ⸢*ṭīṭi*⸣
37′ ÉN ^{d}*Girra šarḫu bukur* ^{d}*Ani ṣalam iṭṭî*
38′ ÉN *keš libiš kedeš ṣalam kupsi*
39′ ÉN *eppušūni eteneppušūni ṣalam iṭṭî ša gaṣṣa ballu*

40′ ÉN *attīmannu kaššāptu ša ina nāri imluʾu ṭīṭaya ṣalam ṭīṭi ša lipâ ballu*

41′ ÉN *attīmannu kaššāptu ša tubtanaʾʾînni ṣalam bīni ṣalam erēni*

INSTRUCTIONS FOR TABLET III

42′ [a]ÉN *kaššāptu muttalliktu ša sūqāti ṣalam ṭīṭi*

43′ *lipâ ina rēš libbiša ēra ina kalâtīša tusannaš*
44′ ÉN *šittā šina mārāt* ^{d}*Ani ša šamê ṣalam lipî*[a] *ḫimmāti*

45′ ÉN *kaššāptu nērtānītu ṣalam iškūri*
46′ ÉN ^{d}*id ellu namru quddušu anāku ṣalam iṭṭ*[*î*]
47′ ÉN *lamânni sutû elamû red*[*ânni*] *ṣalam iṭṭî ša kibrīta* [*ballu*]

48′ ÉN *attīmannu kaššāptu ša iqbû*[a] *amāt lemuttiya*

49′ *ina libbiša ṣalam ṭīṭi ina kunukki arqi pâša t*[*abarram*]

50′ ÉN *attīyē ša tēpušīnni* ^{d}*ištar kubši kinṣi ša ṭīṭi teppuš* [a-]*maḫar šumēliša iṭṭâ tašakkan*[-a]

51′ *ḫaḫâ ša utūni diḫmenna ša diqāri*

INSTRUCTIONS FOR TABLET II

32′ Incantation. "O Grand Nuska, counselor of the [great] god[s": A figurine of tallow].
33′ Incantation. "O Girra, perfect lord": A figurine of b[ronze with sulphur].
34′ Incantation. "O blazing Girra, sc[ion of] Anu": [A figurine of bronze].
35′ Incantation. "O blazing Girra, warlike son of Anu": A figurine of d[ough].
36′ Incantation. "O powerful Girra, wild (fire-)storm": A figurine of clay.
37′ Incantation. "O splendid Girra, scion of Anu": A figurine of bitumen.
38′ Incantation. "*keš libiš kedeš*": A figurine of sesame pomace.
39′ Incantation. "They perform sorcery against me, they keep on performing sorcery against me": A figurine of bitumen mixed with gypsum.
40′ Incantation. "Whoever you are, O witch, who has taken out clay (for a figurine) of me from the river": A figurine of clay mixed with tallow.
41′ Incantation. "Whoever you are, O witch, who keeps on seeking me": A figurine of tamarisk, a figurine of cedar.

INSTRUCTIONS FOR TABLET III

42′ Incantation. "The witch, she who roams the streets": A figurine of clay—
43′ You insert tallow in her epigastrium, cornel in her kidneys.
44′ Incantation. "Two are they, the heavenly Daughters of Anu": A figurine of tallow (and) sweepings.
45′ Incantation. "Witch, murderess": A figurine of wax.
46′ Incantation. "Pure River (and) holy Sun am I": A figurine of bitumen.
47′ Incantation. "The Sutean surrounds me, the Elamite pursue[s me]": A figurine of bitumen [mixed] with sulphur.
48′ Incantation. "Whoever you are, O witch who has spoken an evil word against me
49′ in her heart":[298] A figurine of clay—you [seal] its mouth with a yellow seal.
50′ Incantation. "O you who have performed sorcery against me": You make (a figurine of) a goddess from head to toe(?)[299] out of clay. Put bitumen on her left.[300]
51′ Slag from a kiln (and) soot from a pot

52′ *ina mê tamaḫḫaḫma ana qaqqadiš[a tatabbak]*

53′ ÉN *ša*[a] [b-]*īpušanni ultēpišanni*[-b] [c-]*makur ṭīṭi* [d-]*[šinā ṣalmī ṭīṭi] ina lib[biša]*[-c|-d]

54′ ÉN[a] *makurraya* ^{d}*Sîn ušēpiš*

55′ *[m]akur līš[i* [a-]*šinā ṣa]lmī līši ina [libbiša]*[-a]

56′ ÉN *ḫaṣabti sūqāti ammēni tugda(n)narrênni ḫaṣabti sūq erbetti*

57′ *l[ipâ ta]paššaš* <*na*>*bāš[i t]aka[r]r[ik]*

58′ ÉN *rittumma rit[tu] ritta lipî*

59′ ÉN *rittumma ritt[u ritti iškūri]*

Instructions for Tablet IV

60′ ÉN *bišlī bišlī pallurta qanê ša gisa[llê (teppuš)]*

61′ *šinā qanê ša malû ina muḫḫi aḫameš taparrik*

62′ *ina nirī* [a-]*ṣalmūti qabalš[u]n[u*[-a] *takaṣṣar]*

63′ *šinā ṣalmī lip[î ši]nā ṣa[lmī . . .]*

64′ [a]*ina erba appāti ša pallurti*[!b] *tennīma tašakkan p[all]urti [lipâ] t[apaššaš nabāsa takarrik]*

65′ ÉN *attīmannu kaššāptu*[a] *ša zikurrudâ ippuša*[!b] *šalāšat ḫuṣāb ēri* [c-]*li[pâ tapaššaš nabāsa takarrik]*[-c]

66′ ÉN *nērtiya kaššāptiya u kušāpātīya lipâ*[a] *ubān ṭīṭi t[apaššaš(?) (nabāsa takarrik)]*

67′ [a]ÉN *ša* ^{d}*Šamši mannu abušu* [b-]*mann[u ummašu]*[-b] [c-]*ṭurri šīpāti peṣâti šalāšat kiṣrī takaṣṣar*[-c] *t[abattaq*[d] *ana li]bbi ḫulu[ppaqqi tanaddi(?)]*

68′ ÉN *ippušāni īteneppušāni*

69′ *ṭurri šīpāti peṣâti sebet k[i]ṣrī takaṣṣar*[a] *[tabattaq*[b] *ana libbi ḫuluppaqqi tanaddi(?)]*

70′ ÉN *ruʾuʾa kaššāpat anāku pāširāk erbēšer ḫaṣbāta sūq erbetta ana* x [. . .]

52′ you moisten in water and [pour] on her head.

53′ Incantation. “She who has performed sorcery against me, has had sorcery performed against me”:[301] A boat of clay—[two figurines of clay] insid[e it].

54′ Incantation. “I have had Sîn make my boat”:

55′ A [b]oat of dou[gh—two fig]urines of dough in[side it].

56′ Incantation. “O sherd of the streets, why are you constantly hostile to me?”: A sherd from the crossroad

57′ [you] rub with ta[llow] (and) wra[p up] with <re>d wool.

58′ Incantation. “Hand, hand”: A hand of tallow.

59′ Incantation. “Hand, han[d”: A hand of wax].

Instructions for Tablet IV

60′ Incantation. “Burn, burn”: [(You make)] a cross of reeds from/for a roof rail[ing (made of reeds)].

61′ You lay two “full” reeds one across the other.

62′ At the[ir] intersection [you tie them together] with black string.

63′ Two figurines of tallo[w], two fig[urines of . . .]

64′ You place upside down(?) at the four ends of the cross. The c[ro]ss y[ou rub with tallow (and) wrap up with red wool].

65′ Incantation. “Whoever you are, O witch, who performs *Zikurrudâ*-magic against me”: Three sticks of cornel [you rub with] tal[low (and) wrap up with red wool].

66′ Incantation. “My murderess, my witch, and my sorceress(?)”: Yo[u rub(?)] a finger of clay with tallow [(and wrap up with red wool)].

67′ Incantation. “Of the Sun, who is his father, wh[o is his mother]?”: You tie three knots in a band of white wool, y[ou undo(?) (them) and cast(?) (the band) in]to the cru[cible].

68′ Incantation. “They perform sorcery against me, they keep on performing sorcery against me”:

69′ You tie seven knots in a band of white wool, [you undo(?) (them) and cast(?) (the band) into the crucible].

70′ Incantation. “My friend is a witch; (but) I am a releaser”: Fourteen sherds from the crossroad to . . . [. . .].

INSTRUCTIONS FOR TABLET V

71′ ÉN [a-]*ēpištī*[!] *u muštēpištī*[!-a] [[b-]*ḫašê šam*]*aššammī*[-b] [*(tašarrap)*]

72′ ÉN *mannu pâ iptil pâ* [*tašarrap*]
73′ ÉN *dunnānī dunnānī*
74′ *tābīlu* DUB.MEŠ-[*ak/q*[a] x x x]
75′ ÉN *attīmannu kaššāptu ša tēteneppu*[*šī*[!a]]

76′ *kukra ḫaš*[*ê*] *u pâ tašarrap*
77′ ÉN *zīru ša*[a] ⸢*tēpušāni*⸣ [*tušēpišāni*] ⸢*kibrīta u*(?) *ṭābat*⸣ *amurri* ⸢*tašarrap*⸣

78′ ÉN *att*[*ī*]*mannu kaššāptu ša kīma šūti*
79′ [*ikk*]*imu*[a] *m*[*aṣḫat*]*u qamû*
80′ ÉN *šaruḫ lānī* [a-][*š*]*aruḫ zimī*[-a] *maṣḫatu qamû*

81′ ÉN *šēr*ʾ*ānī tukaṣṣirā* [d]*Ea uptaṭṭer*

82′ *ina ḫuṣāb*[a] *ēri libbi ḫulu*[*pp*]*aqqi tubaḫḫaš*
83′ ÉN *attunu mû ina mê tunāḫ*
84′ ÉN *ēpišūʾa ēpišētūʾa ina mê tunāḫ*

85′ ÉN *ezzētunu šamrātunu ina mê tunāḫ*
86′ ÉN *akbus gallâya ṣalam līši ina šēpīšu ikabbas*

87′ ÉN *ḫūlā zūbā ina nignakki ša maḫar* [d]*Nuska bāb ḫuluppaqqi takattam*

88′ ÉN *šadû liktumkunūši aban šadî*
89′ *ina muḫḫi nignakki ša bāb ḫuluppaqqi tašakkan*
90′ ÉN *isâ isâ imannūma maṣḫata tattanaddi*[a]

91′ [a-]*qil*[*ûtu adi ḫulupp*]*aqqi*[-a] *ana bābi tušeṣṣēma tan*[*assuk*[b]]

92′ *arkišu* ÉN udug.ḫul edin.na.zu.šè *adi bābi kamî tamannūma*

93′ *maṣḫata bābānī teṣṣer*
94′ *ana bīti terrubma*[a] *ašar maqlâ taqlû mê tattanaddi*

INSTRUCTIONS FOR TABLET V

71′ Incantation. “My$^{!}$ sorceress and the woman who instigates sorcery against me$^{!}$”: [(You burn) thyme (and) se]same.
72′ Incantation. “Who has twined chaff together”: [You burn] chaff.
73′ Incantation. “Strong one$^{(?)}$, strong one$^{(?)}$”:
74′ You strew dried plants, [. . .].
75′ Incantation. “Whoever you are, O witch, who keeps on performing sorcery (against me)”:
76′ You burn *kukru*, thym[e], and chaff.
77′ Incantation. “The hate(-magic) that you have performed against me, [have had performed against me]”: [You bu]rn sul[phur and] Amurru-sa[lt].
78′ Incantation: “Whoever you are, O witch, who like the South wind
79′ [has pi]led up[302]”: Parched ro[asted flo]ur.
80′ Incantation. “Splendid is my appearance, splendid is my countenance”: Parched roasted flour.
81′ Incantation. “Ea has (now) unbound the sinews that you have bound up”:
82′ You stir the contents of the crucible with a stick of cornel.
83′ Incantation. “You, O water”: With water you extinguish the fire.
84′ Incantation: “My sorcerers, my sorceresses”: With water you extinguish the fire.
85′ Incantation. “Raging, furious”: With water you extinguish the fire.
86′ Incantation. “I trample down my foe”: He tramples a figurine of dough with his feet.
87′ Incantation. “Melt, dissolve”: You cover the opening of the crucible with the censer that is before Nuska.
88′ Incantation. “May the mountain cover you”: A mountain-stone
89′ you set upon the censer that is on the opening of the crucible.
90′ Incantation. “Be off, be off”: He recites (it), and you then repeatedly pour out roasted flour.[303]
91′ You take the remains [of the burning together with the cruc]ible out through the entrance and then thro[w (it) away].
92′ Afterwards you recite the Incantation “Evil udug-demon to your steppe” [304] to the outer entrance,[305]
93′ and you then draw around the entrances with roasted flour.
94′ You enter[306] the house and then sprinkle water where you performed the Maqlû-burning.[307]

95′ ÉN *anamdi šipta ana puḫri ilī kalāma tama[nnu]*

Instructions for Tablet VI

96′ ÉN ^{d}*Enlil qaqqadī pānūʾa ūmu burāš[a]*^{a} *k[ukra]*
97′ ÉN *ēpišta*^{a} *qumqummat[u] k[ukra] maštaka[l]*
98′ ÉN *kukrumma kukru kukra* ⸢*pâ*⸣ ⸢*nīnâ*⸣ *dikmenna*
99′ $^{a-}$ÉN *kukrumma kukru alkān[im]ma*$^{-a}$ *kukra*
100′ ÉN *ē kaššāptiya elēnītiya kukra*
101′ ÉN *lām* ^{d}*Ningirsu ina māti ilsû* ^{d}*alāla kukra*

102′ ÉN *u[ndu kaššāptu] ukaššipanni kukra*
103′ ^{a}*lipâ lubārī naksūti*
104′ ÉN *att[ī]ʾē ša tēp[ušī k]alāma kukra*
105′ ÉN *kibr[ī]tu elletu*$^{!a}$ *m[ār]at šamê*^{b} *rabûti anāku kibrīta*

106′ ÉN *kibrītu kib[rītu kibrītu] mārat* ^{d}*id kibrī[ta]*

107′ ÉN *kibrītu elletu atāʾišu šammu quddušu anāku*
108′ *kibrīta atāʾiša*
109′ ÉN ^{d}*id qaqqadī kibrītu padattī*
110′ *kibrīta anḫullâ u imḫur-līm*
111′ ÉN ^{d}*id ākul alti*^{a} *kibrīta*
112′ ÉN *ē kaššāptiya elēnītiya īde* ⸢*ul*⸣ *īde kibrīta*
113′ ÉN *attī ṭābtu ša ina ašri elli ibbanû ana muḫḫi kirbān ṭābti imannūma*

114′ *ina muḫḫi nignakki ša qutāri ša ina rēš erši tašakkan*

115′ ÉN *ē kaššāptiya lū raḫḫātiya*
116′ *ana muḫḫi nuḫurti imannūma ina muḫḫi nignakki ša ina rēš erši tašakkan*
117′ *ulinna erša talammi*
118′ ÉN *ē kaššāptiya lū raḫḫātiya ana muḫḫi šinšeret šaʾirrī imannūma ina muḫḫi nignakki*^{a} *ša ina rēš erši tašakkan*

119′ ÉN *ē kaššāptiya elēnītiya* $^{a-}$*ša tattanallakī kalu mātāti*$^{-a}$

120′ *ana muḫḫi šinā [ḫ]uṣāb ēri imannūma*

95′ You reci[te] the Incantation "I am casting an incantation upon the assembly of all the gods."

Instructions for Tablet VI

96′ Incantation. "Enlil is my head, my face is *ūmu*": Juniper, *k*[*ukru*].
97′ Incantation. "My[!] sorceress is a *qumqummatu*": *k*[*ukru*], soapwort.
98′ Incantation. "*kukru, kukru, kukru*": Chaf[f, a]mmi, soot.
99′ Incantation. "*kukru, kukru*, Come hi[ther]": *kukru.*
100′ Incantation. "Ha! my witch, my deceiver": *kukru.*
101′ Incantation. "Before Ningirsu called out the '*alāla*' work-song in the land": *kukru.*
102′ Incantation. "On the d[ay that the witch] bewitched me": *kukru*,
103′ tallow, torn rags.
104′ Incantation. "You who have performed [a]ll kinds of sorcery": *kukru.*
105′ Incantation. "Pure Sulphur, d[augh]ter of the great heavens[308] am I": Sulphur.
106′ Incantation. "Sulphur, Sul[phur, Sulphur], daughter of River": Sulph[ur].
107′ Incantation: "Pure Sulphur (and) *atāʾišu*, the holy plant am I":
108′ Sulphur, *atāʾišu*-plant.
109′ Incantation. "River is my head, Sulphur my physique":
110′ Sulphur, *anḫullû*-plant, and *imḫurlīmu*-plant.
111′ Incantation. "River, I have eaten, I have drunk[309]": Sulphur.
112′ Incantation. "Ha! my witch, my deceiver, whoever you are": Sulphur.
113′ Incantation. "You, Salt, who were created in a pure place": He recites (it) over a lump of salt,
114′ you then place (it) upon the censer for incense that is at the head of the bed.
115′ Incantation. "Ha! my witch, my inseminatrix[310]":
116′ He recites (it) over asafoetida, you then place (it) upon the censer that is at the head of the bed.
117′ You surround the bed with (colored) twine.
118′ Incantation. "Ha! my witch, my inseminatrix": He recites (it) over twelve (wooden) *šaʾirru*s, you then place (them) upon the censer[311] that is at the head of the bed.
119′ Incantation. "Ha! my witch, my deceiver, you who (constantly) roam over all lands":
120′ He recites (it) over two sticks of cornel,

121′ *ina imitti bābi u šumēl bābi kamî tašakkan*
122′ ÉN *ē kaššāptiya elēnītiya*
123′ *ana muḫḫi aban šadî imannūma ina tarbaṣi tanassuk*

124′ *qutārī ša* ÉN[a] ^{d}*Enlil qaqqadī*
125′ *mala ana*[a] *riksī šaṭrū*
126′ *ištēniš taballalma tuqattaršu* ÉN ^{d}*Enlil qaqqadī imannu*

Instructions for Tablet VII

127′ ÉN *rittī* ^{d}*Manzât maṣḫata u billata*

128′ [*ina*] [a-]*la*[*ḫan*]*ni šaḫarrati*[-a] *marṣu iballalma*
129′ *dalta sikk*[*ū*]*ra* [a-]*sippē bābāni*[-a] *iltanappat*
130′ ÉN *araḫḫēk*[*a r*]*amānī akal šamna*
131′ ÉN *šamnu ellu šamnu ebbu akal šamna*
132′ ÉN ^{d}*Enlil qaqqadī* ^{mul}*šukūd*[*u*] *lānī* [a-]⸢*akal*⸣ *šamna*[-a]
133′ [a]*ša*[*m*]*na kala šīrīšu* [*tapaššaš*]
134′ ÉN ^{d}*Nuska apil Ekur ša têrēt ilī r*[*abûti* (x x)]

135′ ^{d}⸢*Nūru*⸣ [*k*]*urab* <*ana* ^{d}*Enlil*>(?) *šutēšer ḫarrānka a*[*na*] *Ek*[*ur tamannūma*]
136′ *arkišu zisurrâ* [*er*]*ša teṣṣer*
137′ ÉN sag.ba sag.ba ÉN *tummu b*[*ītu tamannu*]

138′ *ina sēr*[*i*] *a*[*d*]*i šurpu tašarr*[*ap*]*u*
139′ *šurpu ana bābi*[a] *tušeṣṣēma ta*[*nassuk*[b]]
140′ *arkišu* ÉN *attīmannu kaššāptu ša īpuš*[*u imannu*]

141′ *ṣalam kaššāpti ša qēmi ina libbi namsê teṣṣer*
142′ [a-]*ṣalam* ⸢*ṭīṭi*⸣ *ša kaššāpti ina muḫḫi tašakkan*[-a] *qātīšu ana muḫḫi imessi*[b] *ana bī*[*ti terrub*[c]]
143′ ÉN *bāʾertu ša bāʾirāti*
144′ *ṣalam kaššāpi u kaššāpti*
145′ *ša qēmi ina libbi*[a] *namsê teṣṣ*[*er*]

121′ you then place (them) to the right and left of the outer gate.
122′ Incantation. "Ha! my witch, my deceiver":
123′ He recites (it) over a mountain-stone, you then throw (it) away in the courtyard.

124′ The fumigants for the Incantation(-tablet): "Enlil is my head,"
125′ as many as are prescribed for the ritual arrangements,
126′ you mix together and fumigate him. He recites the Incantation(-tablet): "Enlil is my head."

Instructions for Tablet VII

127′ Incantation. "My hand is the Rainbow": Roasted flour and a dry (substance for producing) beer
128′ the patient mixes [in] a flask[312] made of porous clay,
129′ he then smears (it on) the door, the bar, and the posts of the doors.
130′ Incantation. "I am impregnating you, my self": 1/10 of a liter of oil.
131′ Incantation. "Pure oil, clear oil": 1/10 of a liter of oil.
132′ Incantation. "Enlil is my head, Sirius is my form": 1/10 of a liter of oil.
133′ [You anoint] his whole body with oil.[313]
134′ The Incantation. "Nuska, first-born of Ekur, (the house) of instructions of the [great] gods [(x x)]
135′ (divine) light, salute <Enlil(?)>, make your way directly to E[kur" you recite].
136′ Afterwards you then draw a circle around the [b]ed.
137′ [You recite] the Incantation "Ban, ban" (and) the Incantation "The h[ouse] is adjured."

138′ In the morning, when you burn the fire,[314]
139′ you take the fire[315] out through the entrance[316] and t[hrow (it) away].
140′ Afterwards [he recites] the Incantation "Whoever you are, o witch, who has made."
141′ You draw a likeness of the witch made of flour inside a washbasin,
142′ you place thereon a clay figurine of the witch. He washes his hands thereon. [You enter[317] the ho]use.
143′ Incantation. "Huntress of huntresses":
144′ Likenesses of the warlock and witch
145′ made of flour you dr[aw] inside the washbasin,

146′ *ṣalam ṭīṭi ša kaššāpi u kaššāpti ina muḫḫi* [a-]*ṣalam qēmi*[-a] *tašakkan*

147′ *qātīšu ana*[a] *muḫḫi imessi ina ḫuṣāb ēri ana šalāšīšu ikar*[*rit*]

148′ [a]ÉN *ipšīki epšēteki mīs qātī*
149′ ÉN *kiṣrīki kuṣṣurūti mīs qātī* [a-]*eprī ana libbi namsê tanassuk*[-a]

150′ [ÉN *a*]*msi qātīya ubbab*[a] *zumrī*
151′ [a-][*ana muḫ*]*ḫi ṣalam nigsagilê*[-a] [b-]*qātīšu imessi*[-b]
152′ [ÉN *te*]*bi šēru mise* [a-]*qātīya mīs*[-a] *qātī*
153′ ÉN *ittamra šēru mīs qātī*
154′ ÉN *šērumma šēru mīs qātī*
155′ ÉN *ina šēri mesâ qātāya mīs qātī*
156′ ÉN *amsi qātīya*[a] *amtesi qātīya mīs qātī*

Instructions for Tablet VIII

157′ ÉN *adi tappuḫa bīna maštakal aban suluppi*

158′ *pâ gaṣṣa unuq šubî kukra*
159′ *burāša qātīšu imessi*
160′ [a]ÉN *ittapḫa* [d]*Šamaš akaššad mīs qātī*
161′ ÉN *undu kaššāptu īber nāra mīs qātī*
162′ ÉN *ultu* [d]*Uru ina māti ilsû alāla*
163′ *pâ ana libbi*[a] *ḫaṣbi šaḫarri tanaddīma*
164′ *ina pîšu ana libbi namsê inappaḫ*
165′ ÉN *annû ininnama*
166′ *ṣalam kaššāpti ša ṭīṭi teppušma*[a] *aban šadî ina rēš libbiša tašakkan*

167′ *qātīšu ana muḫḫi imessi*
168′ *ina ḫuṣāb ēri ana šalāšīšu ikarrit*
169′ ÉN *pû idbub lemnāti mīs qātī*
170′ ÉN *ēpištu u muštēpištu* [a-]*muribbat kišpī ruḫê*[-a]

171′ *šinā akalī ištēnâ ṣalam kaššāpi u kaššāpti*
172′ *ša līši teppušma*[a] *ina*[b] *libbi akalī tarakkasma*

146′ you place clay figurines of the warlock and witch upon the likenesses of flour.[318]

147′ He washes his hands thereon. He stri[kes] (them) three times with a stick of cornel.

148′ Incantation. "Your sorcery, your manipulations": Handwashing.

149′ Incantation. "Your tightly knotted knots": Handwashing. You throw dirt into the washbasin.

150′ [Incantation. "I] wash my hands, I cleanse my body":

151′ He washes his hands [upo]n the figurine of the substitute.[319]

152′ [Incantation. "Ris]e up, morning, wash my hands": Handwashing.

153′ Incantation. "Dawn has broken": Handwashing.

154′ Incantation. "It is morning, yea morning": Handwashing.

155′ Incantation. "At dawn my hands are washed": Handwashing.

156′ Incantation. "I wash my hands,[320] I have (now) washed my hands": Handwashing.

INSTRUCTIONS FOR TABLET VIII

157′ Incantation. "Until you rise": (With water in which have been placed) tamarisk, soapwort, date pit,

158′ chaff, gypsum, a ring of *šubû* stone, *kukru*,

159′ juniper he washes his hands.

160′ Incantation. "Šamaš has risen, I reach": Handwashing.

161′ Incantation. "When the witch crossed the river": Handwashing.

162′ Incantation. "After Uru called out the '*alāla*' work-song in the land":

163′ You put chaff inside a potsherd made of porous clay,

164′ with his mouth he then blows (the chaff) into the washbasin.

165′ Incantation. "Now, then, this (one)":

166′ You make a figurine of the witch out of clay and then place a mountain-stone on her upper abdomen.

167′ He washes his hands thereon.

168′ He strikes it three times with a stick of cornel.

169′ Incantation. "The mouth spoke evil": Handwashing.

170′ Incantation. "The sorceress and the woman who instigates sorcery, who sets witchcraft and spittle in motion":

171′ Two loaves of bread, (and) one figurine each of the warlock and witch

172′ you make out of dough and then insert[321] (each) inside (one of) the loaves.[322]

173′ [a-]*ina imittišu u šumēlišu inaššīma*[-a] *šipta imannūma*[b]

174′ *ana kalbi u kalbati tanamdin*
175′ ÉN *attā ṣillī mê burzigalla šaḫarrata*[a] *tumallāma*

176′ ⸢*pānīšu*⸣ *ina libbi immarma*[a]
177′ *ib*[*arri ana ṣ*]*īt šamši tasallaḫ*
178′ [*arkišu* ÉN *anašši*] *gamlīya tamannūma*
179′ *mê tasallaʾ*

180′ [*ṭuppi nēpešī ša Maql*]*û*

173′ He then raises (the two loaves) in his right and left hands and then recites the incantation.
174′ You then throw (them) to a male and a female dog.
175′ Incantation. "You are my reflection": You fill a *burzigallu*-vessel made of porous clay with water,
176′ He then looks at his face in it
177′ and beh[olds (it)]. You sprinkle the water [towards s]unrise.
178′ [Afterwards] you recite [the Incantation "I raise my c]rooks,"
179′ you then sprinkle water.

180′ [The Ritual Tablet of Maql]û

NOTES

MAQLÛ TABLET I

NOTES TO TRANSCRIPTION

line 7 [a] Var.: *amruṣ*.
line 23 [a–a] Var.: line omitted.
line 24 [a] Var.: *terinnat ašūḫi* (so quoted in a commentary).
line 30 [a] Var.: *ruḫê*.
line 33 [a] Var.: *kirbān ṭābti ina mê* | [b] Var.: *liḫḫarmiṭ*.
line 35 [a] Var.: *limlâ*.
line 36 [a] Var.: + [KA.INIM.MA U]Š$_{11}$.BÚRU.DA.[KAM].
line 39 [a] Or perhaps *teppušā*.
line 41 [a–a] Var.: *lā īšâ* | [b] Var.: + [KA.INIM.MA UŠ$_{11}$].BÚRU.DA.[KAM].
line 42 [a] Perhaps read *Ṣappān*.
line 44 [a] Since the parallel entries in lines 44 (^{d}UTU.È … ^{d}UTU.ŠÚ.A) and 45 (*ṣi-it* ^{d}UTU-*ši* … *e-reb* ^{d}UTU-*ši*) refer to the two positions of the sun with different writings and each line does so consistently across all manuscripts, the seemingly logographic writings in line 44 probably represent different Akkadian terms from those found in line 45, and thus the writings in line 44 should perhaps be read as if they were Akkadian words ^{d}*utu-è* … ^{d}*utu-šú-a* (and not *ṣīt* ^{d}*Šamši* … *ereb* ^{d}*Šamši*).
line 63 [a] Perhaps read *qaqqari* instead of *erṣeti*; cf. VII 144 and note there.
line 75 [a–a] Var.: line omitted.
line 79 [a–a] Var.: line possibly omitted in one ms.
line 81 [a] Var.: one ms has the line order 82–81.
line 83 [a] Var.: one ms has the line order 85-83-84.
line 87 [a–a] Var.: one ms has line 95 here instead of line 87.
line 88 [a] Var.: + *ša amēlūti*.
line 95 [a–a] Var.: absent.
line 98 [a] Var.: + *naglab*[*īya*].
line 101 [a] Var.: + *dig*[*līya ušamṭ*]*û ḫasīsīya u*[*ṣabbitū*].
line 109 [a–a] Var.: line absent.
line 113 [a] Var.: *q*[*u*]*rādi* | [b] Var.: + *ina ūmu annê ina d*[*īn*]*iya izizzammu*.
line 115 [a] I have read LÚ.UŠ$_{11}$.ZU *u* MÍ.UŠ$_{11}$.ZU here in line 115 as *kaššāpī u kaššāptī*; for this reading, cf. II 132 and 109. The first-person possessive suffix (.MU) sometimes seems to be implicit in the logographic writing LÚ/MÍ.UŠ$_{11}$.ZU when the noun is in the nominative or the accusative; cf. VII 17.
line 117 [a–a] Var.: line omitted.

line 123 [a] Var.: ^{d}*Ea*.
line 124 [a] Vars.: ^{d}*Ninmen*[*na*], [^{d}*An*]*unnaki*.
line 130 [a–a] Var.: line absent.
line 132 [a–a] Var.: omitted in one ms.
line 139 [a] Var.: + [*ēpiš kiš*]*p*[*ī lemn*]*ū*⸢*ti ruḫê lā*⸣ *ṭābūti* / [*ša ana lemutti*] *ikpudun*[*i*] *yâši*. *ēpiš kišpī lemnūti ruḫê lā ṭābūti ša ana lemutti ikpud*$^{\bar{u}}$/*uni yâši* is a formulaic block insertion. *ēpiš* in *ēpiš kišpī* … here and in II 117–118 can be either singular or plural (pl. *ēpišūt* > *ēpiš*). The singular fits the context of Tablet I, and the plural fits that of Tablet II (for the use of a singular form as the first part of a construct in plural meaning, cf. Werner Mayer, "Sechs Šu-ila-Gebete," *OrNS* 59 [1990]: 452–53). As for *ik*-⸢*pu-du*⸣-*ni*, it can be either plural subjunctive *ikpudūni* (with -*ni* as dative first-person suffix) or singular subjunctive *ikpuduni* (with -*ni* as accusative first-person suffix; see *GAG* paradigm 12a, n. 6). Cf. note on II 117.
line 145 [a] Var.: ÉN *alsīkunūši ilī mušīt*[*i*].

Notes to Translation

1. Lines 4–12 form a causal clause introduced by *aššu* ("because") in line 4; this clause introduces and justifies the request made in lines 13–14.

2. For this translation, see Tzvi Abusch, "*Alaktu* and *Halakhah*: Oracular Decision, Divine Revelation," *HTR* 80 (1987): 15–42.

3. Unlikely alternative: Verily are her witchcraft, her spittle, her enchainment released.

4. Var.: the cone of a pine tree.

5. Var.: the evil spell.

6. That is, the witch's mouth.

7. That is, the witch's tongue.

8. Var.: like a clump of salt in water.

9. Var.: May all of her words fill the steppe.

10. That is, her accusations are dismissed.

11. Var.: + [It is the wording (of the incantation)] to undo witch[craft].

12. For my understanding of the incantations in lines 37–72, see Tzvi Abusch, "The Socio-Religious Framework, Part I," 1–34; "The Socio-Religious Framework of the Babylonian Witchcraft Ceremony *Maqlû*: Some Observations on the Introductory Section of the Text, Part II," in *Solving Riddles and Untying Knots: Biblical, Epigraphic, Semitic Studies in Honor of Jonas C. Greenfield*, edited by Ziony Zevit, Seymour Gitin, and Michael Sokoloff (Winona Lake, IN: Eisenbrauns, 1995), 467–94; and "Ascent to the Stars in a Mesopotamian Ritual: Social Metaphor and Religious Experience," in *Death, Ecstasy, and Other Worldly Journeys*, edited by Michael Fishbane and John J. Collins (Albany: State University of New York Press, 1995), 15–39 .

13. Or, perhaps: you do.

14. That is, the oath. Alternative translation: Whatever my witches do, it (i.e., their oath) will not secure anyone who will overlook, undo, release.

15. Var.: Whatever my witches do, they will not have anyone who will overlook, undo, release (it, i.e., the oath).

16. Var.: + [It is the wording (of the incantation)] to undo [witchcraft].

17. If, in fact, lines 44 and 45 refer to the two positions of the sun differently, the terms in line 44 should perhaps be translated not as "the rising of the sun … the setting of

the sun" (a mythological description) as in line 45, but rather as either "sunrise … sunset" (more naturalistic) or "east … west" (directional).

18. Or: Cast the incantation.

19. Lit., "shall release." I understand the ox and sheep here as offerings to the (divine) judge.

20. That is, may it stand up under scrutiny.

21. That is, may it not prevent mine from being effective.

22. Possible alternative translations for forms designating doers of the action *reḫû (rāḫû, rāḫītu, raḫḫātu)* are "spitter" and "poisoner," the latter of which I prefer.

23. Var.: + of mankind.

24. Could *kadabbedû* denote lockjaw?

25. Lit.: the calming of anger.

26. Var.: + (and) my hips.

27. Or: caused me to turn against myself.

28. Var.: + [Decreas]ed [my vis]ion, i[mpaired] my hearing (lit., "[seiz]ed my ears").

29. Or, possibly: my semen. But the water mentioned here probably refers to water poured out as part of a funerary ritual; see note to IV 44.

30. Var.: the hero.

31. Var.: + On this day, stand by me in my judgment.

32. Earlier I translated *ūmu ezzu* in Maqlû as "brilliant red light/fiery red light/fierce rays" (see Abusch "An Early Form," 16 and 31); I have generally replaced this translation with "raging (fire-)storm." However, I am still not fully convinced that *ūmu* here must refer to storm (so, e.g., *CAD* s.v. *ūmu*) rather than to rays or light. For the possible daylight character of this demonic force, see also the note to VI 1.

33. Lit., "the striking of stones," that is, may their fingers be cut off as if they were smashed by stones. Possible, but less likely, alternatives: "may their fingers be cut back like stones that are smashed," or (so *CAD* G, 53b) "may they trim their fingers like blunted stones."

34. Var.: Ea.

35. Vars.: Ninmenna, Anunnaki.

36. The *lil*-group includes male (incubus) and female (succubus) spirits who attack the living in search of a sexual partner.

37. Var.: + [The doer of] ev[il witchcra]ft, not good spittle, [Who] plotted [evil] against me myself.

38. Var.: The first tablet of "Incantation. I call upon you, Gods of the Night." This alternative title for Maqlû is the incipit of the first incantation in Maqlû.

Maqlû Tablet II

Notes to Transcription

line 14 [a] Var.: *bašâ*.

line 17 [a] Var.: + ÉN.

line 18 [a–a] Var.: rubric omitted in some mss.

line 60 [a] It is possible, but less likely, that the Hand-group entries in lines 60–62 should be rendered *lū qāt ili lū qā[t* ^{d}*ištari] / lū qāt eṭemmi lū qāt [māmīti] / lū qāt amēlūti*, and understood as the causes or powers behind the diseases and not as the diseases themselves.

line 61 [a–a] Var.: *lū šunamerimmakku* and *lū šunamlullukku* transposed in lines 61–62: *lū* ⸢*šu*⸣<*nam*>*l*[*ullukku*] *l*[*ū šunamerimmakku*].
line 76 [a–a] Vars.: KA.INIM.MA *ina muḫḫi ṣalam siparri kibrīti imannu* in one Aššur ms; rubric omitted in some mss.
line 85 [a] Var.: [*a*]*ttā*.
line 86 [a–a] Vars.: *anāku aradk*[*a* …]; *anāku* ^{I}*Aššuršaliṭ mār ilišu ša ilšu* ^{d}[*Na*]*bû* ^{d}*ištaršu* ^{d}*Tašmētu* (Aššur ms).
line 88 [a] We expect *ili šarri kabti u rubê*.
line 95 [a] For a D form of the verb *abāru* with an *e*-vowel, see CH §126, l. 14, cited in *AHw* s.v. *abāru* III D (and note the variant *ūtabbiri* in R. Borger, *BAL*^{2}, 27). Instead, this verb might possibly be read *liddappirūma*.
line 97 [a–a] Var.: line absent.
line 99 [a] Var.: + ^{I}*Aššuršaliṭ* (Aššur ms).
line 104 [a–a] Vars.: KA.INIM.MA *ina muḫḫi ṣalam siparri imannu* in one Aššur ms; rubric omitted in one ms.
line 107 [a] We expect *tadinnu* (cf. note on III 159); var.: *tadinna*.
line 110 [a–a] Var.: line absent.
line 117 [a] *ēpiš kišpī lemnūti u ruḫê lā ṭābūti ša ana lemutti ikpud*^{ū}/*uni yâši* in lines 117–118 is a formulaic block insertion. *ēpiš* in *ēpiš kišpī* … here and in the var. for I 139 can be either singular or plural (pl. *ēpišūt* > *ēpiš*). The plural fits the context of Tablet II (for the use of a singular form as the first part of a construct in plural meaning, see Mayer, "Sechs Šu-ila-Gebete," 152–53), and the singular fits that of Tablet I. As for *ik-pu-du-ni*, it can be either plural subjunctive *ikpudūni* (with *-ni* as dative first-person suffix) or singular subjunctive *ikpuduni* (with *-ni* as accusative first-person suffix; see *GAG* paradigm 12a, n. 6). Cf. note for var. on I 139.
line 125 [a–a] Var.: absent.
line 126 [a–a] Var.: rubric omitted in one ms.
line 134 [a] Var.: absent.
line 135 [a–a] Vars.: [KA.INIM.MA] *ina muḫḫi ṣalam ṭīṭi imannu* in one Aššur ms; rubric omitted in one ms.
line 137 [a] Var.: ^{d}*Šala*.
line 138 [a] Var.: *zikri*.
line 139 [a] Var.: *isq*[*i* (*u nindabê*)].
line 141 [a] Var.: *ayyābī*.
line 142 [a–a] Var.: *mulappit dūr abnī*.
line 144 [a] Var.: + *muʾabbit*/*mulappit lemnūti attāma anāku a*[*radka* …].
line 148 [a–a] Var.: *kaššāpiya u kaššāptiya*, which is erroneous but might suggest that LÚ.UŠ$_{11}$.ZU *u* MÍ.UŠ$_{11}$.ZU of the main text should be construed as *kaššāpī u kaššāptī* (cf. note on I 115) | [b] Var.: + ÉN.
line 149 [a–a] Var.: KA.INIM.MA *ina muḫḫi ṣalam iṭṭî imannu* in one Aššur ms.
line 156 [a–a] Var.: absent.
line 160 [a–a] Vars.: KA.INIM.MA *ina muḫḫi ṣalam kupsi imannu* in one Aššur ms; rubric omitted in one ms.
line 170 [a] Var.: + ^{I}*Aššuršaliṭ* (Aššur ms).
line 181 [a–a] Var.: absent.
line 182 [a–a] Var.: [KA.INIM.MA *ina muḫḫi ṣalam iṭṭî ša gaṣ*]*ṣa ballu imannu* in one Aššur ms.
line 198 [a] Text: *īpušaššimma*.
line 199 [a] Var.: omitted.
line 204 [a–a] Var.: rubric omitted in one ms.

line 215 [a–a] Given the Nippur association of the gods in the surrounding lines, it is more than possible that [[d] x] x should be restored [[d]*en-lí*]*l*.
line 224 [a–a] Var.: [*ša kaššāpiya u kaššāptiy*]*a arḫiš ḫanṭiš.*
line 226 [a–a] Var.: rubric omitted in some mss.
line 228 [a] Var.: ÉN *a*[*lsīkunūši*].

Notes to Translation

39. Lit., who listens to the secret of Enlil.

40. The text has *māliku šadû* (wr. *šá-du-ú*/[KU]R-*ú*) [d]*Igigī*, which translates literally as "the counselor, the mountain of the Igigi," and would seem to refer to Nuska. While sense suggests that *māliku* refers to Nuska and *šadû* to Enlil, which would require the emendation *māliku šadî* [d]*Igigī*, the full title *māliku šadû* [d]*Igigī* appears in this form in *CMAWR* 1, 8.13, line 27, where it clearly refers to Enlil (cf. ibid., p. 371). Accordingly, the title is a frozen form, and our line should probably be translated, "the one who listens to Enlil, (who is) the counselor, (and) the mountain of the Igigi." Cf. II 137: "Offspring of the pure one, the exalted Šalaš" (but see note there).

41. Perhaps better: He who calls your name.

42. For my understanding of this incantation, see Tzvi Abusch "The Revision of Babylonian Anti-Witchcraft Incantations: Analysis of Incantations in the Ceremonial Series *Maqlû*," in *Continuity and Innovation in the Magical Tradition*. Edited by Gideon Bohak, Yuval Harari, and Shaul Shaked, JSRC 15 (Leiden: Brill, 2011), 16–28.

43. See note on I 78.

44. Lit., fallen-from-heaven-epilepsy.

45. The reading *lū šudingirrakku lū š*[*uʾinannakku*], etc., in lines 60–62 assumes that the Hand-group entries refer to diseases. It is not impossible that instead we should read *lū qāt ili lū qā*[*t* [d]*ištari*], etc.; this latter reading assumes that the Hand-group represents the causes or powers behind the diseases. We would then translate "Be it hand of a god, be it han[d of a goddess], Be it hand of a ghost, be it hand [of a curse], Be it hand of mankind."

46. Var.: Transposition of the last entry in line 61 and the first entry in line 62: "be it Ha[nd-of-man]<kind>-disease, Be it [Hand-of-a-curse-disease]."

47. Perhaps: "smites," or "penetrates."

48. Var.: He recites the wording (of the incantation) over a figurine of bronze with sulphur.

49. Var.: "you," instead of "speedily."

50. Vars.: I, your servant [...]; I, Aššuršaliṭ, the son of his god, whose god is Nabu, whose goddess is Tašmētu.

51. Lit., stand before you.

52. We expect: god, king, noble, and prince.

53. Or, perhaps: May they be driven away.

54. Lit., be/go straight.

55. Var.: He recites the wording (of the incantation) over a figurine of bronze.

56. For the translation of *ša* here as a causative particle, compare the use of *aššu* in the similar lines II 22–23 (*aššu attā ana yâši tazzazzuma kīma* [d]*Sîn u* [d]*Šamaš tadinnu dīnu*); for the use of *ša* as "because," see III 164.

57. The objects and location of the action in lines 119–121 refer to grave goods and the grave, respectively.

58. Or, perhaps: cause them not to have rest soon.

59. But *CAD* K, 284 treats *lik-pu-du-šú-nu-ti* as a metathesis for *lipqidušunūti*; if that is correct, translate: deliver them over to evil.

60. Var.: He recites [the wording (of the incantation)] over a figurine of clay.

61. Var.: Šala.

62. Or, possibly: "Pure offspring of exalted Šalaš"; if so, "bright offspring" would be a more appropriate translation.

63. Var.: utterance.

64. Var.: allotment [(and cereal offerings)].

65. Var.: the enemies.

66. Var.: the one who strikes down wall(s) of stone.

67. Vars.: + It is you who are the destroyer of the evildoers. I, [your] se[rvant …]. A variant of the first word of the additional line reads "the one who strikes down" instead of "the destroyer."

68. This probably refers to one (e.g., a vassal) who disregards or tries to change the terms of an agreement supported by an oath.

69. Var.: He recites the wording (of the incantation) over a figurine of bitumen.

70. The emended text refers to the Elamite goddess Narunde and god Naḫḫunte (Naḫundi).

71. Var.: He recites the wording (of the incantation) over a figurine of sesame pomace.

72. Var.: + Aššuršaliṭ.

73. Or, perhaps better: figurine(s).

74. Var.: He recites [the wording (of the incantation) over a figurine of bitumen] mixed [with gyp]sum.

75. That is, a tomb.

76. Text: she.

77. Var.: The second tablet of "Incantation. I [call upon you]."

Maqlû Tablet III

Notes to Transcription

line 5 [a] Var.: + *ša*.

line 6 [a–a] Var.: *isaḫḫur šēpīšu.*

line 7 [a] I am uncertain whether *ip-ta-ra-as* should be treated as a Gt durative in both lines 7 and 14 or as a Gt durative only in line 7 and a Gt preterite in line 14. Is a G perfect in either line possible? For further details, see Tzvi Abusch, "*Maqlû* III 1–30: Internal Analysis and Manuscript Evidence for the Revision of an Incantation," in *Of God(s), Trees, Kings, and Scholars: Neo-Assyrian and Related Studies in Honour of Simo Parpola*, ed. Mikko Luukko, Saana Svärd, and Raija Mattila, StOr 106 (Helsinki: Finnish Oriental Society, 2009), 310, n. 9.

line 8 [a] Var.: lines 8–14 absent in one ms.

line 14 [a] See note to *ip-ta-ra-as*, line 7.

line 17 [a] While the first-person possessive suffix (-MU) sometimes seems to be implicit in the logographic writing LÚ/MÍ.UŠ$_{11}$.ZU when the noun is in the nominative or accusative, this logogram normally takes the possessive marker -MU when the noun is in the genitive; hence the necessity of an emendation here.

line 21 [a] Var.: *amātki.*

line 30a [a–a] Var.: rubric absent in all but one ms.
line 38 [a] Vars.: + ÉN, *te* ÉN.
line 38a [a–a] Var.: rubric absent in all but one ms.
line 45 [a] Var.: *bārītu.*
line 50 [a] Var.: *pī* (sic). *pī* in one ms is a scribal error under the influence of *pī* in the preceding line.
line 55 [a] On interpretive grounds, I consider it to be likely that the original reading was *i-tú-ru-ki (târu)*, i.e., *ittūrūki*, but that *-tú-* was misunderstood as *-tam* and then even resolved as *-ta-am-* or *-ta-ma-*, i.e., *i-tam/ta-am/ta-ma-ru-ka/i.*
line 60 [a–a] Var.: *litēr ana šāri* | [b] Var.: absent.
line 60a [a–a] Var.: rubric absent in all but one ms.
line 61 [a] I have transcribed [d]*íd* as [d]*id* throughout for the sake of simplicity.
line 64 [a] For the 'incorrect' third-person prefix *e-* in lines 64–66, see Abusch, *Mesopotamian Witchcraft*, 201, n. 13.
line 68 [a] Var.: *šadê.*
line 69 [a] Var.: *ētelil (*so quoted in a commentary; perhaps the commentary's *Vorlage* transposed *ētelil* and *ētebib* of lines 68 and 69) | [b] Var.: absent.
line 74 [a–a] Var.: *[d]īnšu lis<sa>ḫerma dīn<ī> līšir.*
line 76 [a] Var.: *šadî* | [b] Var.: + *te.*
line 82 [a] Var.: *nuḫḫu* (probably a mistake for *<i>nuḫḫu*). If the verb is plural (*inuḫḫū),* 'they' would be the subject and not the mountain.
line 83 [a] Var.: + *-ša/šu* | [b] Var.: + *-ša/šu* | [c] Var.: + -[*ša*]/*šu.*
line 87 [a] Var.: *šadê* | [b] Var.: + *te.*
line 87a [a–a] Var.: rubric absent in all but one ms.
line 88 [a] Var.: *ibšû* | [b–b] *ina libbiša* was probably modeled on *ina libbiša* of the following line and inserted here in order to accommodate the change of *iqbû* to *ibšû.*
line 90 [a] Var.: *ibbašû*, which probably preserves the original reading.
line 101a [a–a] Var.: rubric absent in all but one ms.
line 104 [a] Var.: lines 104–107 and 111 absent in one Uruk ms.
line 110 [a] Var.: *tukaṣṣirī*[*nni*] (sic).
line 113 [a–a] Var.: *šīmti u šīmāti* (sic) | [b] Var.: + *u* | [c] Or perhaps *šeʾatu.*
line 114 [a] Var.: *diḫme* (so quoted in a commentary). In Maqlû, this word is sometimes written *diḫmennu*, at other times *dikmennu*; I have transcribed accordingly.
line 115 [a] Var.: + *muḫḫi* | [b] Var.: *uggatu* | [c] Vars.: + ÉN, *te* ÉN.
line 115a [a] Var.: rubric in lines 115a–115b absent in all but one ms.
line 116 [a] Var.: *ukaššipanni.*
line 122 [a] Var.: + *-ma.*
line 124 [a] Var.: *lissaḫer.* Line 124 has been added to the incantation. *lissaḫer* is the more original reading; its replacement by *lissaḫip* is due to *nabalkutu* in the two previous lines. | [b] Var.: + [*te*] | [c] Var.: absent.
line 124a [a–a] Var.: rubric absent in all but two mss.
line 125 [a] Var.: + *ina* | [b] Var.: + *ana.*
line 126 [a] Var.: + *ša.*
line 127 [a–a] Var.: *kaššāpī u kaššāptī.*
line 128 [a–a] Var.: *ēpišī u ēpištī.*
line 129 [a–a] Var.: *sāḫirī u sāḫertī.*
line 131 [a] Var.: *-šina l*[*ibb*]*atiqma* instead of *lippaṭerma*, a reading that was erroneously repeated from the preceding line.
line 132 [a] Var.: omitted in one ms | [b] Var.: + *qabal.*

line 133 [a] Vars.: *lītelli*, *ētel*[*lû*/*i*].
line 135 [a] Var.: + *te*.
line 135a [a–a] Var.: rubric absent in all but two mss.
line 136 [a] Var.: + *ša*.
line 137 [a] Var.: + *yâši*.
line 143 [a–a] Var.: *eṭemmu rēdâka*.
line 147 [a] Var.: *tala''înni* (from *lu''û*).
line 148 [a] Var.: *ta<<ta>>saḫḫirīnni*.
line 149 [a] Var.: lines 149–150 transposed in at least two mss.
line 153 [a] Vars.: + TU$_6$, *te*.
line 153a [a–a] Var.: rubric absent in all but one ms.
line 157 [a] Var.: + *ša* (i.e., *ša kīma*) in lines 157–160 of one ms.
line 159 [a] Text: *i-bar-ru, i-bar-ri, i-ba-ar*, all of which are wrong, since we expect a subordinate form of the preterite (*ibāru*). It is possible that a scribe corrected the mistaken *i-bar* by adding *-ru*, hence *i-bar-ru* (cf. notes on II 107 and VII 161); for abnormal orthographic doubling of consonants, see Werner R. Mayer, "Ein Hymnus auf Ninurta als Helfer in der Not," *Or* 61 (1992): 47–48 and Mikko Luukko, *Grammatical Variation in Neo-Assyrian*, SAAS 16 (Helsinki: The Neo-Assyrian Text Corpus Project, 2004), §3.7 (pp. 31–35).
line 161 [a] Var.: + *ēp*[*iš(u)*] *u ēpištu*.
line 162 [a] Vars.: *līkul* and *lišti* seem to be transposed in one ms: *lišti* … [*līkul*].
line 164 [a] Var.: + ^{d}*Girra*.
line 165 [a] Var.: *lissuḫ*.
line 168 [a] Var.: *rušumtikunu*.
line 170 [a] Var.: + *u* | [b] Could *kišpīkunu ruḫêkunu lemnūti* in line 170 be a scribal abbreviation of *kišpūkunu ruḫûkunu rusûkunu upšāšûkunu lemnūti* (cf. III 151–152)? But note also VIII 34.
line 172 [a] Var.: + *kīma qanî ina api* in two Uruk mss.
line 173 [a] Var.: + *<<aḫi>>*. *aḫi* here is probably due to *aḫi atappi* in the following line.
line 179 [a] Vars.: + ÉN, *te* ÉN.
line 180 [a] Var.: this incantation (lines 180–187) is omitted in one ms.
line 186 [a] Var.: + *u*.
line 187 [a–a] Vars.: *bilī*/*bil rittakima* | [b] Var.: *bilā*. The reading *bilī* in the main text follows a Nineveh (Ass.) ms; however, *bilī*, a second person singular imperative, does not agree with the second person plural addressee (*rittakunuma*) found in that ms. But a southern text, probably from Sippar, reads the expected *bilā* with *rittakunuma*. Note that a text from Aššur correctly has the reading *bilī* together with a second person singular addressee (*rittakima*) | [c] Var.: + *ṣalam* | [d] Following *rittakima*, one ms reads ^{d}*Gir*[*ra* …] instead of, or in addition to, *ana išāti luddi* | [e] Var.: + TU$_6$.
line 187a [a–a] Var.: rubric absent in all but one ms.
line 189 [a–a] Var.: IM 3.KAM.MU | [b] Var.: + *iškār āšipūtu*.

Notes to Translation

78. For my understanding of this incantation, see Abusch, "*Maqlû* III 1–30."

79. Var.: Who.

80. Lit.: she turns (others') feet around. Translation of the variant is difficult; perhaps: she turns around (in respect to) her feet.

81. Var.: your word.

82. All entries in the list are in the feminine form.

83. Var.: Diviner (f.).

84. The verbal form *ú-šar/šá-ru* here is treated as if it were a Š form of *wâru*; but note that a Š form of this verb seems not to be listed in the dictionaries.

85. If my reconstruction of the original reading is correct, then translate: Now then, having turned against you, …

86. Var.: And turn whatever sorcery you have performed into a wind.

87. For my understanding of the incantations in III 61–76, 154–179, and VI 85–97, see Abusch, *Mesopotamian Witchcraft*, 197–216.

88. The Sages (*apkallū*) and the Daughters of Anu are creatures associated with water (see Abusch, *Mesopotamian Witchcraft*, 202–3).

89. That is, free, in lines 68, 76, and 87.

90. Var.: the mountain(s). In lines 68, 76, and 87, the mountain is a prison.

91. That is, innocent. Var.: pure.

92. Var.: May his case be per<ver>ted, but may <my> case go straight (that is, be successful).

93. Var.: the mountain(s).

94. Perhaps: The witch is a Sutean, …, the denouncer is an Elamite, …

95. Or: so that like the mountain they be made quiet by sulphur. Most mss have KUR-*i*, one has KUR-*ú*. The translation in the body of the text assumes *šadû*; but if *šadî* is preferred, then perhaps the translation should follow that given in this note.

96. Vars.: Her witchcraft, her spittle, her enchainment.

97. Var.: the mountains.

98. Var.: "was"; and so translate: in whose heart an evil word was against me.

99. Var.: was created.

100. That is, sallow.

101. Or, possibly translate: "like the whirling of this seal, may your face spin and become yellow" (lines 100–101); see *CAD* Ṣ, 58b.

102. Var.: have knotted [me].

103. Var.: fate and destiny (sic).

104. Var.: anger.

105. Lit., from turban to sh[in].

106. Var.: has bewitched me.

107. Lines 117–118 explicate the first half of line 116, while lines 119–120 explicate the latter half of the line.

108. "Turn over" and "turn back" are both possible translations of *nabalkutu* in lines 122 and 123.

109. Var.: perverted. The variant is the more original reading; the replacement of *lissaḫer* by *lissaḫip* ("to be overturned") under the influence of *nabalkutu* in lines 122–123 supports the translation "to turn over" (rather than "to turn back") for *nabalkutu* in those lines.

110. That is, be successful.

111. Or, possibly: Sîn has had my boat made. Var.: I have had a boat made for Sin. The variant supports the treatment of the verb as a first person form.

112. That is, between its bow and stern.

113. Var.: The witches in this and in the two following lines are defined as "my" (e.g., "my warlock and witch").

114. Var.: + midst of the.

115. Or, possibly (combining lines 138 and 139): O witch, why do the head/beginning of your words reach me again and again so as to seize me?

116. Var.: a ghost, your pursuer.

117. Lit., your heart.

118. That is, so that you lose control over your body.

119. Var.: defile.

120. See note on VI 53. Var.: enchant.

121. Var.: + sor[cerer] and sorceress.

122. Var.: Girra.

123. Or, possibly: … may your body be aflame. This translation suits the intransitive usage of the G of *ḫamāṭu*, but does not take account of the fact that in a variant (see earlier note on this line) Girra seems to be the subject of the same verb with an object (hence transitive).

124. Var.: uproot.

125. Or: May Girra cover your face with smoke.

126. Var.: + like reed in a marsh.

127. Var.: + <<the edge of>>.

128. Or, more likely, another more common blackwood tree.

129. That is, inscribed for life.

130. Var.: + a model of.

131. A variant has Girra here at the beginning of a break, so perhaps: "so that Gir[ra may 'destroy' it]," or less likely, "so that Gir[ra may cast it into the fire]."

132. Var.: + an exorcistic series.

Maqlû Tablet IV

Notes to Transcription

line 1 [a] I am unable to explain the form *qí-de-e* here.

line 2 [a] Text: man-gu.

line 7 [a–a] Var.: *akassīkunūši* and *akammīkunūši* seem to be transposed: [*akammīkunūš*]*i akassīkunūši*; this transposed order also occurs in line 74.

line 33 [a–a] Var.: omitted.

line 47 [a] Perhaps restore *nidût* here in line 47 and *nigiṣ* in line 48 (cf. Tzvi Abusch and Daniel Schwemer, "The Chicago *Maqlû* Fragment (A 7876)," *Iraq* 71 [2009]: 70 and reference there).

line 50 [a–a] Perhaps *š*[*ārat zumriy*]*a*; if not, the occurrence of *mêya* in the preceding six lines suggests that we might restore … [*mêy*]*a* also here | [b] Vars.: *tapqidā*, [*ta-di*]*n-nu*.

line 53 [a–a] Var.: *tē*(*pušāni* …) omitted in lines 53–55 and 58–59 of one ms.

line 55 [a] Var.: ^{múl}*Gula*.

line 56 [a–a] Var.: line omitted.

line 62 [a–a] Var.: omitted.

line 63 [a–a] Var.: [*mi*]*mma šum*[*š*]*u*.

line 64 [a] Var.: absent.

line 65 [a–a] Var.: <*u uḫūli*> *qarn*[*ānî*] | [b–b] Var.: *tē*(*pušāni* …) omitted in lines 65–67 of one ms.

line 68 [a] Var.: one ms has the line order 69-72-71-70-68-73 | [b] Text: ⸢DINGIR<<.MEŠ>>⸣.

line 75 [a] Var.: omitted; alternatively, *qāmî* and *qālî* may have been transposed: [*qālî qām*]*î*.
line 79 [a] Var.: + [KA.I]NIM.MA UŠ$_{11}$.BÚ[R.RU.DA.KAM] in a Babylonian ms.
line 80 [a] Var.: omitted.
line 88 [a–a] Var.: line absent.
line 90 [a–a] Var.: probably absent.
line 94 [a] Var.: + [KA.INIM.MA UŠ$_{11}$.BÚRU(.DA) *šalāšat ḫuṣā*]*b*(?) *<ēri> lipâ* ⌜*tapassaš nabāsa*⌝ *ta*[*karrik*] in an Aššur ms.
line 96 [a] *erṣeti* is a possible, but less likely, restoration.
line 100 [a] Perhaps [*šupulk*]*i*.
line 106 [a–a] Var.: absent.
line 110 [a] Var.: + *u*.
line 114 [a–a] Text: *ana šāri*.
line 116 [a] i.e., *ḫanigalbatâtu*.
line 121 [a] Var.: *qām*[*î*]*ya*.
line 122 [a] Var.: *qālîya* | [b] Var.: *te*.
line 135 [a] Perhaps *āši<bat>*.
line 139 [a] Perhaps emend to *ašapparšināti*; cf. II 191.
line 140 [a–a] Var.: line omitted | [b] I have read LÚ.UŠ$_{11}$.ZU *u* MÍ.UŠ$_{11}$.ZU as *kaššāpī u kaššāptī* in lines 140–141; for this reading cf. II 109–111, and note that Babylonian and Assyrian excerpts read *kaš-šá-pi* here. Also see note on I 115.

Notes to Translation

133. For my understanding of this incantation, see Abusch, "Revision of Babylonian Anti-Witchcraft Incantations," 28–38.

134. All verbs of bewitching in this incantation are second person plural.

135. That is, a mat that is covering water.

136. That is, a channel that is full of water.

137. This water probably refers to the water that is poured out as part of the funerary cult, so too I 108, II 185, and IV 45–49; see Schwemer, *Abwehrzauber und Behexung*, 103. For a different interpretation, see note to I 108.

138. Perhaps: [in the waste]land.

139. Perhaps: [in a crevice] in the earth.

140. Var.: have handed over

141. Perhaps: "h[air from m]y [body]" or, possibly, "[m]y [water]."

142. More precisely, Cygnus, Lacerta, and parts of Cassiopeia and Cepheus (so Hermann Hunger and David Pingree, *Astral Sciences in Mesopotamia* [Leiden: Brill, 1999], 274).

143. Var.: Aquarius.

144. Var.: [You have fed] me all kinds (of food). The objects in lines 63–67 are infused with witchcraft; contact with them causes the victim to be bewitched.

145. Var.: "horned <potash>," i.e., Salicornia.

146. That is, the witches' ritual arrangements and the victim's bonds that are thereby created.

147. Var.: + [It is the w]ording (of the incantation) to un[do] witchcraft.

148. Perhaps: circle dancer.

149. Var.: + [It is the wording (of the incantation) to undo witchcraft: three stick]s <of cornel(?)> you rub with tallow (and) wr[ap up] with red wool.

150. Perhaps: [Yo]ur [depth].

151. That is, the effects of the spittle.

152. Lit., "I send sorcery, rebellion, evil word to (*ana*) the wind." *ana* should almost certainly be deleted as an error.

153. Lit., "daughters of the land."

154. Because *riksū* ("bindings") is a masculine plural, the feminine suffixes in lines 119–121 may refer to the female witches, but both context and the ritual (RT 69′) indicate that the object of the actions should be the bindings.

155. Var.: my burner.

156. Var.: my scorcher.

157. In this incantation, the term "witch," all designations of the witch, and all pronominal suffixes are feminine.

158. Perhaps: The witch is one who <sits> at my gate.

159. Perhaps emend to: I am sending them to a burning stove.

Maqlû Tablet V

Notes to Transcription

line 12 [a] Text: a.

line 14 [a] Text: *i-*[*t*]*a-aṣ-ṣa-ru*.

line 17 [a] For the verb forms in lines 17–18, see note to VII 175.

line 18 [a] Var.: [*iṭ*]*eḫḫûni* | [b] Var.: + [KA.INIM.MA UŠ$_{11}$.BÚRU(.DA) *pâ t*]*ašarr*[*ap*] in an Aššur ms.

line 20 [a] Or perhaps *šūbilte/ī*.

line 26 [a] Var.: lines 26–35 absent in one ms | [b–b] Var.: [*ēpi*]*štu muštēpištu*.

line 27 [a] See note on line 35.

line 34 [a–a] Var.: omitted (haplography).

line 35 [a–a] Var.: *littaḫḫirūšu* [*kišpūšu*] in one ms. | [b] Or perhaps *šapātūša*.

line 36 [a–a] Var.: *ēpištu u muštēpištu*.

line 42 [a] That is, *ētiqu*.

line 43 [a–a] Var.: *ēpišt*[*u*] *muštēpištu*.

line 47 [a] Var.: absent.

line 48 [a] Var.: *tēte<nep>pušī*.

line 49 [a] Var.: *teʾût*.

line 50 [a] Var.: *malât*.

line 60 [a] All nouns in lines 60–67 are written logographically; the first mention of each noun is in the accusative case, but I have rendered the accusative here in *-u* on the analogy of the explicit writings in line 71.

line 66 [a] As in earlier lines, the scribe in lines 66–67 used KI.MIN to represent the verbs, but in these two lines he intended the final KI.MIN to represent plural verbs rather than singular ones.

line 72 [a] The verb should be in the plural (probably feminine *liššaknānikkunūši*, but possibly masculine *liššaknūnikkunūši*), but the scribe simply repeated the form from line 70.

line 78 [a] Var.: + *ana*.

line 83 [a] Restorations for this incantation are drawn from the variant incantation CTN 4,

145 (+ 92+147) i 8″–14″. For the incipit (line 83), see RT 80′.
line 89 [a] Restorations for this incantation are drawn from the variant incantation CTN 4, 92 (+145+147) ii 24–34. For the incipit (line 89), see RT 81′.
line 98 [a] Restorations in lines 98–102 are drawn from K 2467 + 80-7-19, 166 (identified by G. Van Buylaere).
line 102 [a] Or possibly *tâmāti rapšāti*.
line 103 [a] Restorations in lines 103–104 and 108–110 are uncertain; those in lines 105–107 are fairly certain.
line 109 [a] According to Martin Stol ("'To Be Ill' in Akkadian: The Verb *Salā'u* and the Substantive *Sili'tu*," in *Advances in Mesopotamian Medicine from Hammurabi to Hippocrates*, edited by Annie Attia and Gilles Buisson, CM 37 [Leiden: Brill, 2009], 29–46), *salāʾu* and *salāḫu* should not be differentiated from each other; there is only one verb *salāʾu*, "to sprinkle." All the same, I have retained the conventional *salāḫu* when the verb is written either with a *-laḫ* sign (V 109, V 110) or with the logogram SUD (RT 29′ and RT 177′), but have transcribed *salāʾu* when the verb is written with an aleph (VII 143 and RT 179′).
line 111 [a] Var.: + *u*.
line 131 [a] Var.: + *u*.
line 139 [a] Var.: [ ]-*ia m*[*û* …]. The variant reading may be restored [*pī*]*ya m*[*û pīkunu išātu*] and treated as a mistaken repetition of the preceding line (dittography) due to *pīya* at the beginning of both lines. Alternatively, the line may be restored [*libbi*]*ya m*[*û libbakunu abattu*] on the basis of a variant text, but this restoration is contradicted by the suffix *-ia*, for the first-person possessive form of *libbu* is *libbī*, while *-ia* certainly agrees with *pīya*.
line 141 [a–a] Var.: *kipid ša libbiya kipi*[*d*] *ša libb*[*ikunu liballi*].
line 154 [a] Var.: + *šadû linērkunūši*.
line 155 [a] Var.: line absent | [b] The verb is *katāmu*, written explicitly *likattimkunūši* in one ms.
line 169 [a] Var.: + *ana zumriya lā teqerrebā*.
line 177 [a] Var.: + .MA | [b] Var.: É[N *alsīkunūši*].

Notes to Translation

160. Var.: + [It is the wording (of the incantation) to undo witchcraft: yo]u burn [chaff].

161. Or, perhaps: my shipment.

162. Or, perhaps: "Set your feet down in the footsteps of my warlock and my witch!" In either case, the line means: establish yourself in the place of the witches.

163. Or: So that her judge may …

164. Var.: The sorceress (and) the woman …

165. In lines 27–35, the conjunction of verb and noun is based on similar consonantal roots.

166. Var.: Like an asafoetida root may [his witchcraft] cause him to shrivel?.

167. Var.: The sorceress and the woman …

168. That is, sheep dung.

169. Var.: The sorceress (and) the woman …

170. Var.: you who <keep on> performing.

171. *kukru* is an aromatic tree or branch.

172. Var.: nourishment.

173. "that you have performed against me, have had performed against me, I perform against you" in lines 58–59 is represented by the sign for "ditto" referring back to line 57.

174. "you have caused to seize me" in the first half of lines 61–67 and "May … seize you" in the second half of lines 61–67 are represented by the sign for "ditto."

175. For the images in this incantation and the sending of signs as a form of bewitchment, see Tzvi Abusch, "The Witch's Messages: Witchcraft, Omens, and Voodoo-Death in Ancient Mesopotamia," in *Studies in Ancient Near Eastern World View and Society Presented to Marten Stol on the Occasion of His 65th Birthday, 10 November 2005, and His Retirement from the Vrije Universiteit Amsterdam*, edited by Robartus J. van der Spek et al. (Bethesda: CDL, 2008), esp. 57–59.

176. Does *nakāmu* ("to pile up"), a transitive verb, have an understood object here?

177. Alternatively, we may take line 78 as not dependent upon the relative pronoun of line 76 and translate: She has formed a cloud against me.

178. Perhaps translate lines 89–90 as: "You have bound up the sinews, but [Ea has (now) unbound (them)], you have twisted and fettered figurines, but [Asalluḫi has (now) released (them)]."

179. It is possible that lines 115–116 depend on the relative pronoun of line 114, in which case we would translate: "You whose heart has planned evil against me, Who keep on seeking malicious spells against me, Who with evil sorcery have bound my knees."

180. Var.: Restore the variant either as: "My [mouth] is wa[ter, your mouth is fire]" (dittography from preceding line), or less likely as "My heart is water, your heart is stone."

181. Var.: "plot" (twice).

182. Lit., "my (demonic) constable."

183. Translate thus if the verb is a Dtn preterite and is to be treated as a performative preterite, like the preceding three verbs. But if it is a D perfect, then translate: I have (now) annihilated.

184. Var.: + May the mountain kill you.

185. Var.: + To my body draw near not.

186. Lit., "who burns you."

187. Var.: The fifth tablet of "Incan[tation. I call upon you]."

Maqlû Tablet VI

Notes to Transcription

line 2 [a–a] *ilu gít-ma-lu* may be the result of an ancient misreading and reinterpretation and should perhaps be emended to [d]*g<u*[!]*-l>a <<lu>>*; similarly, *pa-ni-ia* may be the result of an ancient misunderstanding of *IGI as *pānū* rather than as the expected *īnu* — therefore read *īnīya*. Emendations yield: [d]*Uraš* [d]*Gula lamass*[a]*/āt īnīya*. (The recently discovered reading [d]Gula in line 3 calls the emendation [d]Gula in line 2 into question.)

line 13 [a] Or perhaps *dan<dan>*[*nu*].

line 24 [a–a] Incipit restored from RT 98′ and the parallel line VI 34.

line 25 [a] Lines 25–28 restored from lines 35–38, the parallel lines in the next incantation. In fact, lines 35–37 are an expansion based upon lines 25–27 (see note on RT 99′) | [b] Perhaps restore here and in line 35: [*āšib*].

line 28 [a] Note the third person fem. singular possessive suffix on *rikissa* in lines 28 and 38, which lines are identical. In view of *ša kaššāpiya u kaššāptiya*, we expect the plural suffix *-sunu* (from *-šunu*). But given the focus on a female witch in lines 29–33, the feminine singular suffix is probably original and the male *kaššāpiya* was secondarily added.

line 49 [a] For the restoration of lines 49–50, cf. VII 4–5.

line 53 [a] Or perhaps [*rāḫīt*]*u*.

line 55 [a] The transcription *ṣillī* for GIŠ.MI assumes that the first-person possessive suffix (.MU) is implicit in the logographic writing.

line 56 [a] For this restoration, cf. II 194; an alternative restoration might be [dTišpak], for which cf. *Šurpu* IV 95.

line 64 [a] Var.: omitted.

line 68 [a–a] Var.: omitted.

line 69 [a] *ilī*, not *šamê*, is expected; perhaps emend accordingly.

line 74 [a] In lines 74 and 75, the alternative readings *qašd*[*ū*] and *qašda*[*t*], respectively, are also possible.

line 77 [a] Var.: omitted.

line 84 [a–a] KI.MIN here is construed in this manner on the basis of the preceding line, but this is not certain, especially in view of the remaining broken signs.

line 87 [a] This form is to be understood as the feminine plural *ēpišētūʾa*, perhaps created under the influence of the masculine plural form in the preceding line and/or as the result of a phonological development (for the latter possibility, see Abusch and Schwemer, "Chicago *Maqlû* Fragment (A 7876)," 80 on lines 20′–21′ = VI 86–87) | [b] Text: *mārat*.

line 89 [a] *al-te-ʾi-ši-na-a-ti* is here construed as a Gtn preterite (contra the opinion earlier expressed in "The Chicago *Maqlû* Fragment (A 7876)," 80).

line 95 [a] Var.: omitted | [b] Var.: omitted.

line 96 [a] Var.: *narqâ*.

line 100 [a-a] Or possibly *tâmātu rapšātu* | [b] Var.: omitted.

line 102 [a] Text: *úḫaluppi*.

line 106 [a] For the *überhängende* vowel *i*, see Luukko, *Grammatical Variation in Neo-Assyrian*, §4.8.2 (pp. 105–8), and esp. §4.8.3 (pp. 108–9).

line 111 [a] Text: mu-šik-ku.

line 113′ [a] Incipit restored from RT 112′.

line 118″ [a] Alternatively, if *kibrītu* of line 117″ is to be construed as the antecedent of line 118″, then perhaps restore [*pāṭirat*] or [*mupašširat*] instead of [*paṭrū*] and read BÚR.MEŠ as *mupašširat* rather than *pašrū* in line 118″.

line 141″ [a] Var.: *kurumm*[*ā*]*t*.

line 159″ [a] Restoration based upon RT 127′ and VII 1.

Notes to Translation

188. According to Frans A. M. Wiggermann, *ūmu* "daylight" is a member of a class of personified time periods and is "imagined as a roaring leonine monsters": see "Some Demons of Time and their Functions in Mesopotamian Iconography," in *Die Welt der Götterbilder*, ed. Brigitte Groneberg and Hermann Spieckermann (Berlin: de Gruyter, 2007), 111 and n. 7 and "The Mesopotamian Pandemonium: A Provisional Census," *SMSR* 77 (2011): 315–16. See also the note to I 117.

189. Emendation yields: Uraš and Gula are the pupils of my eyes.

190. The (heavenly) flock refers to the planets and stars.

191. Possible emendation: strongest.

192. A soap plant.

193. Perhaps restore here and in line 35: [dweller].

194. The literal translation in both line 28 and 38 is "of my warlock and witch break her strong bond."

195. Lit., "May the knot of the heart of my witch be loosened."

196. Possible alternative translations here and in all cases where *raḫḫātu* or *rāḫītu* is the subject of the verb *reḫû*: "the spitter spat upon me" or "the poisoner poisoned me" (see also note on I 78).

197. Alternative restoration: [Tišpak].

198. And she will, therefore, not be able to articulate any further curses.

199. That is, cannot join together or be reattached.

200. Perhaps emend to "great gods."

201. The question in this and the next line is a rhetorical one; the answer is "nowhere on my body have you been able to reach me (because I am identified with Sulphur)."

202. See note on VI 53.

203. That is, to the extent that.

204. The verbs in this and the next line are here construed as stative forms of *kašādu*. Still taking the verbs as derived from *kašādu*, lines 74–75 might also be translated in two additional ways: "As much as the heavens can be reached, so my head (can be reached) / As much as the Netherworld can be reached, so my feet (can be reached)." Alternatively: "The heavens reach as far as my head, the netherworld reaches as far as my feet." In any case, the speaker is saying that it is impossible to reach or harm him, for he is protected above and below, that is, all around, from witchcraft. But note that the verbs in lines 74–75 might instead be construed as stative forms of *qašādu*, 'to be pure,' in which case translate: As much as my head heaven is holy, as much as my feet earth is holy.

205. But we expect an inner entrance or quarter rather than an inner hem.

206. Or, possibly: "sealing," in which case, the verb should be better translated "is applied/placed."

207. For the Sages (*apkallū*) and the Daughters of Anu, see note on III 62.

208. Or, more likely, another more common black wood tree.

209. A less likely reading: ditch (E: *īku*).

210. Var.: Hide yourselves in the ground.

211. Hair (*qimmatu*) here might refer to water grasses, rushes, or the like; the act of shaking the hair may possibly be an aggressive or hostile act performed by powers of water.

212. *ebbā*, "are pure," of line 103 refers not only to the "limbs" in line 103 but also to the "head" and "hair" in line 101.

213. If the alternative reading and restoration are correct, then lines 117″–118″ should probably be translated: […] Sulphur, the daughter of the great gods, [which undoes] your [witchcraft], which releases your spittle on the day of the disappearance of the moon.

214. For inseminatrix here and in line 135″, see note on I 78.

215. Or: "for" instead of "at" in lines 128″, 129″, 136″, and 137″.

216. That is, "Asafoetida is so strong that it will cause all your witchcraft to wither." Note also the play on words between *nuḫurtumma* "asafoetida" and *unaḫḫara* "cause to wither."

217. Offspring refers to the food offerings produced by the roasting (Girra) of grain (Nisaba).

218. Nisaba appears here as a goddess of grains.

Maqlû Tablet VII

Notes to Transcription

line 3 [a] Perhaps [*anāku*].
line 15 [a] Var.: *ēpišātīšunu*.
line 17 [a] Var.: MÍ.UŠ$_{11}$.ZU; but note that the first-person possessive suffix (-MU) sometimes seems to be implicit in this writing, thus MÍ.UŠ$_{11}$.ZU: *kaššāptī*.
line 21 [a] Var.: *tēpušīnni* | [b] Var.: ⸢*ušābil*⸣ | [c] Vars.: + TU$_6$/*te* ÉN.
line 24 [a–a] Or perhaps: *laḫru immerša ṣabītu armâša atānu mūrša*; for the grammatical analysis of this line, see Tzvi Abusch, "Mother and Child or Sexual Mates," in *A Woman of Valor: Jerusalem Ancient Near Eastern Studies in Honor of Joan Goodnick Westenholz*, ed. Wayne Horowitz, Uri Gabbay, and Filip Vukosavović, BPOA 8 (Madrid: CSIC, 2010), 13–17 | [b] Var.: *ḫuzāla*.
line 28 [a] Var.: *lissuḫ*, which may reflect a text form prior to the addition of *ilū rabûtu* (cf. Abusch, *Mesopotamian Witchcraft*, 199) | [b–b] Var.: absent | [c] Vars.: + ÉN, *te* ÉN.
line 31 [a] Var.: [*muš*]*apšeḫ* | [b] Var.: *šerʾānī*.
line 34 [a] Var.: *tapšuḫti*; the writing *tap*[!](text: *pa*)-*šu-uḫ-ti* confirms that *tapšuḫti* is an error—the scribe began to write *pašḫāti* but under the influence of *tapšuḫti* in the preceding line completed the word as if it were *tapšuḫti*.
line 38 [a] Var.: + *u*.
line 39 [a] Var.: *ušapšeḫ*.
line 42 [a–a] Vars.: *rikis rabābu/a*, *riksi rabû/ê*, *qātī rabbāti*. *qātī* in the variant *qātī rabbāti* was introduced by mistake under the influence of the following line.
line 45 [a] Var.: The verb appears at the beginning of the line rather than in the middle in all but one ms. Note that the writing can also be construed as *idīšumma* (imperative). Regardless of placement, the preterite form *iddīšumma* may be a mistake for the imperative; if Ea is the addressee, it is possible that instead of *šipat amāti* (= INIM) *ša balāṭi*, we should read *šipat-ka ša balāṭi* | [b–b] Vars.: *šipat balāṭi*, *šipat amāt* [*balāṭi*]. The phrase *šipat amāti ša balāṭi* seems rather clumsy; I would therefore take *šipatka ša balāṭi* to be a better and more original resolution of the signs.
line 46 [a] Var.: *lišapšiḫū* | [b] Var.: absent.
line 47 [a] Var.: this incantation (lines 47–54) is absent in one ms | [b] Var.: *lānu*. This variant appears in a Nippur ms that seems indifferent to case endings and to the first-person possessive suffix -*ī*; so also lines 48 (*pūtu*), 56 (*lānu*), 57 ([*ga*]*ttu*), and 58 (*nabnītu*).
line 48 [a] Written SAG.KI = SAG.KI(-MU); see above, note on line 17.
line 51 [a] Perhaps insert <*ina ereb*> instead of <*kīma*>.
line 52a [a] Var.: lines 52a and 54a appear in only one ms.
line 55 [a] Var.: NU; perhaps the note on *kaššāptī*, line 17, applies here as well, thus NU: *ṣalmī*. But notice that NU here appears in a Nippur ms that seems indifferent to case endings and to the first-person possessive suffix -*ī* even in syllabic writings; see above, note on line 47.
line 56 [a] Var.: ^{d}LAMMA; perhaps LAMMA: *lamassī* (cf. above, note on *kaššāptī*, line 17).

line 62 [a] Var.: *umaʾʾirannima.*
line 67 [a–a] Var.: *mešrêtīka ubber minâtīka ukassi.*
line 69 [a] I have taken *ipšu* here as a singular because the parallel nouns in the following two lines are in the singular and because a variant reads *ipša.*
line 72 [a–a] Var.: absent.
line 77 [a] Var.: in a Neo-Babylonian (Nineveh) ms, lines 77–79a read:

itti m[ê ša zumriya u musâti ša qātīya]
liššaḫi[ṭma eli ṣalam nigsagilê lillik]
ṣalam nigsagi[lê arnī dinānī lizbil]
sūqu [u sulû lipaṭṭirū arnīya]
ūmu šul[ma arḫu ḫidûti šattu ḫegallaša libila]
[d]*Ea* [[d]*Šamaš u* [d]*Marduk yâši rūṣānimma]*
lippaš[rū kišpī ruḫû rusû upšāšû lemnūti ša amēlūti] \
[u māmītu littaṣi ša zumriya É]N

line 78 [a] Var.: *lillik.*
line 79a [a–a] Var.: line absent in both Nineveh (Assyrian) mss | [b] Vars.: ÉN, *te* ÉN.
line 82 [a–a] That is, *sūqāti nadât.*
line 91 [a] One ms has the line order 94-95-93-91 | [b–b] Var.: line absent | [c] Var.: *qurqurrū.*
line 92 [a–a] Var.: line absent.
line 95 [a–a] Var.: line absent.
line 100 [a] Vars.: *tēteppušu* (2nd masc. sg.); *tēpušā*, which should probably be emended to *tē<tep>pušā* (2nd pl.) | [b] Var.: + T[U$_6$ ÉN].
line 101 [a] Var.: one ms has an incantation order that deviates from that of the standard text: the two incantations *ipšīki epšētīki* (lines 101–106) and *kiṣrīki kuṣṣurūti* (lines 107–113) (the latter of which is destroyed) appear after *amsi qātīya* (lines 114–140), and not between *bāʾertu ša bāʾirāti* (lines 80–100) and *amsi qātīya* | [b] Var.: the heading ÉN is absent in the two main Nineveh (Assyrian) mss (certainly one, but probably both), which, moreover, lack a dividing line between lines 100 and 101 (i.e., between the two incantations *bāʾertu ša bāʾirāti* and *ipšīki epšētīki*).
line 105 [a] Var.: *kīma.*
line 110 [a–a] Var.: *ušābil šāra*, which seems to reflect a change in the text.
line 112 [a] Var.: *[kīm]a.*
line 113 [a] Var.: *te.*
line 114 [a] Var.: in a Neo-Babylonian (Nineveh) ms, the incantation *amsi qātīya* (lines 114–140) reads:

[ÉN *amsi qātīya ubbib]a zumrī*
[ina mê nagbi ellūti ša ina Eridu i]bbanû
[mimma lemnu mimma lā ṭābu ša ina zu]mriya šīrīya
[šerʾānīya b]ašû itti mê ša zumriya
[u musâti] ša qātīya liššaḫiṭma
[ana muḫḫiki u] ana lāniki lillik
[ēnītu līn]ânni māḫertu limḫuranni
[amḫur miḫru lim]ḫurūʾinni ÉN

line 116 [a–a] Var.: *a-kam-mì lemnu.*
line 118 [a] Var.: lines 118–119 transposed in one ms | [b] Var.: *lumnū* in lines 118 and 119 | [c–c] Var.: *ittāti idāti* | [d–d] Var.: omitted in one ms.
line 120 [a] Var.: + *mimma šumšu* x x.
line 128 [a] Var.: *[il]i* | [b] Var.: *ili* | [c] Var.: *[ili].*
line 141 [a] I have treated this verbal form as an imperative; it can also be construed as a

stative. If so, perhaps read the following verb as *mesâ* (stative), but note the oblique form of *qātīya* (in contrast to the nominative form in line 162).

line 143 [a–a] This line seems to be intrusive; the secondary nature of the line might explain the occurrence of a female witch in the first part of the line and a male in the latter part | [b] Var.: [*ī*]*pušanni*.

line 144 [a] Var.: *bilamma*, which is either an imperative form or an error for *<li>bilamma* | [b] I have taken KI-tim here as representing not KI-*tì*: *erṣetu*, but rather a Neo-Assyrian writing for *qaqqaru* (KI.TIM); in favor of reading *qaqqaru* here is *qaq-qa-ru* of line 142. (KI-tim in I 63 may possibly also represent *qaqqaru*; cf. *KAR* 71 rev. 2.) Elsewhere in Maqlû, KI-*tì* represents *erṣetu* not only in the expected genitive case (e.g., III 48, V 12, 15) but also in the nominative (VI 75, VII 25) and accusative (VII 25) | [c] Var.: + TU$_6$ É[N].

line 147 [a] Or perhaps *ēzib bītišu*.

line 152 [a] Vars.: + [É]N, T[U$_6$ ÉN].

line 155 [a] Var.: [*ula*]*ppat*.

line 156 [a] The reading of the name of the god ^{d}IGI.DU is not certain (cf. Manfred Krebernik, "^{d}PĀLIL(IGI.DU)," in *RlA* 10 (2003), 281 and Rykle Borger, *MZl*^{2}, 408).

line 158 [a] Var.: lines 158–159 omitted in one ms.

line 160 [a] Var.: omitted.

line 161 [a–a] Var.: *utār kišpīki ana pîki* | [b] Var.: *utarrū* in one ms (this ms also writes GUB-*zu* in line 157); *utarrū* is probably an error that was made under the influence of plural *uṣabbatūki* later in the line. But this writing could also be an example of unexpected orthographic consonant doubling, for which see references in note to III 159 | [c–c] Var.: absent.

line 164 [a] Var.: + *u*.

line 166 [a] Var.: [*lišš*]*akin*.

line 167 [a–a] Var.: omitted.

line 168 [a] Var.: omitted in one ms.

line 170 [a] Citations of this incipit in all mss of the Ritual Tablet (line 156′) give this word as *qātīya*, but the fact that *qātīya* would then occur twice in this one line renders this reading suspect and supports the partially preserved reading *pīya* found in one ms of Tablet VII.

line 175 [a] The verb forms in lines 175–177 are in the singular (similarly, V 17–18); in VII 12–13, *ṭeḫû* appears in the plural with these nouns (but without *qerēbu*), as does the variant *iṭeḫḫûni* in V 18.

line 177 [a–a] Var.: absent | [b] Var.: + possibly a rubric in one ms: [KA.INIM.MA UŠ$_{11}$.BÚ]R(?).⌜DA(?).KE$_4$⌝.

Notes to Translation

219. Scorpion refers to the constellation of that name; Rainbow probably refers to a star.

220. Or, possibly: "sealing," in which case, the verb should be better translated "is applied."

221. There is some uncertainty regarding the identity of the referent of the pronominal suffixes in lines 14–16. The pronominal suffix in line 14 may refer to either the sorcery or the sorcerers; the former seems more likely. In line 16, the suffix certainly refers to the sorcerers. The identity of the referent in line 15 depends on which of the two extant

readings is chosen. Overall, it would appear that lines 14–15 refer to the sorcery, while line 16 (in conjunction with line 17) refers to the sorcerers; this pattern is strange and calls for an explanation.

222. Var.: May they (i.e., the sorcery) turn back and capture their sorceresses. This reading is inferior.

223. Or: clamp down (on them).

224. Var.: The wind has carried off.

225. Var.: you (sing.).

226. But if the female animals (the mothers) are construed in the nominative (rather than in the accusative), then translate: The ewe (received) her lamb, the gazelle her young, the jenny her donkey foal. For this line, see Abusch, "Mother and Child."

227. Var.: And may it (i.e., the spell) extirpate …

228. For my understanding of this incantation, see Tzvi Abusch, "Blessing and Praise in Ancient Mesopotamian Incantations," in *Literatur, Politik und Recht in Mesopotamien: Festschrift für Claus Wilcke*, ed. Walther Sallaberger, Konrad Volk, and Annette Zgoll (Wiesbaden: Harrassowitz, 2003), 4–6 and "Notes on the History of Composition of Two Incantations," in *From Source to History: Studies on Ancient Near Eastern Worlds and Beyond Dedicated to Giovanni Battista Lanfranchi on the Occasion of His 65th Birthday on June 23, 2014*, ed. Salvatore Gaspa et al., AOAT 412 (Münster: Ugarit-Verlag, 2014), 5–10.

229. Vars.: comforting bandage; great bandage; soothing hands.

230. Possible var.: "O Ea, cast" (imperative); if so, perhaps read: "your incantation of healing," instead of "the incantation of the word of healing."

231. Var.: the incantation of healing.

232. That is, the constellation Auriga.

233. We expect a heavenly referent. Can the writing here be a play on *is lê* = α Tauri + Hyades?

234. Perhaps: You, O great gods, shine forth in the sky <at the setting of> the sun.

235. For my understanding of this incantation, see Tzvi Abusch, "Ritual and Incantation: Interpretation and Textual History: A Consideration of Maqlû VII: 58–105 and IX: 152–59," in "*Sha'arei Talmon*"*: Studies in the Bible, Qumran, and the Ancient Near East Presented to Shemaryahu Talmon*, ed. Michael Fishbane and Emanuel Tov (Winona Lake, IN: Eisenbrauns, 1991), 367–80 and "A Neo-Babylonian Recension of *Maqlû*," 1–16.

A line division of lines 55–68 that is organized not by ancient line divisions but by sense, would read as follows:

> Incantation. Whoever you are, O witch, who has made a figurine of me—
> Who has looked at my form and created my image,
> Who has seen my bearing and given rich detail to my physical build,
> Who has comprehended my appearance and reproduced my features,
> Who has bound my body,
> Who has tied my limbs together,
> Who has twisted my sinews.
> As for me, Ea, exorcist of the gods, has sent me,
> And before Šamaš I draw your likeness—
> I look at your form and create your image,
> I see your bearing and give rich detail to your physical build,
> I comprehend your appearance and reproduce your features with pure flour,
> I bind your body,
> I tie your limbs together,
> I twist your sinews.

236. Lit., "Nisaba."

237. Var.: I bind your limbs, I tie your body.

238. Var. of lines 77–79a in a Neo-Babylonian (Nineveh) ms:

With the wa[ter of my body and the washing of my hands]
May it rins[e off and come upon a figurine of a substitute],
[May the] figurine of the substit[ute bear my sin as a replacement],
[May] street [and way undo my sins],
[May] the day [bring] well-[being, the month joy, the year its prosperity].
Ea, [Šamaš, and Marduk, help me so that]
[Witchcraft, spittle, enchainment, evil machinations of mankind] be relea[sed],
[And oath go forth from my body. É]N

239. For my understanding of this incantation, see Abusch, "Ritual and Incantation," 370–75.

240. That is, "I am calling forth."

241. Or, perhaps: I am calling forth … so that I may break your bond.

242. Var.: metalworkers.

243. This is done so that the witch will be unable to talk.

244. Lit., "causes water to carry off."

245. Var.: like.

246. Lit., "causes water to carry off"; var.: causes the wind to carry off.

247. Var.: like.

248. For my understanding of this incantation, see Abusch, *Babylonian Witchcraft Literature*, 13–44 and "A Neo-Babylonian Recension of *Maqlû*."

249. Var. of the incantation *amsi qātīya* (lines 114–140) in a Neo-Babylonian (Nineveh) manuscript:

[Incantation. I wash my hands, I clean]se my body
[In the pure spring water that] was formed [in Eridu].
May [everything evil, everything unfavorable that i]s [in] my [bo]dy, my flesh,
[and my sinews] rinse off with the water of my body
[and the washin]g of my hands
and come [upon your head and] upon your body.
[May a substitute s]tand in for me, may one who encounters (me) take (it) over from me,
[I have encountered an ominous encounter; may] they [t]ake (it) over from me.

250. Var.: The evils, here and in the beginning of line 119.

251. That is, the evil portended by.

252. Var.: + of any sort x x.

253. The relative pronoun *ša* at the beginning of line 121 ("that I have looked at daily, …") either refers to understood but unstated objects portending evil that are seen daily or are stepped on in the street, thus introducing a new entry, or resumes the evil signs and portends mentioned in line 118 (*lumun šunāti* …); in any case, line 121 does not seem to continue the divinatory sequence of lines 119–120 (*lumun šīrī* …).

254. Vars.: "god" for "gods" in the first three phrases of one manuscript.

255. The curse here probably refers to a curse that results from a broken oath.

256. That is, the various evils.

257. If the verbs are stative, translate: Morning has appeared, my hands are washed.

258. Note, however, that *petû* is usually transitive; but the transitive translations that I can imagine seem contextually less appropriate. Moreover, the parallelism, noted below, between this line and 144b supports this translation.

259. Var.: has performed sorcery against me.

260. Line 143 is probably a secondary addition; it does not fit the context. The incantation is then easily understood, especially once one realizes that lines 141–142 and 144 are parallel (i.e., 141 // 144a and 142 // 144b). But if line 143 is part of the original incantation, then perhaps the relative pronoun *ša* introducing line 143 refers back to the sin of the preceding line and should be translated "with which."

261. Var.: Šamaš, bring me release.

262. Or, perhaps: The one who leaves his house.

263. See note on VI 53.

264. Var.: Over a whole mile.

265. Var.: be made favorable.

266. Var.: "my [ha]nds," in the citation of the incipit in the Ritual Tablet.

267. Lit., "complete your awesome power for me."

Maqlû Tablet VIII

Notes to Transcription

line 1 [a] Restorations based upon RT 157′ and VII 178.

line 5 [a] Or *šigar[š]a*.

line 16 [a] It is possible that the line endings of the few preserved lines in A 7876 rev. iii belong in the break between lines 16 and 17′.

line 24′ [a] Alternatively, the second half of lines 24′ and 25′ (without the emendation—a correction of the omission due to haplography—in line 24′) may be construed as: … *abi māti* … *abi mātāti*.

line 26′ [a] Or perhaps [*ina napāḫik*]*a*.

line 27′ [a] Or perhaps [*šaptāya*].

line 35′ [a] Var.: this incantation (lines 35′–52′) is absent in a Babylonian (Nineveh) ms.

line 40′ [a] Or perhaps [*imḫurū*]*šima*.

line 42′ [a] *uṭ-ṭa-a* can also be construed as *liḫ-da-a* (*liḫdâ*); if that reading is correct, then one would probably restore [*liša*]*sḫipši* in line 43′ and [*l*]*itēr* in line 44′.

line 45′ [a] Perhaps rather *idâ* (imperative).

line 53′ [a–a] Incipit restored from RT 162′.

line 57′ [a–a] The restoration *ša yâši u ramān*[*iya*] is also possible, but the lack of a verb and the awkwardness of the phrase suggest that *ramān*[*ī īpuša*] is a more reasonable restoration.

line 68′ [a] Or perhaps É]N-*ki*: *šip*]*atki*.

line 81″ [a] Or [d]*Ni*[*n*-.

line 82″ [a] Perhaps [d]*Ereš*[*kigal*.

line 84″ [a] For the restoration of lines 84″–85″, cf. I 33 and 35.

line 91″ [a] For restorations in lines 91–95, cf. III 56–60.

line 96″ [a] A less likely alternative is to read *lem-na-ti* as *ši-na-ti*, i.e., -*šināti* ("them"); but if so, *lemnāti* should not be restored in line 97″.

line 97″ [a] *imtala* (G perfect) is also possible | [b] Var.: *umt*[*alli*].

line 99″ [a–a] Var.: *ša eššebê eššepât*[*išina*], a reading which is probably corrupt.

line 100″ [a] As in line 96″, *lemnāti* in lines 100″–101″ can also be read -*šināti*.

line 104″ [a] Var.: *yâši taltapparāni* of lines 104″–105″ omitted.

line 106″ [a] Var.: + [x x x -*n*]*i*.
line 108″ [a–a] Restoration and emendation (text: *mu-ru-bat*) based upon RT 170′ as well as CTN 4, 145 ii 2′ + CTN 4, 147 obv! ii 1′.
line 109″ [a] Restorations in lines 109″–110″ derive from CTN 4, 145 ii 3′ + CTN 4, 147 obv! ii 2′ and CTN 4, 147 obv! ii 3′ | [b] We expect *eṭlūti* (cf. line 119‴), but perhaps the restoration *ḫābilat* is wrong.
line 117‴ [a] Or perhaps *nakkapt*[*i*].
line 124⁗ [a] Or perhaps *ana*.
line 136⁗ [a] Var.: + [*ē tamḫur zikurr*]*udâ*.

Notes to Translation

268. Or: her bolt.
269. Lit., "have."
270. See note on VI 53.
271. Alternative reading of the latter half of lines 24′ and 25′ (without the emendation in line 24′): … the father of the land, … the father of the lands.
272. Alternative restoration: [at y]ou [rising].
273. Alternative restoration: [My lips].
274. The second-person referent is the plant mentioned in the previous line.
275. Instead of "against" in lines 29′ and 30′, perhaps translate *ana* as "to," if the preposition in these two lines has the same function as *ana* in line 28′.
276. "Knot" here may refer to a knot of people bound together in hostility in addition to, or even instead of, its literal meaning.
277. That is, cause the heart not to be angry.
278. Or: the ford.
279. Alternatively, lines 37–38 may be translated: "Sitting in the ferry/ford, [the one who instigates] sorcery against me [has (now) engul]fed the qua[y]."
280. Alternative restoration: The sages of the *apsû* [received] her.
281. Alternative reading and restoration of the verbs in 42′–44′ yield: "May [Ea], king of the *apsû*, welcome her (i.e., drown her), [May he over]whelm her with *bennu*-epilepsy, confusion, (and) trembling, [May he] turn back her terror."
282. Alternative grammatical analysis yields: [O Riv]er, cast her (own) fear upon her.
283. That is, innocent.
284. A farmer-god.
285. Alternative restoration: O witch of mine and of [my] very person—.
286. If *rēš* is to be restored immediately before *libbiša*, then translate "her [epi]gastrium" rather than "her heart."
287. Perhaps: your [incanta]tion.
288. Or: "has been ful[l …]" (G perfect).
289. Var.: The ecstatic pow[ers] of the ecstatics.
290. The mouth and tongue of line 102″ are the subjects of the verbs in lines 100″–101″.
291. We expect "young men."
292. That is, may Ereškigal not allow the witch to find a place in the netherworld after death.
293. Var.: + [Do not accept *Zikur*]*rudâ*-magic.
294. That is, the evil portended or caused by.

Maqlû Ritual Tablet

Notes to Transcription

line 1 [a–a] This line is destroyed in all mss of the Ritual Tablet; it is found in a catalogue in which the tablets of Maqlû are listed by their first line.
line 4′ [a] Emending u + mul to ŠUḪUB: *ikabbas*.
line 9′ [a–a] Or perhaps *ṣalmu* ⸢*ša*⸣ *lipî*.
line 10′ [a] Var.: omitted.
lines 14′–18′ [a] In my notes to the Nineveh (Bab.) text, presented as the main text of lines 14′–18′, I have occasionally introduced a Sultantepe reading where it seems certain. It is possible that the Babylon text is not a ms of the Ritual Tablet of Maqlû but belongs to a similar ritual text. All the same, I have incorporated its sparse testimony into the reading of lines 20′–24′.
line 14′ [a] The line begins: *ana bīti* [*tatârma*/*terrubma* …] | [b] Probably] *ana maḫar* […] *riksa tarakkas*.
line 15′ [a] Or perhaps] x *uppa*.
line 17′ [a] This instruction was preceded by ÉN[N …].
line 21′ [a] Var.: *akt*[*ali*].
line 25′ [a] It is possible to read [… *līš*]*i* (i.e., NÍG.LAG.G]Á? in the Sultantepe ms rather than [… *līši ina muḫḫ*]*i* (i.e., UG]U?); if so, read: … *ṣalam lī*[*š*]*i ḫuluppaqq*[i]/*ī* …
line 26′ [a–a] Var.: absent.
line 29′ [a] For the spelling of this verb in the RT, see note to V 109.
line 32′ [a] Restorations of the ritual instructions for Tablet II are drawn from the rubrics in that tablet.
line 33′ [a] Var.: omitted.
line 42′ [a] Restorations of the ritual instructions for Tablet III are drawn from the rubrics in that tablet.
line 44′ [a] Var.: + *u*.
line 48′ [a] Var.: *ibšû*.
line 50′ [a–a] Var.: apparently *maḫar šumēliša* and perhaps even *iṭṭâ tašakkan* are absent (in the break) in all but one ms.
line 53′ [a] Var.: omitted | [b–b] Var.: *ippušanni īteneppušanni* | [c–c] Var.: omitted in one ms | [d–d] Var.: probably omitted in the break in all other mss (see below, note on line 55′).
line 54′ [a] Var.: + *ina*.
line 55′ [a–a] Var.: probably omitted in the break in the same mss in which the comparable section in line 53′ is omitted.
line 62′ [a–a] Var.: *ina qabliš*[*u*]*n*[*u*].
line 64′ [a] Restoration based upon the Aššur rubric for the next incantation (IV 94a for IV 80–91), which ends with KI.MIN, indicating that the rubric, i.e., the ritual for the preceding incantation (IV 1–79, ÉN *bišlī bišlī*), had the same text as the following one | [b] Text: *pallurta*.
line 65′ [a] Var.: omitted | [b] Text: *ippuš* | [c–c] Restoration based upon the rubric for this incantation in IV 94a.
line 66′ [a] Var.: *ina* in one ms; in that variant ms it is likely that *lipâ* was omitted and *ina* added in its place. The same ms probably did not have the expected *lipâ* in line 64′.
line 67′ [a] Var.: the incipit and the second half of the ritual instructions in line 67′ are transposed in one ms, which ms, moreover, omits the first half of the ritual instructions, the

incipit in line 68′, and the second half of the ritual instructions in line 69′ | [b-b] Var.: absent | [c–c] Var.: omitted (see note a on this line) | [d] Or perhaps *t*[*apaṭṭar*].

line 69′ [a] Var.: + *-ma* | [b] Or perhaps [*tapaṭṭar*].

line 71′ [a–a] Text: *ēpišta u muštēpišta* | [b–b] For the restoration, cf. V 4.

line 74′ [a] Regarding DUB.MEŠ(-)[…]: the logogram DUB may represent *sarāqu*, *šapāku*, or *tabāku*; the dictionaries seem not to recognize a Gtn for *sarāqu*.

line 75′ [a] Text: *tēteneppu*[*š*].

line 77′ [a] Var.: omitted.

line 79′ [a] Var.: + *ūmī ḫamiššeret*.

line 80′ [a–a] Var.: absent.

line 82′ [a] Var.: omitted.

line 90′ [a] Var.: *tanaddīma* (ŠUB-*di-ma*).

line 91′ [a–a] Var.: *nappa*[*ṭa*] | [b] Var.: *in*[*a*]*ssukma*.

line 94′ [a] Var.: *tatârma*.

line 96′ [a] Var.: omitted in error.

line 97′ [a] We expect *ēpištī*.

line 99′ [a–a] The Ritual Tablet preserves the original incipit of the incantation; the text of the incantation (VI 34–39) has been expanded by dittography (or perhaps intentional repetition) of VI 25–27 in VI 35–37.

line 103′ [a] For lines 103′–104′, I follow the order of a single Babylonian ms against all others. These others quote the incipits in lines 102′ and 104′ in adjoining lines and then place the ritual prescription (line 103′) after the latter. I follow the single text that places the ritual instructions after the first incipit (line 102′) because the relevant ritual acts are mentioned in that incantation.

line 105′ [a] Text: *elleti* | [b] *ilī*, not *šamê*, is expected; perhaps emend accordingly.

line 111′ [a] Var.: + *appašiš*.

line 118′ [a] Var.: + *ša qutāri*.

line 119′ [a–a] Var.: absent.

line 124′ [a] Var.: omitted.

line 125′ [a] Var.: *ina*.

line 128′ [a–a] Var.: part of the name of the vessel was probably omitted by mistake in one ms: *la*<*ḫanni*> *šaḫarrati*; if this is not an omission, then read: *ḫaṣbi šaḫarri*.

line 129′ [a-a] Var.: apparently absent in the break in one ms.

line 132′ [a–a] Var.: omitted by mistake in the main Nineveh Assyrian ms.

line 133′ [a] Lines 133′–137′ follow the Nineveh Assyrian ms; all other mss do not contain lines 133′–135′ and 137′, and instead read: *šipāti annâti imannūma*, followed by line 136′.

line 139′ [a] Var.: ⸢*nāri*⸣ | [b] Var.: omitted.

line 142′ [a–a] Var.: absent; this shorter text probably reflects a more original and correct text | [b] Var.: *imessīma* | [c] Var.: [*tatâr*].

line 145′ [a] Var.: absent.

line 146′ [a–a] Var.: absent.

line 147′ [a] Var.: *ina*, a mistake in the main Nineveh Assyrian ms.

line 148′ [a] Var.: for the three entries in lines 148′–151′, a Sultantepe ms has the line order 150′-151′-148′-149′ (which agrees with the order of a Nineveh Babylonian ms of Tablet VII).

line 149′ [a–a] Var.: absent.

line 150′ [a] *ubbab* (durative) seems to be a mistake for the expected *ubbib* (preterite); the text of this incantation (VII 114) has the expected *ubbib*(*a*) (so all mss, with the exception of one from Nippur).

line 151′ a–a Var.: absent | b–b Var.: *mīs qātī*.
line 152′ a–a Var.: omitted by mistake in the main Nineveh Assyrian ms.
line 156′ a All mss read *qātīya*, but see note on VII 170; *qātīya* should probably be emended to *pīya*.
line 160′ a Var.: the two entries in lines 160′–161′ are absent in Sultantepe and Babylonian mss.
line 163′ a Var.: absent.
line 166′ a Var.: *teppuš*.
line 170′ a–a Var.: absent.
line 172′ a Var.: absent | b Var.: *ana*.
line 173′ a–a Var.: absent | b Var.: *imannu*.
line 175′ a Var.: absent.
line 176′ a Var.: *immar*.

Notes to Translation

295. That is, I 32.

296. The manuscripts for these lines are too fragmentary to be coordinated in synoptic fashion. I present a partial translation of the Nineveh (Bab.) text supplemented by a few Sultentepe readings:

14′ [You return] to the house […]; before […] you set up the ritual arrangement.
15′ […] … you set
16′ …
17′ […] The incantation … you recite three times, then
18′ […] you prostrate yourself.

297. Alternative reconstruction: … a figurine of dough [on] the crucible …

298. Var.: "was" instead of "has spoken" in line 48′; and so translate the second part of line 48′ through the first part of 49′: O witch in whose heart an evil word was against me.

299. Lit., "from turban to shin."

300. Var: "Put bitumen on her left" seems to be absent in all but one ms.

301. Var.: She performs sorcery against me, she keeps on performing sorcery against me.

302. Var.: + for fifteen days.

303. Var. for the final clause in line 90′ and for line 91′: " … you then pour out roasted flour / and then take the brazier out [through the gate], and he then throws (it) away, then … "

304. The incantations mentioned in lines 92, 95, 134–135, 137, and 178 are cited only by incipit in the RT, and their text is not given in the incantation tablets of Maqlû; for the significance of these incantations, see Abusch, "Mesopotamian Anti-Witchcraft Literature," 253–55, esp. n. 11.

305. A comparison with a similar passage (UET 6/2, 410 obv 25′–26′ [*CMAWR* vol. 2 8.16 44′–45′]) suggests that, having discarded the remains of the burning outside the estate, the officiant recites the incantation on his way back to its outer gate.

306. Var.: return to.

307. That is, the ritual and incantations of the first five tablets of the Maqlû series.

308. Perhaps emend to "great gods."

309. Var.: + I have salved myself.

310. See note on I 78.

311. Var.: + for incense.

312. Var.: If the variant is not a mistake, then translate: sherd.

313. All non-Nineveh Assyrian mss do not contain lines 133′–135′ and 137′, and instead read: "he recites these incantations and then," followed by line 136′.

314. *Šurpu*. Is the *Šurpu* ceremony, or a form thereof, intended here? Note that Maqlû and *Šurpu* are often cited together in ritual tablets and catalogues.

315. *Šurpu.*

316. Var.: to the river.

317. Var.: [and you then return to …].

318. Var.: "thereon" instead of "upon the likenesses of flour."

319. Var.: "Handwashing" instead of "He washes his hands upon the figurine of the substitute."

320. Var.: "my mouth," following the incipit of this incantation in Tablet VII.

321. Lit.: "attach."

322. Var: " … (and) one figurine each of the warlock and witch of dough you insert … "

Bibliography

Works with Major Sections on *Maqlû* and Related

Abusch, I. Tzvi. "Ascent to the Stars in a Mesopotamian Ritual: Social Metaphor and Religious Experience." Pages 15–39 in *Death, Ecstasy, and Other Worldly Journeys*. Edited by Michael Fishbane and John J. Collins. Albany: State University of New York Press, 1995 (= Pages 271–86 in Abusch, *Mesopotamian Witchcraft*).

———. *Babylonian Witchcraft Literature: Case Studies*. BJS 132. Atlanta: Scholars Press, 1987.

———. "Blessing and Praise in Ancient Mesopotamian Incantations." Pages 1–14 in *Literatur, Politik und Recht in Mesopotamien: Festschrift für Claus Wilcke*. Edited by Walther Sallaberger, Konrad Volk, and Annette Zgoll. Wiesbaden: Harrassowitz, 2003.

———. "Considerations When Killing a Witch: Developments in Exorcistic Attitudes to Witchcraft." Pages 191–210 in *The Dynamics of Changing Rituals: The Transformation of Religious Rituals within Their Social and Cultural Context*. Edited by Jens Kreinath, Constance Hartung, and Annette Deschner. TStR 29. New York: Lang, 2004 (= Pages 65–78 in Abusch, *Mesopotamian Witchcraft*).

———. "The Demonic Image of the Witch in Standard Babylonian Literature: The Reworking of Popular Conceptions by Learned Exorcists." Pages 27–58 in *Religion, Science, and Magic in Concert and in Conflict*. Edited by Jacob Neusner, Ernest S. Frerichs, and Paul V. M. Flesher. New York: Oxford University Press, 1989 (= Pages 3–25 in Abusch, *Mesopotamian Witchcraft*).

———. "Dismissal by Authorities: *Šuškunu* and Related Matters." *JCS* 37 (1985): 91–100.

———. "Divine Judges on Earth and in Heaven." Pages 6–24 in *The Divine Courtroom in Comparative Perspective*. Edited by Ari Mermelstein and Shalom E. Holtz. BibInt 132. Leiden: Brill, 2014.

———. "An Early Form of the Witchcraft Ritual *Maqlû* and the Origin of a Babylonian Magical Ceremony." Pages 1–57 in *Lingering over Words: Studies in Ancient Near Eastern Literature in Honor of William L. Moran*. Edited by Tzvi Abusch, John Huehnergard, and Piotr Steinkeller. HSS 37. Atlanta: Scholars Press, 1990 (= Pages 113–62 in Abusch, *Mesopotamian Witchcraft*).

———. "Exorcism. I. Ancient Near East and Hebrew Bible/Old Testament." Pages

513–19 in *The Encyclopedia of the Bible and Its Reception*. Vol. 8. Edited by Hans-Josef Klauck et al. Berlin: de Gruyter, 2014.

———. "Illness and Healing in Ancient Mesopotamia." Pages 456–59 in *Religions of the Ancient World: A Guide*. Edited by Sarah Iles Johnston. Cambridge: Belknap Press of Harvard University Press (HUP Reference Library), 2004.

———. "An Incantation-Prayer: Gods of the Night 1." Pages 157–67 in *Reading Akkadian Prayers and Hymns: An Introduction*. Edited by Alan Lenzi. ANEM 3. Atlanta: Society of Biblical Literature, 2011.

———. "The Internalization of Suffering and Illness in Mesopotamia: A Development in Mesopotamian Witchcraft Literature." Pages 49–58 in *Magic in the Ancient Near East*. Edited by Paulo Xella. *SEL* 15. Verona: Essedue, 1998 (= Pages 89–96 in Abusch, *Mesopotamian Witchcraft*).

———. "Lists of Therapeutic Plants: An Observation." Pages 1–3 in *If a Man Builds a Joyful House: Assyriological Studies in Honor of Erle Verdun Leichty*. Edited by Ann K. Guinan et al. CM 31. Leiden: Brill, 2006.

———. "*Maqlû*." *RlA* 7 (1989): 346–51 (= Pages 287–92 in Abusch, *Mesopotamian Witchcraft*).

———. "*Maqlû* III 1–30: Internal Analysis and Manuscript Evidence for the Revision of an Incantation." Pages 307–13 in *Of God(s), Trees, Kings, and Scholars: Neo-Assyrian and Related Studies in Honour of Simo Parpola*. Edited by Mikko Luukko, Saana Svärd, and Raija Mattila. StOr 106. Helsinki: Finnish Oriental Society, 2009.

———. "*Maqlû* Tablet II: Its Literary Frame and Formation." In *Memorial Volume for Avigdor Hurowitz*. Edited by Shamir Yona et al. Winona Lake, IN: Eisenbrauns, 2015.

———. "Mesopotamian Anti-witchcraft Literature: Texts and Studies. Part I: The Nature of *Maqlû*: Its Character, Divisions and Calendrical Setting." *JNES* 33 (1974): 251–62 (= Pages 99–111 in Abusch, *Mesopotamian Witchcraft*).

———. *Mesopotamian Witchcraft: Toward a History and Understanding of Babylonian Witchcraft Beliefs and Literature*. AMD 5. Leiden: Brill/Styx, 2002.

———. "Mother and Child or Sexual Mates." Pages 13–17 in *A Woman of Valor: Jerusalem Ancient Near Eastern Studies in Honor of Joan Goodnick Westenholz*. Edited by Wayne Horowitz, Uri Gabbay, and Filip Vukosavović. BPOA 8. Madrid: CSIC, 2010.

———. "A Neo-Babylonian Recension of *Maqlû*: Some Observations on the Redaction of *Maqlû* Tablet VII and on the Development of Two of Its Incantations." Pages 1–16 in *Festschrift für Gernot Wilhelm anläßlich seines 65. Geburtstages am 28. Januar 2010*. Edited by Jeanette C. Fincke. Dresden: Islet, 2010.

———. "Notes on the History of Composition of Two Incantations." Pages 1–10 in *From Source to History: Studies on Ancient Near Eastern Worlds and Beyond Dedicated to Giovanni Battista Lanfranchi on the Occasion of His 65th Birthday on June 23, 2014*. Edited by Salvatore Gaspa et al. AOAT 412. Münster: Ugarit-Verlag, 2014.

———. "The Promise to Praise the God in Shuilla Prayers." Pages 1–10 in *Biblical and Oriental Essays in Memory of William L. Moran*. Edited by Agustinus Gianto. BibOr 48; Rome: Editrice Pontificio Istituto Biblico, 2005.

———. "The Revision of Babylonian Anti-Witchcraft Incantations: The Critical

Analysis of Incantations in the Ceremonial Series *Maqlû*." Pages 11–41 in *Continuity and Innovation in the Magical Tradition*. Edited by Gideon Bohak, Yuval Harari, and Shaul Shaked. JSRC 15. Leiden: Brill, 2011.

———. "Ritual and Incantation: Interpretation and Textual History: A Consideration of *Maqlû* VII: 58–105 and IX: 152–59." Pages 367–80 in *"Sha'arei Talmon": Studies in the Bible, Qumran, and the Ancient Near East Presented to Shemaryahu Talmon*. Edited by Michael Fishbane and Emanuel Tov. Winona Lake, IN: Eisenbrauns, 1991 (= Pages 185–96 in Abusch, *Mesopotamian Witchcraft*).

———. "The Ritual Tablet and Rubrics of *Maqlû*: Toward the History of the Series." Pages 233–53 in *Ah, Assyria ...: Studies in Assyrian History and Ancient Near Eastern Historiography Presented to Hayim Tadmor*. Edited by Mordechai Cogan and Israel Eph'al. Scripta Hierosolymitana 33. Jerusalem: Magnes Press, Hebrew University, 1991 (= Pages 163–83 in Abusch, *Mesopotamian Witchcraft*).

———. "The Socio-Religious Framework of the Babylonian Witchcraft Ceremony *Maqlû*: Some Observations on the Introductory Section of the Text, Part I." Pages 1–34 in *Riches Hidden in Secret Places: Ancient Near Eastern Studies in Memory of Thorkild Jacobsen*. Edited by Tzvi Abusch. Winona lake, IN: Eisenbrauns, 2002 (= Pages 219–47 in Abusch, *Mesopotamian Witchcraft*).

———. "The Socio-Religious Framework of the Babylonian Witchcraft Ceremony *Maqlû*: Some Observations on the Introductory Section of the Text, Part II." Pages 467–94 in *Solving Riddles and Untying Knots: Biblical, Epigraphic, Semitic Studies in Honor of Jonas C. Greenfield*. Edited by Ziony Zevit, Seymour Gitin, and Michael Sokoloff. Winona Lake, IN: Eisenbrauns, 1995 (= Pages 249–69 in Abusch, *Mesopotamian Witchcraft*).

———. "Some Reflections on Mesopotamian Witchcraft." Pages 21–33 in *Public and Private Religion in the Ancient Near East*. Edited by Adele Berlin. Bethesda: CDL, 1996.

———. "Water into Fire: The Formation of Some Witchcraft Incantations." Pages 27–63 in *Mesopotamian Witchcraft: Toward a History and Understanding of Babylonian Witchcraft Beliefs and Literature*. AMD 5. Leiden: Brill Styx, 2002.

———. "Witchcraft and the Anger of the Personal God." Pages 83–121 in *Mesopotamian Magic: Textual, Historical, and Interpretive Perspectives*. Edited by Tzvi Abusch and Karel van der Toorn. AMD 1. Groningen: Styx, 1999 (= Pages 27–63 in Abusch, *Mesopotamian Witchcraft*).

———. "Witchcraft, Impotence, and Indigestion." Pages 146–59 in *Disease in Babylonia*. Edited by Irving L. Finkel and Markham J. Geller. CM 36. Leiden: Brill, 2007 (= Pages 79–88 in Abusch, *Mesopotamian Witchcraft*).

———. "Witchcraft Literature in Mesopotamia." Pages 373–85 in *The Babylonian World*. Edited by Gwendolyn Leick. New York: Routledge, 2007.

———. "Witches and Demons in Ancient Mesopotamia." *Studi e Materiali di Storia delle Religioni* 77/2 (2011) [= *Demoni mesopotamici*]: 342–56.

———. "The Witch's Messages: Witchcraft, Omens, and Voodoo-Death in Ancient Mesopotamia." Pages 53–68 in *Studies in Ancient Near Eastern World View and Society Presented to Marten Stol on the Occasion of His 65th Birthday, 10 November 2005, and His Retirement from the Vrije Universiteit Amsterdam*. Edited by Robartus J. van der Speck et al. Bethesda: CDL, 2008.

Abusch, Tzvi and Daniel Schwemer. "Das Abwehrzauber-Ritual *Maqlû* ('Verbrennung').” Pages 128–86 in *Omina, Orakel, Rituale und Beschwörungen*. Edited by Bernd Janowski and Gernot Wilhelm. TUAT NF 4. Gütersloh: Guetersloher Verlagshaus, 2008.

———. “The Chicago *Maqlû* Fragment (A 7876).” *Iraq* 71 (2009): 53–87.

———. *Corpus of Mesopotamian Anti-Witchcraft Rituals*. Vol. 1. AMD 8/1. Leiden: Brill, 2011.

———. “RIAA 312 (O 193) Revisited.” *Akkadica* 130 (2009): 103–9, 211.

Biggs, Robert D. ŠÀ.ZI.GA. *Ancient Mesopotamian Potency Incantations*. TCS 2. Locust Valley, NY: J. J. Augustin, 1967.

van Binsbergen, Wim and Frans Wiggerman. “Magic in History: A Theoretical Perspective, and Its Application to Ancient Mesopotamia.” Pages 3–34 in *Mesopotamian Magic: Textual, Historical, and Interpretive Perspectives*. Edited by Tzvi Abusch and Karel van der Toorn. AMD 1. Groningen: Styx, 1999.

Böck, Barbara. “‘When You Perform the Ritual of “Rubbing”’: On Medicine and Magic in Ancient Mesopotamia.” *JNES* 62 (2003): 1–16.

Ebeling, Erich. “Beschwörungen gegen den Feind und den bösen Blick aus dem Zweistromlande.” *ArOr* 17/1 (1949): 172–211. (Pages 185–95 are reedited in *CMAWR* 1)

———. “Eine Beschwörung der Gattung Ušburruda.” *Or* 22 (1953): 358–61. (To be reedited in *CMAWR* 2)

Falkenstein, Adam. *Die Haupttypen der sumerischen Beschwörung literarisch Untersucht*. Leipzig: Hinrichs, 1931.

Farber, Walter. *Beschwörungsrituale an Ištar und Dumuzi*. Wiesbaden: Steiner, 1977. Esp. pages 218–60. (To be reedited in *CMAWR* 2)

Frahm, Eckart. *Babylonian and Assyrian Text Commentaries: Origins of Interpretation*. Guides to the Mesopotamian Textual Record 5. Münster: Ugarit-Verlag, 2011. Esp. pages 121–23, 268–70, and 384–96.

Frankena, Rintje. “Girra und Gibil.” Pages 383–85 in *RlA* 3 (1957–1971).

Geller, Markham J. “A New Piece of Witchcraft.” Pages 193–205 in *DUMU-E_2-DUB-BA-A: Studies in Honor of Åke W. Sjöberg*. Edited by Hermann Behrens, Darlene Loding, and Martha T. Roth. Occasional Publications of the Samuel Noah Kramer Fund 11. Philadelphia: University Museum, 1989. (To be reedited in *CMAWR* 2)

Gurney, Oliver R. “A Tablet of Incantations Against Slander.” *Iraq* 22 (1960): 221–27. (To be reedited in *CMAWR* 2)

King, Leonard W. “The Meaning and Use of *ḳutaru* in Assyrian Magic.” *PSBA* 33 (1911): 62–67.

Kinnier Wilson, James. “An Introduction to Babylonian Psychiatry.” Pages 289–98 in *Studies in Honor of Benno Landsberger on His Seventy-Fifth Birthday, April 21, 1965*. AS 16. Chicago: University of Chicago Press, 1965.

Köcher, Franz. “Die Ritualtafeln der magisch–medizinischen Tafelserie ‘Einreibung.’” *AfO* 21 (1966): 13–20.

Kunstmann, Walter G. *Die babylonische Gebetsbeschwörung*. LSS NF 2. Leipzig: Hinrichs, 1932.

Lambert, Wilfred G. “An Incantation of the *Maqlû* Type.” *AfO* 18 (1957–58): 288–99. (Reedited in *CMWAR* 1)

Maul, Stefan M. *Zukunftsbewältigung: Eine Untersuchung altorientalischen Denkens anhand der babylonisch-assyrischen Löserituale (Namburbi)*. BaF 18. Mainz: von Zabern, 1994.

Maul, Stefan M. and Rita Strauss. *Ritualbeschreibungen und Gebete I*. Mit Beiträgen von Daniel Schwemer. KAL 4. WVDOG 133. Wiesbaden: Harrassowitz, 2011. Esp. nos. 24–37.

Mayer, Werner R. *Untersuchungen zur Formensprache der babylonischen "Gebetsbeschworungen."* Studia Pohl. Series Maior 5. Rome: Pontifical Biblical Institute, 1976.

Meier, Gerhard. *Die assyrische Beschwörungssammlung Maqlû*. AfOB 2. Berlin, 1937.

———. "Studien zur Beschwörungssammlung *Maqlû*." *AfO* 21 (1966): 70–81.

Reiner, Erica. *Astral Magic in Babylonia*. TAPS NS 85/4. Philadelphia: American Philosophical Society, 1995. Esp. pages 97–118.

Ritter, Edith K. "Magical-Expert (=*āšipu*) and Physician (=*asû*): Notes on Two Complementary Professions in Babylonian Medicine." Pages 299–321 in Studies in Honor of Benno Landsberger on His Seventy-Fifth Birthday, April 21, 1965. AS 16. Chicago: University of Chicago Press, 1965.

Rollin, Sue. "Women and Witchcraft in Ancient Assyria." Pages 34–45 in *Images of Women in Antiquity*. Edited by Averil Cameron and Amélie Kuhrt. Detroit: Wayne State University Press, 1983.

Schollmeyer, Anastasius. "Zur *Maqlū* Serie." *ZA* 32 (1918/1919): 73–77.

Schwemer, Daniel. *Abwehrzauber und Behexung: Studien zum Schadenzauberglauben im alten Mesopotamien* (*Unter Benutzung von Tzvi Abuschs Kritischem Katalog und Sammlungen im Rahmen des Kooperationsprojektes Corpus of Mesopotamian Anti-witchcraft Rituals*). Wiesbaden: Harrassowitz, 2007.

———. "Empowering the Patient: The Opening Section of the Ritual *Maqlû*." Pages 311–39 in *Pax Hethitica: Studies on the Hittites and their Neighbours in Honour of Itamar Singer*. Edited by Yoram Cohen, Amir Gilan, and Jared L. Miller. Wiesbaden: Harrassowitz, 2010.

———. ""Forerunners" of *Maqlû*: A New *Maqlû*-Related Fragment from Assur." Pages 201–20 in *Gazing on the Deep: Ancient Near Eastern and Other Studies in Honor of Tzvi Abusch*. Edited by Jeffrey Stackert, Barbara N. Porter, and David P. Wright. Bethesda: CDL, 2010.

———. *Rituale und Beschwörungen gegen Schadenzauber*. KAL 2. WVDOG 117. Wiesbaden: Harrassowitz, 2007.

———. "The Ritual Tablet of *Maqlû*: Two New Fragments." *JCS* 63 (2011): 105–9.

Scurlock, JoAnn. "Magical Uses of Ancient Mesopotamian Festivals of the Dead." Pages 93–107 in *Ancient Magic and Ritual Power*. Edited by Marvin Meyer and Paul Mirecki. RGRW 129. New York: Brill, 1995.

Tallqvist, Knut L. *Die Assyrische Beschworungsserie Maqlû: Nach den Originalen im British Museum*. 2 vols. ASSF 20/6. Leipzig: A. Pries, 1895.

Thomsen, Marie-Louise. *Zauberdiagnose und schwarze Magie in Mesopotamien*. CNIP 2. Copenhagen: Museum Tusculanum Press, 1987.

Weißbach, Franz H. "Zur Serie Maḳlu." *BA* 4 (1902): 155–67.

CPSIA information can be obtained
at www.ICGtesting.com
Printed in the USA
BVHW031436160719
553535BV00008B/13/P